Quality Function Deployment and Systems Supportability

This book presents not only the overall development of Quality Function Deployment (QFD) and what it has been used for to date but also a new product support orientation by which it can be employed. It is product and service "system"-focused and presents how blending the processes and elements of supportability and analysis into a QFD Modeling methodology can achieve optimal cost savings and performance efficiency and effectiveness. In addition, a working model is provided that will assist those that elect to use such an approach to current/new product and/or service development.

QFD is widely spreading throughout the world because of its outstanding usefulness. It is aimed to fulfill the customer's expectation of a product or service design. Organizations of all sizes are using it to (1) save product and service design and development time, (2) focus on how the product or service might satisfy the customer, and (3) improve communication at all levels of an organization during the development process.

Based on these three reasons, today's traditional QFD can be divided into three branches and analyzed. First, QFD can be implemented effectively for developing new products and designs by establishing the linkage between design stages through the manufacturing environment. However, research has found that traditional QFD is quite weak in implementing modifications to existing product and service design during its predicted life-cycle. Second, most research to this point has been squarely focused on the "voice of the customer" for prioritizing customer needs. While certainly needed, the "voice of the system" that is being used to produce the product/service and how to operate during its intended life-cycle have been given less attention. Third, QFD is often viewed as overly labor-intensive, thus costly, and, because of its team-based development logic, manual in nature by those involved during its development and implementation.

Research has shown that life-cycle sustainment planning and support for current or proposed products and/or services require a seamless and balanced life-cycle support methodology. To achieve this type of support, 12 functional elements have been identified that form the product support infrastructure. A new approach, one that views product support as an integrative activity where all 12 product support elements are assessed over the entire product and/or service life-cycle, is being deployed.

With this deployment comes a need to ensure that key performance parameters (KPPs) are achieved and functional alignment obtained by balancing supportability element cost and provisioning throughout the entire product and/or service life-cycle, not just during the development stage, and to view the system as the "customer" and thus listen to the "Voice of the System" when assessing supportability requirements. QFD is such a tool.

This book contains four sections. Section 1 provides an initial overview of QFD origins and history, and highlights some of their use today. It addresses how QFD fits within the organization, increasing revenue and reducing cost. It outlines a step-by-step strategy for successfully deploying QFD within the organization. Section 2 examines the evolving product and/or service requirement, creating the design solution using QFD, assessing supportability characteristics using QFD, and performing functional supportability analysis using QFD. Section 3 provides a guide for developing the life-cycle supportability solution using QFD methodology on an ongoing basis, and managing processes throughout the system's life-cycle. Section 4 addresses using QFD in an imperfect world and will provide insight into how to use QFD beyond the standard "house of quality" concept.

Quality Function Deployment and Systems Supportability

Achieving Key Performance Parameters and Ensuring Functional Alignment

John Longshore, Angela Cheatham, and Jim Gibson

Routledge
Taylor & Francis Group

A PRODUCTIVITY PRESS BOOK

First published 2024
by Routledge
605 Third Avenue, New York, NY 10158

and by Routledge
4 Park Square, Milton Park, Abingdon, Oxon, OX14 4RN

Routledge is an imprint of the Taylor & Francis Group, an informa business

ISBN: 9781032372518 (hbk)
ISBN: 9781032372501 (pbk)
ISBN: 9781003336044 (ebk)

DOI: 10.4324/9781003336044

Typeset in Garamond
by Apex CoVantage, LLC

Contents

Part 2

Part 4

Foreword

Congratulations on achieving this wonderful milestone, by describing the key deliverables of Quality, Supportability, and Life-Cycle Costs, which stimulates value and reduces costs, while increasing revenue simultaneously.

These are well-described elements through your writings and examples to the reader, with the opportunity to test given applications, tailored to their own organization in a real-world situation.

It's been my pleasure over the past six years to experience your knowledge and understanding of this subject matter presented to us in this document through my involvement at the Embry Riddle Aeronautical University's, David B. O'Maley College of Business. It's been a greater honor to get to know you individually, and to develop personal friendships along the way.

Each of the authors has the exact experience required for this document to be concise and to be utilized in business or in education from the standpoint of quality assurance, Lean Six Sigma, or quantitative analysis.

In my 50+ year business aviation career, I could have utilized a tool such as this many times to predict accurate supportability elements, easily and efficiently, if it would have been available.

Embrace the knowledge provided in this document and offer the benefits to your customer.

Roger W. Smeltzer, Sr.
President, Smeltzer Aviation Solutions, Inc.
Retired, Textron Aviation (2019)

Author Bios

John Longshore, DBA

Dr. John Longshore is a professor of management within the David B. O'Maley College of Business at Embry Riddle Aeronautical University's Daytona Beach Campus. His academic teaching responsibilities include systems engineering management, project management, production and operations management, quantitative methods in business, Lean Six Sigma, and other related business courses. Dr. John Longshore is a designated naval aviator with over 4,000 hours of operating and command experience in fixed and rotary-wing aircraft. Over a 22 years career in the Marine Corps, Dr. John Longshore developed and managed the introduction of numerous aircraft systems, including the CH-53E, AV8A/B, and MV-22. Upon his retirement from the Marine Corps, Dr. John Longshore oversaw the introduction of the F/A-18A and F-117 aircraft systems into the international inventory via the Middle East introduction in Kuwait. Working with Booz-Allen and Hamilton, Dr. John Longshore developed numerous fleet logistical readiness models, which continue to be employed today. After joining Northrop Grumman as director of Aeronautical Systems, Dr. John Longshore served as the production manager for the Aerostructures division in Nashville, Tennessee, and then the Vought Aircraft Manufacturing site in Dallas, Texas. Selected as a vice president of operations for a joint venture between Northrop Grumman, Lockheed Martin, and Sikorsky Aircraft Corp., Dr. John Longshore planned, built, and managed a regional maintenance, repair, and overall facility in the United Arab Emirates.

Dr. John Longshore holds a BS degree in industrial Engineering from the Naval Post Graduate School, a BS degree in aviation management, an MBA/A from Embry-Riddle Aeronautical University, an executive MBA from the Wharton School, and a Ph.D. from Nova Southeastern University. He is professionally certified as a Six Sigma Master Black Belt, Lean Six Sigma Sensei, Master Professional Logistician, Supply Chain Professional, Project Management Professional, Airframes and Power Plants Mechanic, Scrum Master, Blockchain Professional, Society of Quality Assurance Professional, and American Society of Appraisal (ASA) Appraiser.

Angela Cheatham, Ph.D.

Dr. Angela Cheatham is an associate professor of management with the O'Maley College of Business at Embry-Riddle Aeronautical University. She teaches supply chain management from a logistics perspective, Lean Six Sigma for aviation and aerospace, management, project management for aviation and aerospace, and transportation. Throughout her career, she has worked with the development and implementation of processes and policies related to management and operations, supply chain, logistics, and curriculum.

Dr. Angela Cheatham holds a BS in technical management and MS in management with a specialization in integrated logistics from Embry-Riddle Aeronautical University. She earned her Ph.D. in business administration with a concentration in homeland security, leadership, and policy. Her research focus is U.S. Space Policy and space operations, logistics management, supply chain, and continuous improvement. She holds a Black Belt in Six Sigma and has participated in Federal Aviation Administration (FAA) and industry projects focusing on commercial space integration, supply chain, and lean processes.

Jim Gibson, Ph.D.

Dr. Jim Gibson is an FAA Flight Test Pilot supporting eVTOL, airplane, helicopter, and UAS projects. Jim is an adjunct professor of engineering management with the College of Business at Embry-Riddle Aeronautical University. His academic teaching responsibilities include engineering management, quantitative analysis, and business analytics. He is a retired U.S. Marine Corps naval aviator rated in the KC-130 and V-22, squadron commander, and experimental test pilot. Following the Marine Corps, Jim worked for Bell as an experimental test pilot and simplified vehicle operations technical lead supporting the V-280, V-247, BH525, Nexus, and APT programs. His research focuses on energy economics and sustainability in urban air mobility. In addition, he works with organizations in East Africa and India to assist subsistence farmers in growing trees to generate carbon offsets. Jim is a US Naval Test Pilot School graduate and earned a Ph.D. in systems and engineering management from Texas Tech University and an MBA from Duke University's Fuqua School of Business.

Introduction

Congratulations on your purchase of *Quality Function Deployment and Systems Supportability: Achieving Key Performance Parameters and Ensuring Functional Alignment.*

Life-cycle sustainment planning and support for current and proposed products or services require a seamless life-cycle sustainment support methodology. To achieve this sustainment support, 12 integrated product support (IPS) elements have been identified that form the foundation by which a comprehensive product support strategy can be developed for a product or service over its intended life-cycle. These IPS elements are product support management, design interface, sustaining engineering, supply support, maintenance, planning support management, packaging, handling, storage and transportation, training and training support, manpower and personnel, facilities and infrastructure, and computer resource. Historically, the management of product or service activities was assessed just prior to distribution. Now, with the focus squarely on balancing product or service performance, support, and cost along with environmental sustainability measures, a new approach, one that views supportability as an interactive and integrative activity where all IPS elements are assessed as the product or service moves through its development life-cycle, is being deployed.

With this deployment comes a need for key performance indicators (KPIs) to be developed and key performance parameters (KPPs) measured not just in the beginning stages of the products or services life-cycle but also progressive throughout its life-cycle. Quality Function Deployment (QFD) is such a tool.

The book is structured into four parts.

Part 1, Chapters 1 through 3, first provides an overview of QFD origins and its history, and provides highlights of how it is being used today. It then addresses how QFD fits within organizations and aids then in their product or services planning and/or redesign of processes by increasing value and reducing cost. Lastly it presents a step-by-step strategy for successfully planning, deploying, and implementing QFD within their organization and provides templates to aid in that process.

Part 2, Chapters 4 through 6, takes the reader first through the process of translating supportability aspirations into measurable criteria that can be used in building a QFD model. It addresses that the supportability challenge facing every organization is to ensure that future support of a system and its cost of ownership receives the same importance during development and acquisition as performance. It then introduces the reader to supportability assessment, which is responsible for the identification of the physical resources required to support a product and/or service. It explains how assessments are performed as interrelated activities in the building of product and/or service systems. Section 2 concludes with a contrast between the supportability assessment function and the supportability analysis function. The former is performed during the building of the product and/or service, the latter, when that product and/or service is nearing its completion and being readied for deployment. It also introduces the reader to the three-stage process of physical supportability analysis: (1) identification of the complete range of resources required to support the product and/or service system; (2) the optimal support infrastructure and maintenance solution to achieve a balance between performance, support, and cost of ownership; and (3) determination of the minimum quantity of each resource identified to support the system at a pre-stated usage rate.

Part 3, Chapters 7 through 9, acts as a pivot for the reader and takes them into the realm of the systems development life-cycle process. It initially presents the reader with a real-world system acquisition case study, which will serve as a thread throughout the section. It requires the reader to assess a chosen system by its IPS elements and determines how they should be prioritized and packaged during its forecasted life-cycle. Because the packaging and prioritization of those elements require an understanding of how they were initially conceptualized and architected during each of its life-cycle development phases, they will be walked through *QFD Life-Cycle Modeling* approach where the results will act as a guide to the QFD Acquisition Model development. The section concludes with the development of a *QFD Acquisition Model* and how the data derived from its use is interrupted to provide adequate IPS support for a system through its operational life-cycle.

Part 4, Chapters 10 and 11, will initially address how organization management, both level and structure, influences a QFD project execution. The reader is walked through the development process of a QFD project in a step-by-step manner with examples that illustrate how each management level influences and guides a QFD project deployment. It guides the reader through the forming of the "QFD Action Team" and presents nine actions that are collectively management's responsibility in forming those teams. The section concludes by presenting the reader with editable templates and forms that can be used by their own QFD Action Teams to implement, manage, and monitor QFD project execution.

PART 1

PART

1

Chapter 1

Quality Function Deployment; Its Origins and Objectives

Quality Function Deployment Defined

What do we mean when we use the word "*Quality*"? As an adjective, *Quality* means "excellent." Because the customer expectations determine quality, you cannot have a quality product or service without first identifying your customers and then defining "What" their needs and expectations are. The second word *Function*, as a verb, means "to work or operate in a proper or particular way." This means "How" customers' expectations will be met or how the product or service will function to meet them. Finally, *Deployment* defines how you will manage the flow of development efforts to make certain customers' expectations drive the product or service effort.

Quality Function Deployment (QFD) is a planning and management quality process tool that drives optimal product and service development. It is a structured product or service planning method that enables development teams to specify a customer's needs clearly. It then can be used to systemically evaluate the products or services capabilities in terms of impact on those identified needs. A key benefit of QFD, because of its structural design, is that it assists product development teams in communicating to decision makers exactly "What" needs to be developed and "How" it needs to be developed. It allows organizations to evaluate early on in the conceptual stage of the product or service development life-cycle whether it is worth the investment.[1,2]

DOI: 10.4324/9781003336044-2

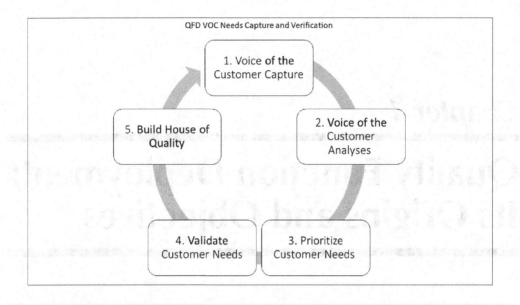

Figure 1.1   Quality Function Deployment VOC Needs Capture and Verification.

The QFD process tends to vary from practitioner to practitioner. However, one constant element required by all QFD efforts is an accurate assessment of the customer's needs. This process begins with listening to the voice of the customer (VOC), gathering information on the identified needs, and ends with validating those needs. An illustration of this front-end work is provided in Figure 1.1.[3]

Understandably, several steps must be followed to determine customer needs before actual matrices construction can proceed. It all starts with listening to the VOC, then analyzing obtained information, prioritizing it, validating it, and lastly, building the matrices. The first of the matrices (often called quality tables) constructed is called the House of Quality (HOQ). Figure 1.2 illustrates a basic HOQ structure with generic attribute identification that practitioners typically use as a starting period. It displays the customer's wants and needs (the VOC) along the left.

The matrix consists of several sections, or sub-matrices joined together in various ways, each containing information related to the others.[4]

Each labeled section (1 through 8) shown in Figure 1.2 is a structured, systematic expression of a product or process development team's perspective on an aspect of the overall planning for a new product, service, or process. The numbering suggests one logical sequence for populating the matrices.

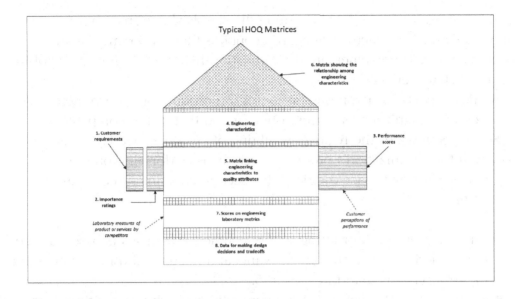

Typical HOQ Matrices

6. Matrix showing the relationship among engineering characteristics

4. Engineering characteristics

1. Customer requirements

3. Performance scores

5. Matrix linking engineering characteristics to quality attributes

2. Importance ratings

Laboratory measures of product or services by competitors

7. Scores on engineering laboratory metrics

Customer perceptions of performance

8. Data for making design decisions and tradeoffs

Figure 1.2   Typical House of Quality Matrices.

The first section, "customer requirements," is a structured section of customer needs and wants. Generally, this structure is determined through qualitative research. Data is often presented in a tree diagram format.

The second section, "importance ratings," contains relative customer-driven importance ratings as determined by sampling the customer base for their priorities.

Section 3, "performance scores," contains two main types of information:

■ Quantitative market-oriented data to include customer satisfaction levels with the organization's product offering and its direct competitor's current offering.
■ Strategic goals for the new product or service.

Section 4 contains the organizations' technical language (generally generated from the customer's wants and needs recorded in section 1) and a high-level description of the product or service planned for development.

Section 5 links engineering characteristics with the customers' quality attributes rankings based on the development team's judgments of the strength of the relationship between each element of its technical response and each customer's want and need.

Section 6, "technical correlations," is half of a square matrix split along its diagonal and rotated 45°. This is the roof of the matrix, which led to the term "house of quality," thus becoming the standard designation for the entire QFD matrix structure. Section 6 contains the development team's assessment of the implementation interrelationships between elements of the technical characteristics.

Section 7 contains a comprehension of the product or service metrics between the organization's current offering and that of the competitors.

Section 8 provides the relative weighting of customer needs versus how well the organization's product or service is performing on the relevant product or service metrics. This section contains three types of information:

■ The computer rank ordering of the technical responses is based on the rank ordering of the customer's wants and needs found in section 2 and the relationships found in section 5.
■ Comparative information on the competition's technical performance.
■ Technical performance targets.

Beyond the initial HOQ, QFD optionally involves constructing additional matrices to plan further and manage the detailed decisions that must be made throughout the product or service development process. In practice, most development teams stop after the base HOQ is developed for the initial planning phase. However, a lot is missed by stopping here. The benefits provided by using additional QFD processes and their related matrices can be significant throughout the development process and useful throughout a product's or service's life-cycle. Figure 1.3 shows a possible configuration of a collection of interrelated matrices along with a standard QFD technique for carrying information from one matrix into another.[5]

The first matrix labeled *Product Planning* has *Whats* labeled on the left of the matrix. This term is generally used to denote desired benefits or objectives the development team wants to achieve. Whats normally comprise customer needs and VOC data, but it can be the development team's own objectives. Whats are prioritized as part of the QFD process based on research data performed by the development team members.

The development team next generates the *Hows* and places them along the top of the initial matrix. Generally, Hows are any set of potential responses aimed at achieving the identified Whats. Hows are normally technical measures of performance of the proposed product or services.

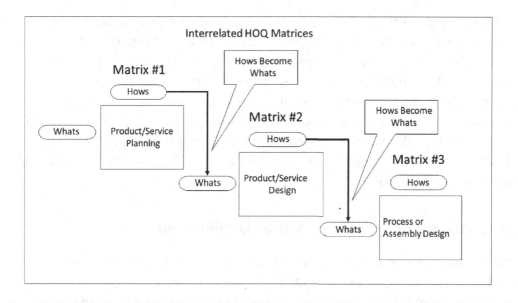

Figure 1.3 Interrelated HOQ matrices.

Relating Whats and Hows is crucial because assumptions often creep in that are unwarranted.

Based on the weights assigned to Whats and the amount of impact each How has on achieving each what, the Hows are given priorities or weights written at the bottom of the HOQ diagram. These weights are a principal result of the HOQ process.

The second matrix, Product Design or Service Design, links matrix one by placing the Hows from matrix one on the left side of matrix two, thus becoming *Whats* of that matrix. The development team then develops a more detailed set of *Hows* placed at the top of the second matrix. Finally, as was done in matrix one, the team used the weights from matrix two Whats to arrive at weights or priorities for matrix two *Hows*.

Matrix two is then linked to matrix three in the same manner as one was to two. The *Hows* from two become *Whats* to matrix three, and new matrix three *Hows* are generated. Each matrix in the chain represents a more specific or technical description of the product or service.

Other multiple-matrix QFD schemes are considerably more elaborate than the matrix model depicted in Figure 1.3. Some schemes involve as many as 30 matrices that use the VOC's priorities to plan multiple levels of Design Detail, Quality Improvement Plans, Process Planning, Manufacturing Equipment Planning, and various Value Engineering plans.[6]

Depending on the benefits a development team needs or is willing to work through, it will construct just the initial HOQ, a large collection of interrelated matrices, or something in between. Teams will then further customize their matrices to solve "knotty" design problems. From my perspective, it does not matter what detail is used as long as it fits the decision criteria the organization and development team requires to reach a sound design decision. To quote what one of my training mentors said about the use level of QFD matrices employed, "QFD is QFD, it is just what practitioners do, period."[7]

Early History of Quality Function Deployment

"By the time design quality is determined, there should already exist critical quality assurance (QA) points that are needed to ensure certain qualities. Why then, could we not note these critical points on a QC process type chart as predetermined control points or check points for production activity, prior to production startup?" (Yoji Akao).[6] These words gave birth to what today is called QFD.

QFD was conceived in Japan in the late 1960s when Japanese industries broke from their post–World War II mode of product development through imitation and copying and moved to product development based on originality. QFD was born in an environment as a method or concept for new product development under the umbrella of Total Quality Control. During this time, between 1960 and 1965, Yoji Akao first presented the concept and method of QFD. The Japanese automobile industry was amid rapid growth, going through new product development and model changes. At that time, the following two issues became the seeds out of which QFD was conceived:

■ People started to recognize the importance of design quality, but how it could be done was not found in any books.
■ Companies were already using quality control (QC) process charts, but the charts were produced at the manufacturing site after the new products were being churned out to the customer.

Akao's original QFD design, shown in Figure 1.4, represents his vision of how quality and customer characteristics should be blended into product development before the production process.[6]

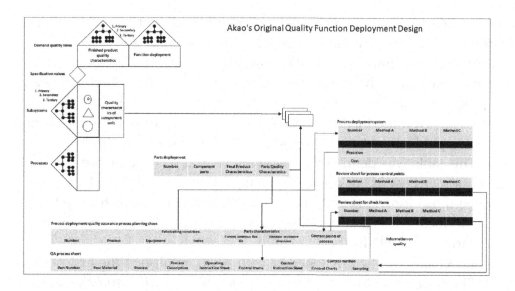

Figure 1.4   Akao's Original Quality Function Deployment Design.

The model was designed to illustrate a methodology that would ensure quality assurance and customer satisfaction design could be integrated into a product before it is manufactured. Two main objectives drove its need:

- To convert the users' needs for product benefits into substitute quality characteristics (SQCs) at the design stage of product and/or service development
- To deploy the SQCs identified at the design stage to production activities, establishing the necessary control points and check points before production start-up

If these two objectives were met, the result would be a product designed and produced that met the user's needs.

In 1966, a process assurance items table was presented by Kiyotaka Oshiumi of the Bridgestone Tire Corporation. Akao immediately saw that this table showed the links between the SQCs and process factors. Akao added a field called "Design Viewpoints" to this process assurance table and tried to get the new table used in new product development.[8]

This idea was taken to various companies for trials, but initially did not generate much public attention. Then in 1972, Akao assembled his concept and experiences and published an article entitled "*New Product Development and Quality Assurance,"* where the approach was described with the term, *hinshitsu tenkai* (quality deployment), for the first time.[9]

Before startup, important quality assurance points needed to ensure design quality throughout the production process are advocated. However, this proved still inadequate in terms of setting the design quality.

What resolved the inadequacy was a quality chart table that was created and made public by the Kobe Shipyards of Mitsubishi Heavy Industry in 1972. This table was defined the following year as a "table of systematized true customer's needs" in terms of functions that showed the relationship between those functions and the quality characteristics, which were the SQCs. All these ideas and developments were integrated and eventually helped to shape QFD further.[10]

In 1978, Sigueru Mizuno, together with Akao, published the first book on QFD, *The Customer-Driven Approach to Quality Planning and Development.* Coinciding with this publication, Toyota Auto Body developed a quality table with a roof-like structure affixed to the base matrices. The term "house of quality" was subsequently used to describe the overall quality table. This vocabulary was passed on via the American Supplier Institution by Yasusshi Furukawa, who was originally with Toyota Auto Body, as the "House of Quality," which became the name it is known by today. Figure 1.5 illustrates this original "House of Quality."[9]

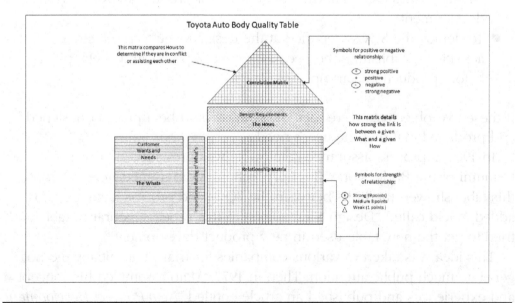

Figure 1.5   Toyota Auto Body Quality Table.

In 1983, QFD was introduced to America and Europe when Akao Yoji, Akashi Fukuhara, and Kogure Masao hosted a four-day seminar on companywide quality control in Chicago. Subsequently, development and refinements at the Toyota Auto Body led to interest on the part of the Ford Motor Company. Donald Clausing of Xerox introduced QFD to Ford. Larry Sullivan (the founder of the American Supplier Institute) and John McHugh shortly after that set up a QFD project with Ford Body Assembly and its supplier. Two Ford suppliers, the Budd Company and Kelsey-Hayes, were the first to develop a case study on QFD outside. Also in the United States, Robert Adams spearheaded the North American QFD Symposium in 1989, contributing greatly to the advancement of QFD by providing a place for QFD research and case study reports. In 1994, Glenn Mazur, Richard Zultner, and John Terninko founded the QFD Institute, which later instituted the Akao Prize in 1996.[10]

In Europe, Akao was allowed to lecture on QFD at Galgano and Associates in Italy in 1987. Subsequently, Italy became the first to implement QFD in Europe, and Galgano and Associates were the first to host a QFD Symposium in 1993. Meanwhile while in Korea, from 1978 to 1985, lectures were given at the Korean Standards Institute; however, these did not lead to practical application. In January 1996, a QFD research committee was created in Korea. In Taiwan, QFD was introduced in 1982, but the actual application occurred in 1996 with the Chinese Productivity Center leading the way. In mainland China, where the importance of new product development was gaining attention, the Quality Bureau from the State Bureau of Technical Supervision invited Akao to give seminars in Peking and Shanghai in 1994. In Brazil, QFD was introduced in 1989 in Rio de Janeiro. Then in Australia, the first Pacific Rim Symposium on Quality Deployment was organized in 1994 by Bob Hunt and hosted the third International Symposium on QFD in 1996.[11]

All these ideas and developments were integrated and helped further define the QFD methodology that "converts used demand into substitutes quality characteristics, determines the design quality of the finished product, and systematically deploys this quality into component quality, individual parts quality and process elements and their relationships."

Katsuyoshi Ishihara expanded this thinking into business process functions and showed how the two paths of value engineering and QFD could be merged. Business process function deployment subsequently became linked to what now is called "narrowly defined" QFD (see Figure 1.6).[12]

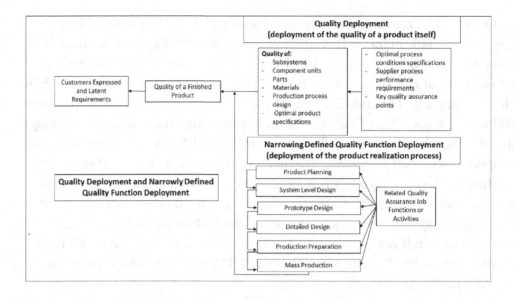

Figure 1.6 Quality Deployment and Narrowly Defined Quality Function Deployment.

A narrowly defined QFD was derived by extending the concept of value engineering that was originally applied to defining the functions of a product to the deployment of business process functions. The word "function" in QFD referred to the job functions of a product development process rather than the functions of the product itself. The job functions used to create product quality are called "quality functions." The purpose of the narrowly defined QFD was to establish a procedure network formed by various planning and operational quality assurance activities and procedures flow to achieve product quality. The network includes all activities at all stages of the product realization process, from product and technology development planning, system-level design, prototype design, and detail design to production preparation and production.

QFD Objectives

QFD focuses on deploying the attributes of a product or service desired by the customer throughout all the appropriate functional components of an organization. It provides a structured mechanism for graphically showing the deployment process. However, many refer to QFD as yet another quality tool. It is, in fact, neither a tool nor solely associated with quality. It is a product/process planning tool. Doing the planning well can help deliver a higher-quality product or service to the customer. QFD is all about taking input from the customer and translating it into technical specifics that can be acted upon. It then establishes a means to measure and monitor how well the technical specifics have been accomplished.

QFD is not new! The approach and associated matrices have been used for over a quarter of a century. It is, in a way, advanced proactive cause-and-effect analysis. Once American auto makers saw the results Japanese auto companies were getting from using QFD, they too began using it and adapting it for their needs, mostly designing products.[13]

QFD is not difficult to use! It is an effective way of taking input from the users and customers (ideas, concepts, ways the product, services, or process is utilized) and using those inputs to create highly focused offerings.

QFD is an awkward name for a wonderfully well-thought-out, integrated, synergistic set of activities. However, what is not awkward is how QFD melds three powerful concepts into a single design process model:[14]

- *Transition from customers' direct input into technical specifications.* QFD provides a structured transition from the customer's general, often not defined, expressed wants and needs into technical specifics that aid the engineer and technician designing a product and/or service into an offering with considerable customer satisfaction opportunity.
- *Rational representations of linkages between the customer and the design.* QFD uses a representation of the transitions or linkages that is easy for an individual or team to relate to and understand because it is both graphical and rationally structured.
- *Knowledge gained from a multifunctional, interactive design team.* A QFD team that is diverse, knowledgeable, and interactive will produce a more robust product. QFD team members are often co-located to assist in an ongoing exchange of information, thus increasing the probability of product and/or service design success.

QFD Benefits and Implementation Issues

Using QFD can result in the development of better products, brought to market earlier and at a price the customer is willing to pay. Based on its application in various organizations, the following three key improvements can be expected: (1) vastly improved customer satisfaction, (2) a substantial reduction in product lead times, and (3) improved communications through structured teamwork.

Documented tangible benefits, common when QFD is applied properly, are a 30–50% reduction in engineering changes; 30–50% shorter design cycles, 20–60% lower startup costs, and 20–50% fewer warranty claims.[15,16]

Conversely, empirical studies conducted have identified some QFD implementation problems. Results have shown that there is often a problem in western organizations associated with "working in teams."[5] Problems have also been noted in maintaining a commitment to the methodology and an unsuitable "organizational culture." Declared one of the most frequently cited issues facing the deployment of QFD is organizational circumstances like project definition and project management as well as team selection and team building.

What Is QFD Being Used for Today

As with any versatile tool, the applications of QFD are limited only by one's imagination. The original intent of QFD was to provide product developers with a systematic method for "deploying" the VOC into product or service design. The requirement to evaluate potential responses against needs is universal, however. In the United States, many applications have been developed that do not fit the original model intent.

The following are some examples of QFD use models that fit into this category:

■ *Course Design*—Curriculum design is a natural extension of the QFD application. Here, what are the needs of students for acquiring skills or knowledge in a certain area? The *Hows* are course modules and course teaching style elements.[17]

■ *Corporate Service Group Strategy*—Assisting organizations to assess their internal service group strategy is a natural fit for the QFD tool. The *Whats* here are the business needs of the individual members of the service client cohorts. The *Hows* are elements of the service group's initiatives.[1]

■ *Product Development Strategy*—Acting as a template for the organization to build multi-year product development plans is a fit for the QFD tool. The *Whats* are generic needs of the organization's customer cohorts. The *Hows* are product offerings planned during the planning horizon.[18]

Time and again, QFD has been extended or modified. The following are some that demand honorable mention, which will be initially introduced in this chapter but reviewed in depth in later chapters.

- *Fuzzy Logic QFD (FL-QFD)*—This is an innovative method of determining the optimum rating of engineering characteristics by simulating the QFD matrix for randomized customer attributes in the fuzzed range.[19]
- *Kano QFD (K-QFD)*—Sustainable supply chain management plays a critical role in today's organizations. K-QFD is an integrative approach where decision-making and trail laboratory (DEMTEL) is integrated with QFD through a nonlinear design that transforms customer requirements into risk factors and then into resilience measures.[18]
- *Analytic Hierarchy Process Integrated QFD (AHP-QFD)*—This decision framework uses Zero-one Goal Programming (ZOGP) to determine the design requirements an organization must possess to achieve a sustainable supply chain structure.[20]
- *Project QFD (P-QFD)*—Gaining use in both industry and academia, provides an advanced product definition methodology based on QFD principles to identify and minimize the risks of project failures due to alignment with the voice of the business (VOB).[21,22]
- *Total Quality QFD (TQ-QFD)*—This blend of Total Quality Management and QFD presents highly compatible and powerful techniques for translating the VOC into technical parameters and values. One of the most unique features is that the solution is practically implemented through the development and execution of work instructions.[23]
- *Constraint Satisfaction Problems and QFD (CSP-QFD)*—CSP-QFD uses optimization blended with QFD to generate an optimized product model during the early design stages. Scores from the QFD matrix are used to weight the sub-objectives of the optimization so that the solving strongly depends on the customers' demands.[24]

As we conclude this chapter, the last new method of employing QFD is the one that serves as the foundation for this book. A *Model-Based (MB) QFD approach to Product or Service Life-Cycle Management. MB-QFD* is a new strategy of product and/or service life-cycle management (PLM) based on computer-aided data transition. MB-QFD transforms the simple gathering of geometrical datasets from disparate repositories during the initial planning stages of a product and/or service to collecting, analyzing,

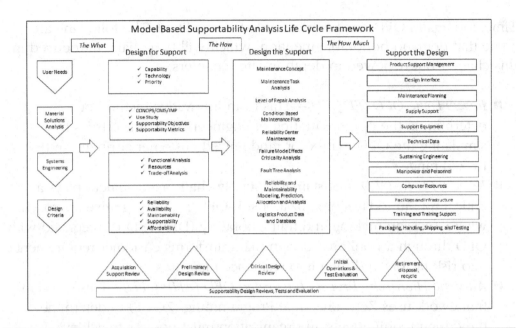

Figure 1.7 Model-Based Supportability Analysis Life-Cycle Framework.

and predicting product and/or service supportability element requirements throughout the life-cycle of that product and/or service. Figure 1.7 provides a notional representation of this MB-QFD Supportability Analysis Life-Cycle Framework.

Summary

Chapter 1 has identified that two related objectives drove the need for QFD. One is the need to convert users' needs (or customers' demands) for product benefits into SQCs at the design stage. And two, to deploy the SQCs identified at the design stage to the production activities, thereby establishing the necessary control and check points "prior" to production startup. It then addressed that the concept of quality deployment was first proposed by Yoji Akao in 1966 and expanded in his 1969 article "Quality Featuring Characteristics of Quality Control." It then guided the reader through QFDs introduction into the United States in 1983 by Yasushi Furukawa, Masao Kogore, and Yoji Akao. The chapter then introduced the reader to the fact that only one's imagination limits the application of QFD. By holding to its original intent of providing product developers with a systematic method for "deploying" the VOC into product design, it is now being used increasingly for applications that do not fit the exact "model" of product development. The chapter concluded with a discussion on what QFD is being used for today and highlighted honorable mentions of the initiative of how QFDs' uses are being expanded. A notional MB-QFD Support Analysis Life-Cycle Framework was presented and informed the reader that it will serve as the book's basis.

Chapter 2

Using Quality Function Deployment to Drive Organizational Excellence

Managing the Organization's Value

The challenges to every organization are varied, but all organizations, regardless of size or product and service offering, must compete with others within their market grouping. One area of the competition is how the organization conducts *value management*. *Value management* is concerned with creating sustainable value for its products and/or services. It can be defined as all the managerial and support processes that operate in an organization to keep it functioning properly. The primary benefits of a comprehensive value management system are that the organization gets a crystal-clear definition of what all organization stakeholders mean by value and an opportunity to balance needs and expectations between stakeholders to improve organizational performance. Value management comprises three interlocking activities: *Value Proposition Creation*, *Value Proposition Design*, and *Value In-Use Delivery*. Figure 2.1 illustrates the process flow, activities, and measurable outcomes associated with each exercise step.[25]

Because of the complex nature of the many activities associated with executing a *value management exercise*, QFD has become an instrumental tool of use. Long recognized for its attributes and uses in the *value proposition creation activity* of a product and/or service, it has more recently been applied to rapidly redefine/redesign an organization's value proposition

 DOI: 10.4324/9781003336044-3

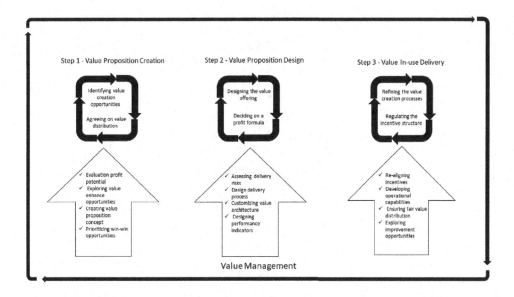

Figure 2.1   Value Management Process Flow.

as it relates to customer in-use delivery phases of value management. QFD, when applied at the earliest point in the decision-making process, ensures a mutual understanding of the context, scope, and required outcomes by the customers/users and ensures the project team has clearly defined "What" the customer wants/needs and "How" the organization can provide sustained value in product or service delivery.[26]

During the execution of this value management exercise, the needs of three diverse groups must be met. First, the customers, second, the owners, and, third, the employees. Each of these groups has varied and changing needs and expectations of the product and/or service at differing times during its life-cycle. Figure 2.2 illustrates how these groups help shape the value management exercise.[27]

Without customers, organizations cease to exist. Customer groups have varied and changing needs and expectations. Because most organizations have a wide range of customer sets with constantly changing requirements, product and/or service change is common. Owners and stakeholders have expectations of increasing organizational growth, profits, market share, and overall company performance. Employees additionally have expectations for success, job growth, a good work environment, equal pay for performance, and job security. Outside groups such as regulating, financial, recording keeping, privacy, and environmental sustainment have voices that must be considered. A tool such as QFD, with its ability to address multiple,

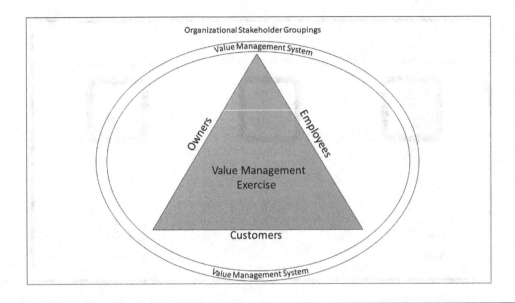

Figure 2.2   Organizational Stakeholder Groupings.

broad-ranging requirements, tracking the needs for analysis while creating value or changing how value is managed or delivered, is well-suited for the challenge.

Increasing Revenues; Decreasing Cost

All organizations, be they public or private, must provide ever-increasing value to their customers and the markets they serve to stabilize and grow. A balance is required between four organizational challenges, which must be addressed simultaneously by the organization. There are multiple needs to grow revenue, keep costs in step with market pricing, deal with shifting markets, and laser focus on the stakeholders' needs. Figure 2.3 illustrates how each of these elements directly influences the value management process.[28]

The foremost challenge in addressing these complex and multiple needs is *Revenue Growth*. Growing the top line of an organization's income statement is a formable way to address a multitude of inherent value needs of various stakeholder groups. Value, of course, is measured by each customer but, in all cases, includes quality components. Developing new products or redeveloping old ones to increase desired qualities and remove cost increase overall value. QFD can play an important role in planning, managing, and directing new value propositions from idea to product or service launch.

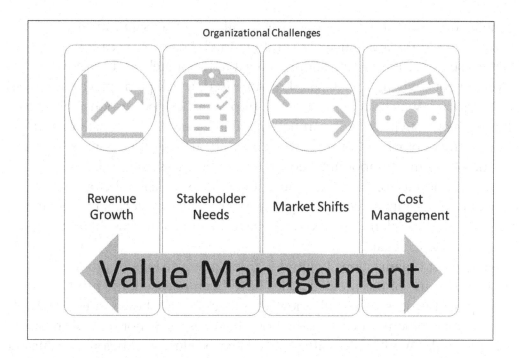

Figure 2.3   Organizational Challenges.

A second but no less daunting challenge for the organization is *Cost Management*. Here the organization must be able to keep costs in step with market pricing by appropriately designing and managing the value management process, especially the value delivery process. Some of these are non-recurring development costs, while others are contained in recurring value-delivery and value-management processes. Costs can be designed out of products, delivery, and support processes. As a management tool, QFD can focus development efforts in the right areas, thus avoiding wasted time and materials on non-customer-valued pursuits. It warrants mentioning here that this is also an attribute and focus area of Six Sigma. We will explore how QFD and Six Sigma work together and are complementary in Chapter 11.

Dealing With Market Shifts and Cycle-Time Reduction

The third major challenge organizations regularly face dealing with *Market Shifts*. Broadly defined, a market shift is a significant change in the structure of an industry. It may range from how a product and/or service is designed, manufactured, distributed, or sold, potentially affecting sales. Ideally, these market shifts are anticipated and planned; however, occasionally, they do surprise. For organizations to react appropriately and quickly to developments, whether anticipated or surprised, a risk plan (playbook) must be developed, which identifies step-by-step activities and responsibilities for all mitigating activities. QFD can help plan, align tasks, direct action, and manage the deployment of resources ensuring successful responses.[29]

One of the most important "moves" in the business "game" is for an organization to make new products or services available before the competition. By introducing new products or services before a competitor can offer an equivalent one, the organization can rob market share that may be impossible to regain.

Since most organizations begin designing new versions of products or services as some of the previous ones have been released, the product development process is usually viewed as a "cycle" as shown in Figure 2.4.[26]

The development process, like all other processes, is not quite as neat as a simple circle. Work often starts on the next product well before the current product is ready to be sold. It is not abnormal for several processes to be executed simultaneously or "concurrently" (more on this in Chapter 3).

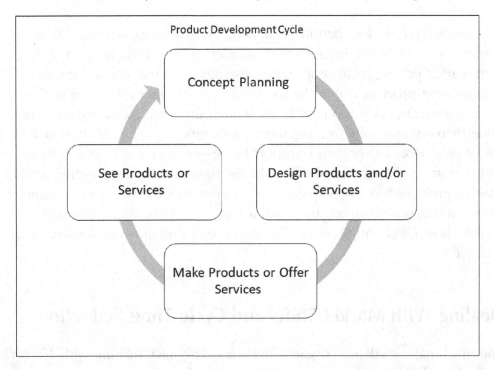

Figure 2.4 **Product Development Cycle.**

QFD, by its nature, is an important key to "cycle" time reduction. QFD helps development teams make key decisions early in the development process when the cost of a decision is relatively low. Some of the ways QFD contributes to reduced cycle time are:[26]

- *Reduces Midcourse Changes*—Midcourse changes, such as shifts in priorities, key vendor replacements, or replacement of key technologies, cause considerable havoc on development schedules. QFD provides linkages between all elements required to produce the product, thus making it easier to evaluate potential impacts on associated product elements before final commitment.
- *Provides a Summary-at-a-Glance of a Project Strategy*—When a project has been planned using QFD, the HOQ and matrices are used to provide a summary-at-a-glance of the project. A well-done QFD planning process will lay out all project needs.
- *Helps Reduce Errors in Implementation*—By working through the QFD process, the development team ensures a common vision of customer needs and responds to them. This common vision and detailed planning starting from the same plan results in consistent follow-through across the entire development team.

QFD—A Rapid Product Development and Communication Tool

A key to competitiveness is rapidly responding to the competition by producing new products and services. Often an organization reverts to "Rapid Product Development" (RPD) to aid them in this process. RPD can be defined as developing new products in the shortest timescales possible while ensuring that the criteria of desirability, feasibility, and viability are met. Many challenges are encountered when executing RPD. Figure 2.5 illustrates the process steps that are normally taken when performing RPD.[12]

There are many challenges to effectively executing these RPD process steps for products and/or services. However, QFD has proven itself a very effective tool that can be used to minimize these challenges and effectively facilitate the RPD process. By RPD process, here are some ways QFD can aid the development process.

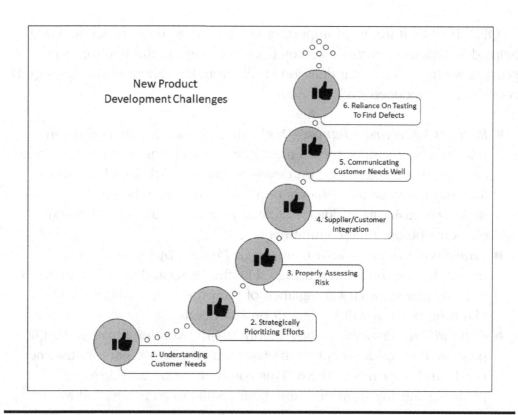

Figure 2.5 New Product Development Challenges.

- *Understanding Customer Needs*—Inadequate research into customer needs leads to varied, uniformed opinions. This leads to disagreement among the development team members and creates delays in decision-making and individuals working at cross-purposes. QFD provides a standardized method of representing customer needs. A standardized method of mapping customized needs for product or service development decisions helps reduce differences of opinion.
- *Strategically Prioritizing Efforts*—One key to cycle time is to invest in what is important and resist investing in what is not important. Failure to take time to work on capabilities important to the customer leads to noncompetitive products. QFD helps developers decide on the relative importance of their choices by deriving *their* proprieties from their *customers'* priorities.
- *Properly Assessing Risk*—Product developers often plunge into projects with unnecessary risk built in. These risks typically relate to design that cannot be effectively manufactured or would be unserviceable. Developers often feel forced to commit to schedules they cannot meet

and those who would build the product offering feel forced to commit to volumes, quality levels, and cost limitations that cannot be met. QFD can help make these risks more visible, and such related tools as Failure Mode and Effects Analysis, which is inherent to the QFD tool, can be applied for risk reduction and mitigation. Also, Pugh's Concept Selection Process, which is adjunct to QFD, can help development teams to identify and synthesize less risky alternatives.

■ *Supplier/Customer Integration*—A product or service is typically conceived by a core team. After developers have worked out the details to a certain point, they decompose the design into subsystems or sub-services. They then decide whether those subsystems or sub-services will be purchased from external or internal suppliers.

Regardless of whether an external or internal supplier is chosen to design the subsystem or subservice, interaction with that supplier is "at arm's length," meaning that regular meetings and communications are conducted at designated intermediate points, and when the task is finished, the result is presented to the core team. Such a "throw it over the wall" method often leads to unsatisfactory, even disastrous results, because the suppliers' subsystem or sub-service may not meet the ultimate customer's needs.

QFD has proven to be an excellent tool in minimizing and often alleviating this problem. Development teams comprise representatives from external and internal organizations vested in the product or service being developed.

■ *Communicating Customer Needs*—Ensuring that the core team is appropriately represented by all parties who have a vested interest in developing a product or service is critical to ensuring the customer needs are front-and-center. Equally as critical is the method by which these needs are conveyed. The normal method by which it is done is by a "specification."

A specification by itself, whether verbal or written, a page of text or a thousand pages, can never express all required to build an error-free product or service. Developing a product or service by simply meeting a specification is like flying an aircraft without visual or instrument reference; you are "flying blind." Too many details, speed, other aircraft, and weather conditions cannot be readily discerned.

QFD is a tool that can help in this area by providing a means for the development team's discussion and for the translation of customers' needs to each team member using terminology and language appropriate to that level. In this respect, the resulting discussion is as important as the specification interruption because it carries with it all the subtle nuances of meaning that qualify and elaborate on the static language of the specification. QFD makes a specification come "alive."

■ *Reliance of Testing to Find Defects*—Testing programs can find numerous defects in products or services. As a developer of complex aeronautical systems in trying to meet tight deadlines, I have submitted work to a tester that I know would have problems. In designing complex hardware and software products, many defects are usually found during internal testing, and developers spend a great deal of time debating which to fix by process changes and which to contain through inspection. However, testing often comes only at the end of the design and development cycle. The truth is that more than 70% of defects are design related, and by the time they are found, it can be too late to fix the design. Assembly or delivery goals must often be compromised in lieu of implementing a design change. Therefore, design-defect management remains an unhappy fact of life.

Despite all the internal testing, we often hear customers complain about the defective product or service they have been offered. Six Sigma methods create the means to measure, analyze, and improve the incident of defects caused by faulty design and processes and then verify when they are eliminated. This defect elimination must be considered an *input* to the next design iteration or any related designs to cease dependence on inspection and thus lower iteration cost.[26]

QFD provides a method for linking customer needs and their relative importance to all development activities, including testing and defect elimination. As a result, it can be readily applied to prioritize testing and repair activities to meet customer needs best.

QFD's Role as a Communication Tool

In our discussion on how QFD supports RPD, we reviewed many challenges encountered in product or service development. In dealing with those challenges, a recurring theme that tends to cause delays in product development initiatives is communications.

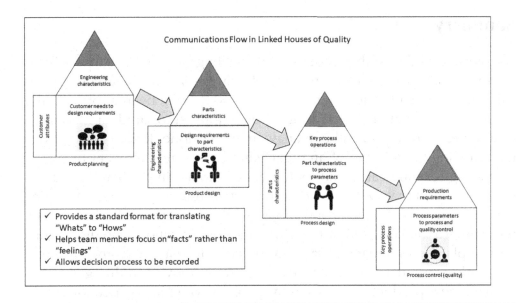

Figure 2.6   Communications Flow in Linked Houses of Quality.

QFD provides a method for individuals involved at various steps of the development process to communicate with one another. It does this by translating the language of one development phase into the language of the next and leaving a "golden thread" to follow should any questions arise. The fact that representatives from each phase perform these translations "together" increases the likelihood that everyone will understand the translation. Figure 2.6 illustrates the communication flow in linked Houses of Quality (HOQs).[30]

Once the development team has completed its translation and recorded it in a QFD matrix, it can be presented and explained to others who were not present during the scheduled QFD workshop. These team members can examine the translation process in minute detail if required, focusing on areas of special interest to them.

QFD's contribution to improving communication is then threefold:

■ It provides a standard format for translating "Whats" to "Hows."
■ It helps development team members focus on the facts rather than feelings.
■ It allows the decision process to be recorded in the matrices, where it can be re-examined, re-visited, and even modified at any time.

Summary

Chapter 2 introduced the reader to the challenges in which almost all organizations must compete in terms of value creation, value delivery, and value management. And, while QFD has traditionally been applied in the value-creation area, it is increasingly being applied to rapidly redesign how value delivery and value management are done. It then addressed that growing the top line of an organization's income statement thus increasing revenue can be attributed directly to adding "inherent value" to customers, and that QFD played an important role in planning, managing, and directing new "value propositions" while simultaneously showing a reduction to the cost side of the profit-and-loss equation. The discussion then explained that markets can shift quickly once a new competitor enters the market and that one of the most important "moves" in the "game" is to make new products or services available before the competition. It then emphasized that QFD, with a key focus on "cycle time reduction," helped development teams make key decisions early in the development cycle. Finally, the chapter concluded with a discussion of the challenges of RPD and how QFD contributed by standardizing customer needs, prioritizing efforts, providing risk assessments, and providing enhanced communications.[31-34]

Chapter 3

Step-by-Step Quality Function Deployment

Using Sequential and Concurrent Design

In using the QFD methodology to design a product, service, or process, the design team is expected to obtain and apply information not acquired by other design approaches. Just as market modeling and testing are necessary to answer certain questions, QFD activities allow organizations to formulate and answer questions that have not been considered. In addition, the knowledge gained gives the creators of the product/service/process a much better understanding of the customer's needs and wants and the operational environment.

It is assumed that the goal of any design project is to move from a defined market segment (or related product concept) to a fully ramped production posture as rapidly as possible using an optimal mix of resources all while keeping the current product laser focused on the target market. This must be accomplished with as few modifications to design after release, often called Engineering Change Orders.[29]

Breaking Down the Walls of Product or Service Design

Ever wondered how many people it took to bring that shiny new product or service you purchased from an idea to the actual offering? It likely took a team comprised of many disciplines to include industrial design, mechanical and manufacturing engineering, logistics engineers, along with supply chain

DOI: 10.4324/9781003336044-4

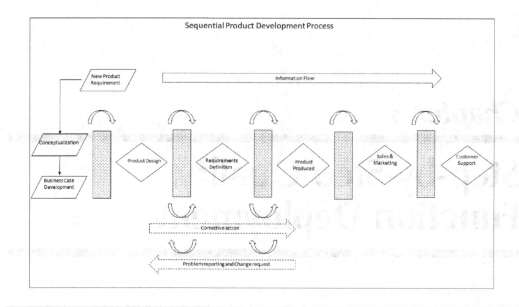

Figure 3.1 Sequential Product Development Process.

professionals, graphic designers, packaging design engineers, financial specialists, human resource specialists, sales and marketing specialists, and more, to come together to turn a great idea into a product that will excite you and hopefully satisfy your need or want.

How these roles interact with one another and at what point in the product or service development the roles interact makes a huge difference in the overall development timeline, cost, and even quality of the end product or service.

The sequential design approach, often called the "over-the-wall" approach," came about after the Industrial Revolution, with the introduction of the assembly line and task specialization.[12] Figure 3.1 illustrates the sequential product development process. In the "over-the-wall approach" to product or service design, each development team member performs his or her task and then passes that collateral on to the next team members. The term "over-the-wall approach" came about because each team member's work is handed over to the hypothetical (or actual) cubicle wall to the next person. This methodology relies on tasks being performed sequentially, with little need for communication or collaboration.

The primary advantage of this method is that it makes a highly complex project easy to understand and track. It also makes it easy to identify underperformers. For this method to work effectively, each person in the development chain has to be given all of the right deliverables and/or specifications from the previous development team member and his/her task exactly as required before passing it off to the next team member. Of course, things do not always go as planned. When an issue arises, the work has to be passed backward over the wall and then sent forward over the wall again. This is called reverse flow and is a major source of this method's inefficiency.

In the concurrent product or service approach, development team members from different job functions collaborate early in the design process and often.[12] In this approach, there are no "walls," and everyone works together. Figure 3.2 illustrates a concurrent product development process flow.

The general idea behind this approach is that by collaborating, team members can identify and solve issues early in the design process and create efficiency by having different team members work on a task simultaneously.

To successfully use the concurrent approach to product development, more structure is required. In addition, more discipline is required to avoid missing tasks and subtasks. The QFD methodology is an excellent tool here because it breaks down the overall design process into discrete tasks so it can overlap major activities. Also, the QFD structure assists the design team by guiding team members through the sequence of tasks in an orderly manner, so none gets overlooked.

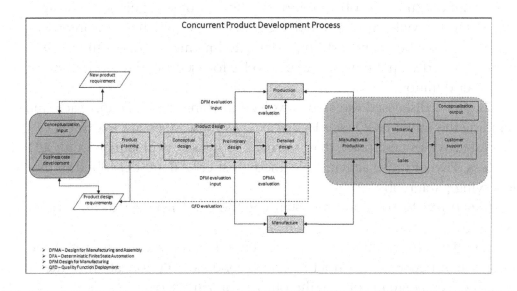

Figure 3.2   Concurrent Product Development Process.

When QFD is being used on product design, a typical cross-functional team would include design engineering, process (manufacturing) engineering, research and development (R&D), marketing/sales, quality assurance, and test, field and customer service, manufacturing, supply chain, and logistics, and if the project is project-driven, project engineering.

Developing a Design Process

Individuals who have had exposure to the product design process often muse on what it would be like to A, have a design process without the constant pressures of time deadlines and B, have unlimited access to the best and brightest personnel in the organization as well as those with specialized knowledge from outside the organization. However, no matter how much we wish otherwise, the actual design process is driven by the internal and external realities of the customer. The competitive marketplace and the availability and use of an organization's limited resources drive the product design process. Time to market is almost always critical for market share, either to gain market or to maintain it. Introducing a product today will yield the largest sales volume. Each day that passes after a competitor has introduced a product reduces market share for all later entries.

Additionally, there is always a limit on the hours available for knowledgeable personnel to work on product or service issues. The maximum output to be obtained in the shortest time requires the design process to be well-organized and structured with guidelines for internal, core team members, and external contracted members. Using the QFD approach to design allows the issues to be focused on and worked on over a shorter duration.

Chapter 1 discussed the steps involved in using the QFD approach and building the initial HOQ (see Figure 1.2). As these steps are executed, several activities take place that is crucial to a successful launch of a QFD process. Five of those activities deemed most critical are described in the following paragraphs.[34,35]

Activity one focuses on understanding the customer's needs and wants (see Figure 3.3).

Data derived from this analysis are refined, and a second subset of the information becomes the input for the second step. Prioritization of the customer segment(s) is one of the outputs of activity one.

Activity two involves gathering the VOC and understanding the context in which the customer makes a statement (see Figure 3.4).[19,35]

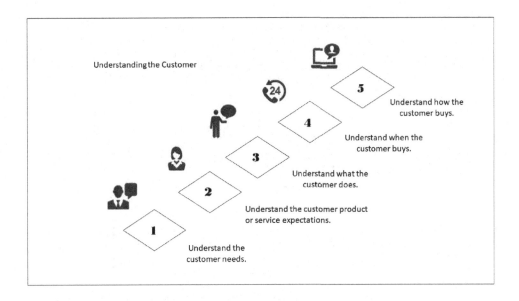

Figure 3.3   Understanding the Customer.

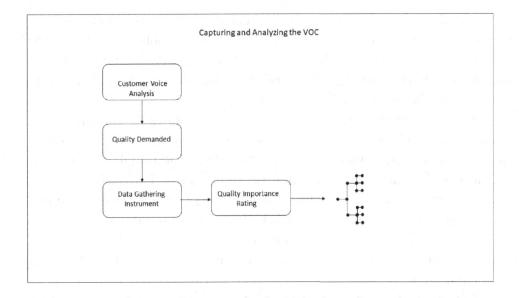

Figure 3.4   Capturing and Analyzing the VOC.

Contextual information clarifies the customer's verbatim information. The purpose of this activity is to establish a clear understanding of requirements. These subjective performance requirements are often referred to as demanded qualities. Each QFD analysis builds on these demand qualities and often becomes the foundation of further activities such as questionnaires, one-on-one interviews, focus groups, and so forth.

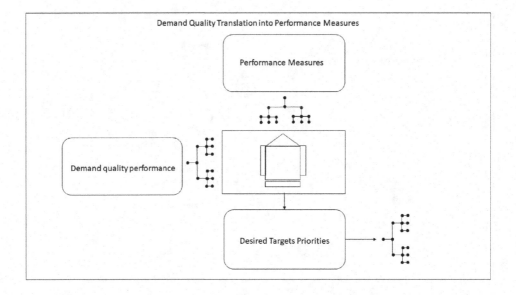

Figure 3.5   Demand Quality Translation into Performance Measures.

Activity three translates the customer's statements and evaluations into a design team's performance measures, language, and priorities (see Figure 3.5).[19,35]

This translation is especially important because it typically takes the customer's language, such as ("comfortable" and "user friendly,") and turns it into technical language for the designer.

The design team sets priorities for demand qualities by combining organizational priorities with the customer's (importance ranking). The team then transforms customer's subjective demanded qualities into technical performance measures that become output. Performance measures are also used to establish desired target values for the design. These target values form the "wish list" that drives the design and development effort. If the translation from subjective to objective is done here, the technicians and engineers have a better chance of hitting technical targets.

Activity four often employs a Stuart Pugh system for generating and comparing new concepts (see Figure 3.6).[19,21,35]

Target costs are often integrated into the generation cost. The output from the previous demand quality and performance measure becomes the input for this activity. The selected "best" concept and associated specifications are linked to the manufacturing process and the subsequent database.

Activity five, the final activity, links the production specifications to the manufacturing conditions (see Figure 3.7).[19,35,36]

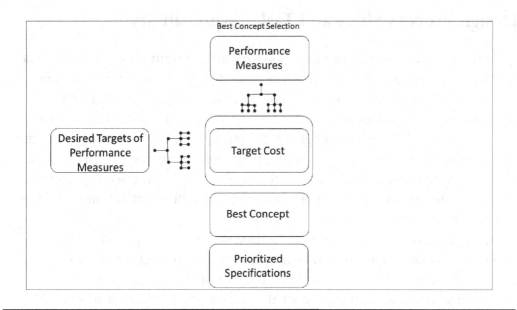

Figure 3.6   Best Concept Selection.

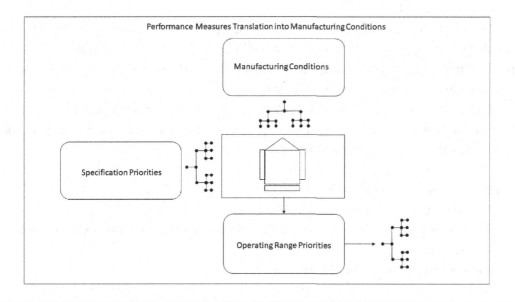

Figure 3.7   Performance Measures Translation Into Manufacturing Conditions.

Identifying the knowledge base for the relationship between operating conditions and knowledge base for the relationship between operating conditions and product performance is part of the manufacturing database. The output of this activity becomes part of the quality control systems or procedures for assuring that the manufacturing process is consistent with variability.

Design Process Steps and Task Responsibility

QFD does not replace an organization's existing design process, nor should it. You can integrate QFD into a sequential design process, a concurrent design process, or your unique design process. The point is that QFD is a supporting tool that can add value at any point in the product or service design process. Adding any single QFD activity will aid in the understanding of the input being used. For example, you could merely apply QFD to the production process. Taking that approach, you might produce a product or service the customer does not want, but you will inevitably improve the production process.

As organizations contemplate how they should employee QFD, it is equally important that the standardization of the product development process be addressed. It is necessary and important that organizations standardize and maintain a product development process that meets measurement criteria in both its repeatability and reproducibility. The following is a process that I have used over the years, which is very practitioner oriented.

As a first step, I find that structuring design activities acts as a catalyst for the planning process. Since QFD is aligned closely with quality management/assurance using the Deming/Shewart cycle (see Figure 3.8) so it works well to create a design flow.[37]

The *Plan-Do-Check/Study-Act (PDCA)* cycle is a four-step problem-solving iterative technique used to improve business processes. Each element possesses the following characteristics:

Plan—create a model to be tested
Do—Try out the model
Check/Study—Compare the actual results obtained with the expected/pre-dicted results
Act—Modify or solidify the theory

Using a cyclic flow like the one depicted in Figure 3.8 reveals the relationship between a design process flow and the organization's functions. It additionally introduces a different way of looking at the design process, often generating new and useful insights.

Employing the PDCA cycle approach in creating a design process requires adapting its elemental terms and altering its process from proactive to reactive.

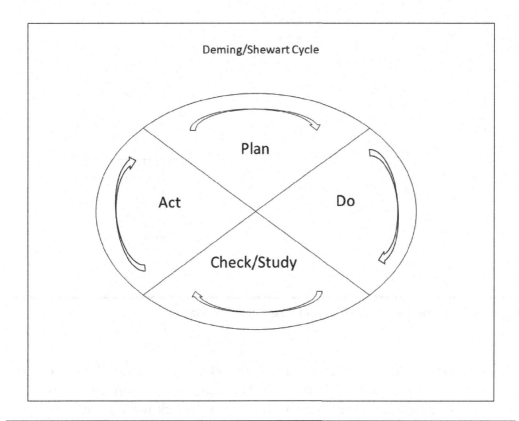

Figure 3.8   Deming/Shewart Cycle.

In the following terms, adaptations apply:

- The P (plan) integrates and translates all technology and concept-relevant data from the VOC into design requirements (performance measures).
- The D (do) includes integrating those technologies and concepts and confirming that the design satisfies the requirements.
- The C (check/study) verifies the product benchmarking performance against competitors.
- The A (act) helps determine whether the design cycle is completed, or modifications must be made to correct deviations noted in step C.

Since the PDCA cycle is a proactive process that attempts to determine what problems may exist before they occur and create a structure that can deal with problem causes and prevent them from happening. The design modeling process requires a reactive cycle because analyses are performed

Design Process Steps and Responsibility Matrix

	Process Steps Responsibility	Marketing/Sales	Personnel	Finance	Quality Control	Engineering	Production/Operations	Logistics
	◉ Primary ○ Secondary							
C	Competitive Assessment	◉	○	○				
A	Define New Product Concept or Improve Existing Design	◉			○	○		
P	Define Technology Concept					◉	○	
D	Define Concept Requirements				○	○	◉	
	Design Process Steps				Responsibility Matrix			

Figure 3.9   Design Process Steps and Responsibility Matrix.

after they occur. Therefore, the order of the PDCA process is altered to start with the last two steps, Check and Act. This mirrors the more traditional approach to product design and can be used to check the current performance of existing products.

The CAPD cycle can be used to identify the tasks needed to design a product. An example of a CAPD cycle element alignment with the design step is illustrated in Figure 3.9.[35,38]

Design Process Steps

Within each cycle element, several steps must be completed. Each of these steps has one or more tasks associated with it. For example, the Plan element should include defining technology concept requirements. The process may also include additional tasks besides those that have been part of a traditional design process. Though they may have been performed informally in the past, these tasks perhaps were missing from the formalized design process. In creating a design process, all steps should be recognized and included in the formal procedure.

Responsibility for Design Process Steps

Once cycle elements have been formalized, the primary responsibility requires assignment to the appropriate organizational function. A notional

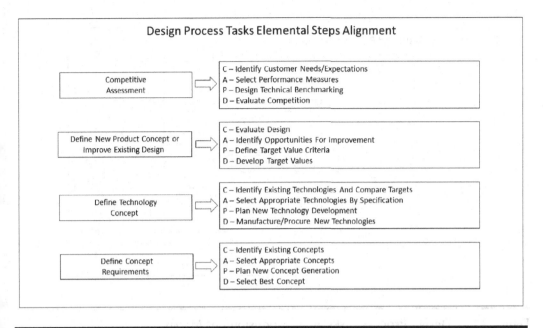

Figure 3.10   Design Process Tasks Elemental Steps Alignment.

responsibility matrix like the one shown in Figure 3.9 (right-hand panel) is often useful for summarizing these function/responsibility alignments. The functional group responsible for the function determines when it is complete and the time to move on to the next elemental step.

Identifying Tasks Within the Design Element Steps

The CAPD cycle can now be used to identify key tasks for each elemental step in the design process. Each step has one or more tasks assigned. Figure 3.10 illustrates the alignment of a task to elemental steps.[35,38]

Depending upon the steps of the design process, key tasks may differ. For more complex design processes, it may be necessary to use an additional CAPD cycle, similar to a Work Breakdown Structure (WBS), to identify sub-tasks within key tasks.

Functional Responsibility for Key Tasks

Using the same responsibility matrix design presented in Figure 3.9, the organization identifies the functional responsibility for each key task. A notional illustration of this is shown in Figure 3.11.[35,38]

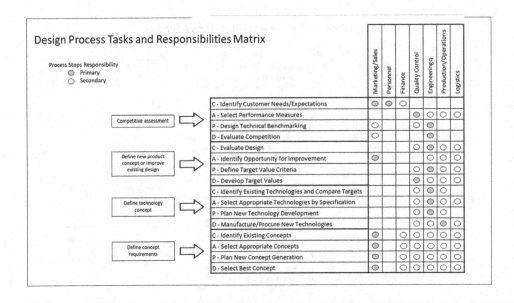

Figure 3.11   Design Process Tasks and Responsibilities Matrix.

The Design Process Steps, Tasks, Responsibilities, and Process Flow

Once the alignment of elemental steps, design tasks, and responsibilities has been accomplished, a Design Process can be created. A notional illustration of a Design Process Steps, Tasks, Responsibilities, and Process Flow is presented in Figure 3.12.[35,38]

Figure 3.12 has rows that contain the elemental design steps and key tasks. The columns represent first the task by organizational function and then by activity. The rectangles identify activities, and the location of the rectangle the functional participation in the activity. The arrows illustrate the flow of documents or decisions.

The Design Process Steps, Tasks, Responsibilities, and Process Flow mapping show the design team members. During product development, the design team needs many documents, such as market analyses, customer requirements, and specifications. These reports would generally be regarded as reports within the design process and are shown in the right-hand column of Figure 3.12. However, for clarity, these documents have been excerpted, and only a sample of QFD documents is shown. These documents align QFD activities with organizational product development functional activities, so the team can take the design process and the QFD

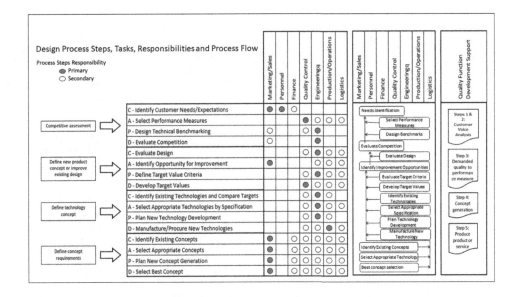

Figure 3.12   Design Process Steps, Tasks, Responsibilities, and Process Flow.

methodology step by step and allow those involved in design activities to add QFD where it is felt appropriate.

Summary

The overall theme of Chapter 3 was to familiarize the reader with how QFD can fit in their organization. It began with a discussion of comparing and contrasting sequential and concurrent design processes then, addressing how QFD is used in each to compress the total time from market identification and concept selection to fully ramped production. It then addressed the product design process, concerning time and resources, then by discussing the QFD design and process steps, key tasks, and the responsibilities for each of those tasks. Five major QFD process steps were introduced, defined, and illustrated by example, discussing how they are employed. A step-by-step process flow was provided that would aid the reader in their QFD initiatives. The chapter concluded with a discussion of several types of process charting examples: design process tree, design process task responsibility, product design process, and recommended sequencing chart of QFD activities.

Figure 3.11. Design Process Steps, Tasks, Responsibilities, and Procedures.

Summary

PART 2

Chapter 4

Translating Supportability Aspirations Into Measurable Characteristics

The System Supportability Challenge

Supportability planning and execution activities are interwoven with the technical disciplines of reliability, maintainability, and testability. Because each of these disciplines is equally important, it is often difficult for the supportability practitioner to determine where the actions of one discipline stop and another's start. Actually, this is the way it should be! Producing a system requires a joint effort by all organizational disciplines who must work together as one team, each having a stated role in the overall objectives of the development team. Supportability in this context is defined as "the inherent characteristics of the system and the enabling system elements that allow effective and efficient sustainment throughout the system's life-cycle." Inherent characteristics must be measurable, so predictions can be made on how best to support the system within a predefined environment and usage profile.

For something to be predicted or measured, it must be intrinsically measurable. This can be considered the core of the historical indifference given to supportability assessment and planning for a system starting in the conceptual development stage. Supportability was viewed as something that happened after the system was placed into service. It could not be adequately determined until sufficient system usage had occurred to see

DOI: 10.4324/9781003336044-6

Table 4.1   Supportability Requirements Stated as Aspirations

Supportability Requirements Stated as Aspirations
➤ Be easy to maintain.
➤ Be cost effective to maintain.
➤ Be safe to maintain.
➤ Minimum requirements for staffing.
➤ Minimum requirements for test equipment.
➤ Maximum use of existing tools and support equipment.
➤ Minimum requirements for new resources.
➤ Maximum use of existing facilitates.
➤ Maximum use of standard parts.
➤ Quickly prepared for ship or transport.
➤ Can be transported by standard modes
➤ Can be interfaced with existing support systems

what was needed. Descriptions of support requirements were stated as aspirations rather than measurable realities. Table 4.1 illustrates some of these unmeasurable support aspirations.[7,39,40]

There is nothing wrong with the way these issues are stated. They are all valid. The problem is that none of them are measurable. If a requirement is not measurable, it cannot be tested, and therefore its achievement can never be completely realized or verified. The challenge for the supportability planning professional is to take aspirations and translate them into measurable requirements that can be integrated into the system design process. This will allow supportability characteristics to be included as measurable requirements like performance characteristics.

Easy to Maintain

The requirement for a system to be easy to maintain is common sense. However, easy can be defined in several ways. What is easy for one customer may not be easy for another. "Easy" often suggests that the maintenance of an item can be done in a short period of time, using simple techniques, with few resources and little chance of not doing the maintenance properly. The most important of these attributes is the speed of completing the maintenance action.

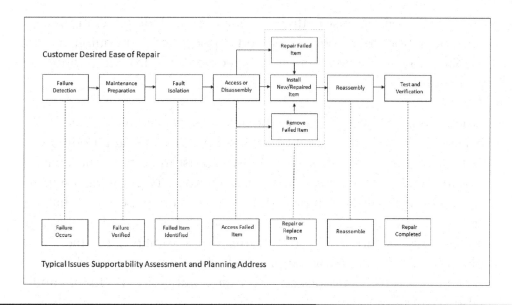

Figure 4.1   Customer Ease of Repair and Supportability Assessment and Planning Issue Address.

Translating "easy" into clearly measurable criteria is a challenging task. Figure 4.1 illustrates a typical maintenance process flow of the activities a customer desires to be done easily and the typical issues supportability assessment and planning address for each maintenance action.

Maintainability considers the maintenance process in developing the mean time to repair (MTTR), which is the weighted average time to return the system to operable condition. It is assumed by maintainability that the resources needed to repair or replace the failed item will be available in the right quantities and at the right location. Supportability planning then addresses each failure issue and plans accordingly to ensure that overall system design is optimal. The following is a logic walk-through of the process followed by the supportability planning team:

■ *Failure occurs*
The maintenance process begins with some detection that a system failure has occurred. The system's design must be such that an unambiguous alert of failure has occurred. Inspection must lead to the identification of the failed item. This process is called "troubleshooting," the accuracy of which is critical. The troubleshooting procedure should have as few and simple as possible. Supportability assessment

and planning must ensure that all resources, including technical documentation, tools, personnel, and support and test equipment, are available to resolve every possible outcome of the troubleshooting procedure.

■ *Fault isolation*

Troubleshooting should lead to the actual item that failed. More complex systems have self-diagnostics capability through a built-in test (BIT). A system with self-diagnostics must indicate a failure and isolate the failure to a single item (avoid ambiguity groupings) which can then be repaired or replaced. However, there is potential that any self-diagnostics can give a false indication and erroneously indicate that a failure has occurred. Because of this, supportability assessment and planning follow the following protocol when accessing troubleshooting procedures, self-diagnostics accuracy rate, ambiguity resolution, and false alarm rate.

■ *Spares, repair parts, and materials*

If the fault isolation results indicate, an item has failed and requires replacement, a repair/replacement must be affected. Recall that MTTR is calculated assuming necessary resources are available to support system maintenance. Therefore, supportability assessment and planning must link repair requirements to develop a "resource package" unique to the item requiring repair.

■ *System design for maintainability*

I remember vividly the first time I assisted my crew chief in the removal of a blade on the rotor head of our aircraft. I smashed my knuckles several times against the drop-stops and was very upset that I could not get a full range of motion in turning the ratchet. A system should be designed so that any item that must be repaired/removed can be reached with minimal steps and as much ease as possible. To minimize the time and cost of maintenance, supportability assessment and planning should ensure that the system is designed to accommodate the needs of maintenance. It has been my experience that following seven simple rules when initially designing a system can dramatically affect the MTTR of a failed item.[41-45]

The first of these is *standardization*. The smallest number of parts should be designed into the system with as much compatibility as possible. Also, keeping the design simple is often difficult, and the payoff is fewer parts, fewer tools, less complexity, and fewer physical resources needed to affect a repair. The second is *modularization*.

The system should comprise as many standard sizes, shapes, and modular units as possible. Lego bricks come to mind! Supportability personnel often work side by side with reliability and maintainability (R&M) personnel. This is to ensure that if different configurations are required, a standard structure should be considered so that interchange of compatible parts can alter functionality without changing the majority of the product. The third feature is *functional packaging*. Again, working alongside R&M personnel, a "kitting" process can be developed where materials needed to affect the repair are gathered together in one package so that the task can be completed quickly and completely. The fourth feature is *interchangeability*. Minimize the drive to create a system that requires unique components. Supportability planning and R&M specialists must reject the "customer form factor" and select interchangeable components. Also, it is critical to manage and control the dimensional functional design tolerances. The fifth feature is *accessibility*. This goes back to my bruised knuckles example. If a component requires replacement or adjustment, then it should permit access. Supportability assessment and planning should consider tooling, lighting environment, and experience of personnel affecting the action. The sixth feature is *malfunction annunciation* goes hand in hand with that system self-diagnostics, a key step in performing any maintenance is knowing what caused the problem or which parts require replacement. Minimizing the need for inspection tools and diagnostics minimizes the time/cost of any corrective procedures. The seventh feature is *identification*. They are naming the parts with unique identifiers where possible aids in streamlining documentation, procedures, and maintenance tasks. Supportability planning must be mindful of being consistent and providing meaningful or memorable naming conventions to avoid confusion.

■ *Repair or replace*
The decision as to whether an item should be repaired or replaced is often determined by two criteria: time and resources. The MTTR for an item indicates the average time to return it to an operable condition. The maximum time to repair MAXTTR is a limitation on time to perform any single action. Any item approaching MAXTTR should be a candidate for replacement vice repair. The other consideration when making a repair or replacement decision is that of resources. For example, there may be times when the removal of the next higher assembly is timelier and requires fewer resources.

- *Disassembly and reassembly*
  The design of a system should consider requirements for physical disassembly and reassembly. Modularization of the design, where items are divided into compact segments that can be easily and rapidly exchanged with a replacement module, should be used. Captive fasteners should be used to lessen the number of nuts and bolts.
- *Verification accuracy*
  The test required to verify that a maintenance action has been successful should be accurate. Therefore, it is suggested that the same test used for fault isolation be used for fault repair verification. This eliminates the requirement for an additional type of test.

Systems whose design characteristics achieve these seven areas have proven to be much more supportable during their lifetime.

Cost-Effective to Maintain

As far as user requirements go, this may be the hardest actually to translate into measurable criteria. In many respects, system effectiveness is measurable; cost-effectiveness is not. The best way to view this aspiration is from the standpoint of functional system value compared to having a system that is not functional due to maintenance requirements. The situation must be addressed regarding the value a customer places on having a system operational vice in-operable.

Safe to Maintain

System safety assessment and planning are responsible for identifying potential hazards that may cause injury. This is normally done by examining maintenance actions after the design is completed. However, several design characteristics can be included in a system specification to avoid potential hazards. Most of these tend to be common sense. However, they deserve to be mentioned and addressed. Figure 4.2 illustrates some of the more common safety design characteristics to consider.[7,39,46]

The system must be constructed using inherently safe materials. Designs containing caustic or other hazardous materials should be avoided unless necessary. Systems constructed of nonhazardous materials may require hazardous materials for maintenance. Using some solvents, degreasing compounds, flushing fluids, and lubricants may create a hazardous situation

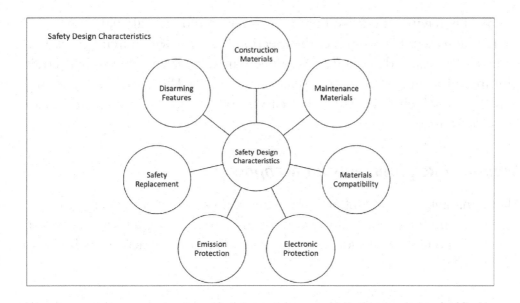

Figure 4.2   Safety Design Characteristics.

for maintenance personnel. For example, I remember limiting the exposure of methyl ethyl ketone (MEK) to maintenance personnel as they were preparing areas to be painted.

In certain cases, two safe materials can be hazardous when combined. For example, this can happen when designing a system such as an aircraft jet fuel starter (JFS), and varying types of metals are used in its construction. A materials compatibility expert should be one to make the call in such circumstances.

A system must be designed to protect those performing maintenance from electrical shock. Systems should be designed with a positive mechanical switch to shut off all power. However, in circumstances where maintenance can be performed while systems are operating, the system must possess one of two characteristics: the ability to isolate a component from the power source or design the system so that removal of the component can be performed without exposure to electrical shock. This is called "hot swapping."

The technology baseline of a system indicates if it presents the potential for hazardous emissions. I recall the time spent trimming engines while the aircraft was operating. While I truly love the "smell of jet fuel" it can be overwhelming if taken in large doses. Other examples of hazardous emissions include gas, vapors, radiation, electrostatic discharge, and liquids.

Systems having explosive components create additional challenges for maintenance. For example, the ejection seats on wing aircrafts have cartridge-activated devices (CADs), which are explosive devices that require pinning (disarming) before any seat maintenance. The same is true for the wing racks, which have CADs that can be blown off the aircraft in a case of hung ordinance.

Minimum Requirements for Manpower

Maintainability assessment and planning analyze a system's design to minimize the time required to perform the maintenance activity. However, the determination of personnel required to perform the activity is based on five criteria:

- How often must each maintenance action need to be performed?
- How long would it take to perform the maintenance action?
- How many personnel would it take to perform the maintenance action?
- Number of systems supported by the maintenance action.
- System usage rate.

The frequency of performing a maintenance action results from reliability predictions. The duration it takes the maintenance action comes from the maintainability predictions. The number it takes to perform the maintenance depends upon largely on its physical characteristics. Human factors assessment and planning will be involved in establishing these parameters.

These issues, combined with the number of systems to be supported in a specific location and the usage of a system, can result in personnel requirements. Figure 4.3 illustrates a notional labor hour calculation for a fleet of aircraft.[30]

This, however, relates exactly to the number of personnel needed to perform the maintenance activity. This is where the challenge arises. How many personnel must be present at any one time to provide the necessary labor? In theory, if each system failure occurs independently at different times, then only two people are required. But the reality is that several systems may require maintenance simultaneously. The establishment of operational availability goals generally addresses this. The other way is to create design-to goals that will result in a system that does minimize manpower requirements. Two statistics are key to this approach: mean

Notional Labor Hours Calculation

$$\frac{\text{Number of Systems X Usage Rate}}{\text{Mean time between failure (MTBF)}} = \text{Estimated Number Of Failures}$$

Estimated number of failures x mean time to repair (MTTR) x average person per task = labor hour requirements

Example: Number of systems supported by a location   90
Usage rate each system per year   2500 hours
Mean time between failure (MTBF)   240 hours
Mean time to repair (MTTR)   2.25 hours
Average number of persons per action   1.5

Results: Approximately 3164 labor hours required to maintain the fleet

Figure 4.3   Notional Labor Hour Calculation.

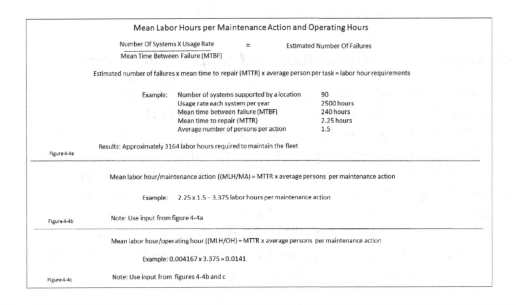

Figure 4.4 a, b, c   Mean Labor Hours per Maintenance Action and Operating Hour.

labor hours per maintenance action (MLH/MA) and mean labor hours per operating hour (MLH/OH). Figure 4.4b and c shows how this statistic is multiplied by the system failure rate to produce MLH/OH. Both these statistics are design-to goals that can be specified as system requirements.

Maximum Use of Existing Personnel

Generally, the customer desires to retain the same mix of personnel currently supporting the system vice having to replace personnel. Normally, this only becomes a problem when the new system's technology is superior to that of the one being replaced. Should the customer desire to have the current mix of personnel support the newer system is to an assessment can be conducted by using the process outlined in Figure 4.3. If the old system required 0.01 MLH/OH, if the current design meets this requirement, the existing number and skillset should be fine.

Minimum Requirements for Test Equipment

"No test equipment required" would be the statement we would like to hear, right? Unfortunately, this is not usually the case. It is based solely on the types of technology the system is based on. Test equipment for an electronic system may be all but eliminated through the use of self-diagnostics. Where it is required, the design should be standardized.

Maximum Use of Existing Tools and Support Equipment

"Use only existing tools and support equipment" is the mantra we would like to plan for consistently when designing a system. However, as described in the *Minimum Requirements for Test Equipment* section, it is not always possible to do so. The systems requirements study, addressed in the previous chapter, contains a section for identifying tools and equipment available to support the new system. This list is generally provided to the design engineering assessment and planning with instructions that only those items supplied in the list will be used to support the new system. The final design solution can then be measured against this list to determine whether the new design meets this requirement.

Minimum Numbers of Resources

It goes without saying that resources to support a system are required, period. However, resource requirements are driven by the technology baseline of the design. Where the new system technology is similar to the existing one, keeping the same number for the new one is achievable. If different, resources to support the system may differ in many ways. The customer must assess the need for a technology change and weigh the value of increased capability with the cost of providing different resources. If it is determined that the trade-off is worthwhile, a vigorous standardization effort should limit the number of resources needed to support the system.

Maximum Use of Existing Facilitates

Facilities represent a long-term investment for the organization and are a significant contributor to the cost of ownership. Therefore, every effort should be made "not" to create requirements for new facilities. The logic here is identical to using existing tools and support equipment. The smart way of initially planning the design of the system is stating that no new facilities are required. The system requirement study would identify all existing facilities available to support system design. Supportability assessment and planning assist systems engineering, not design engineering, in creating a design solution that does not exceed existing facilities' capabilities. Of course, if a new technology is envisioned, the discussion goes into whether an existing facility can be modified, upgraded, or expanded to fulfill requirements.

Maximum Use of Standard Parts

First of all, let us ensure we have a clear definition of a standard part. It is generally defined as a part used by many systems, with multiple sources from which to procure and conform to a specified material content, physical dimension, and functional capability. In addition, there are established standards publications that provide authenticity for standard parts. Therefore, applicable standards must be selected for the technology of the system design being pursued, and a statement can be made, "use only parts that conform to selected standards," in the system design solution.

Quickly Prepared for Shipment or Transport

This requirement normally applies to systems that frequently move to various locations. The customer is saying in this requirement that the design should allow the system to be transformed from its original operational configuration to its shipping configuration with minimal effort. An example of this would be an aircraft engine. When removed from an aircraft, further disassembly is required before it can be placed in the shipping container.

Removal of fragile parts, subassemblies that protrude at awkward angles, and draining residual fluids. Holding fixtures must be attached to the engine to keep it upright and prohibit movement during transport. The actual movement of the engine into the container requires a special harness. Once into the container, the engine is bolted into place in a cradle-like fixture that prohibits any chance of movement during the transport process.

Transported by Standard Modes

The desire here again is to use something standard. Transport has many facets: transport of the system to various locations, transport of support materials to the system, transport of failed items to places of repair, and transport of resources. Each of these situations potentially requires a different type of transport. The issue of deciding which means of transport is best starts with identifying the transportation modes used for the system being replaced and those used by its support infrastructure. A notional grouping of various transport modes is illustrated in Figure 4.5.

The objective is to ensure the final design solution of the system can be transported using the existing transport modes used by the current system.

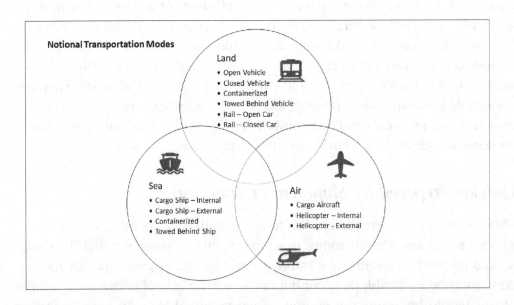

Figure 4.5 Notional Transportation Modes.

Interface With Existing Support Systems

A new system is being acquired and introduced to replace an older one. The customer has an existing support system that sustains all the systems currently in use, not just the one being replaced. The customer desires to introduce the new system into the current support system configuration with little or no impact.

The process that is generally followed to support the customer's request in this situation is called Interface Management (IxM). IxM is related to support requirements and configuration management. It is a technical systems engineering activity focused on the interface's architecture, design, and implementation. Often, it is applied more specifically to the management of interfaces as a sub-component of information and communications technology (ICT) systems. However, because it is integral to the initial supportability assessment planning, it can and is, in a more general manner, directly to situations like the one requested by the customer.

For example, the replaced system currently shares a maintenance facility with another system. The new system will not require facility use due to reduced maintenance requirements. This means the shared portion will become excess when the new system goes into service. The maintenance facility would still be required, but the amortization of its annual cost will be totally on the other system and increase the ownership cost.

Another example would be one that several of the fixed-based operations (FBOs) face when acquiring a new system to support. The customer has a fuel delivery system mechanism common to all current systems in inventory. The new system must be able to accept fuel from the same system delivery mechanism. If a change were to be needed, it could create a significant cost escalation in the infrastructure.

Restating the Requirements

The customer's aspirations for a supportable system, as stated in Table 4.1, can now be restated into understandable and measurable facts. This process is critical to accurately building the QFD mapping association process. Table 4.2 shows how these original aspirations are now restated into clear design goals. Understandably, some of these may be physically unattainable; however, each gives the systems design assessment and planning design team goals to achieve. Supportability assessment and planning are

Table 4.2 Design Supportability Requirements Restated

Design Supportability Requirements Restated	
➤ Fault detection 100% accuracy	➤ No hazardous materials required for maintenance
➤ Error free troubleshooting procedures	➤ All hazards to maintainer eliminated
➤ Fault isolation to single failed item 100% accuracy	➤ Do not exceed existing number of personnel
➤ BIT/BITE coverage 100% of FMECA failure accuracy	➤ Do not exceed MLH/OH
➤ Spares for every fault isolation result	➤ Do not exceed MLH/MA
➤ All items accessible without removal of other item	➤ No test equipment
➤ Modular design	➤ Use only currently existing tools and support equipment
➤ All replaceable items attached with captive fasteners	➤ Use only existing facilities
➤ Color coding of all connections	➤ Use only parts to a recognized and agreed standard
➤ Reassembly reverse of disassembly	➤ No preliminary preparation for transport
➤ Repair verification using diagnostic test	➤ Use current transportation modes
➤ No hazardous materials in system design	➤ Use existing support systems unless justified by technology change

responsible for assisting the customer in refining the goals and then assisting the design of the entire system in achieving them.[30,46]

Figure 4.6 illustrates a completed single QFD modeling methodology that uses the initial characteristic of unmeasurable aspirations as the "What" is needed, and those same aspirations are restated in Table 4.2 as the "How" they can be measured.

Each originally stated functional supportability aspiration has been linked with each restated measurable criterion. Under the ranking room, each unmeasurable aspiration has a level of importance ranking assigned. Of note in this ranking is both "ease to maintain" and "cost-effective to maintain" are tied with the highest ranking of 5. While "safe to maintain" is ranked at a 4. This means that the development focus will squarely be building a safe and maintainable system. A priority ranking has also been assigned that directly supports the level of importance of rank order. Each measurable criterion has been assigned a direction of improvement that clearly supports the importance and priority rankings. The correlation matrix in the HOQ roof shows a strong positive to neutral association between the criteria, and interestingly, there are no negative associations. Contained within the summary statistics, the "technical importance rating" shows a strong emphasis on "build for supportability" and "testing" with scores exceeding 500 in BIT/BITE coverage and diagnostic testing. Also of interest is the balance of "relative weight" percentages. This signals that

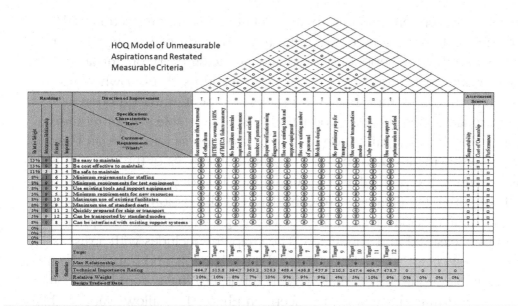

Figure 4.6   HOQ Model of Unmeasurable Aspirations and Restated Measurable Criteria.

the development team is focused and knowledgeable on design dynamics. In the room adjunct to the relationship matrix titled assessment scores, the three criteria of supportability, performance, and cost of ownership are measured as needing to be maximized, held on target, or decreased. Note the clear emphasis on holding the cost of ownership in check followed by the emphasis on supportability. While these statistics are included in a measurable metric, they act as a signal for development. The final statistic of interest is located at the bottom of the matrix, design trade-off data. Like the assessment scoring, these data elements are not included in a measurable metric but do act as visual cue as the system proceeds through its development life-cycle. The trade-offs are continually assessed.

Summary

This chapter began by pointing out that historically systems architecting, and engineering processes have focused primarily on performance with supportability and cost of ownership being a secondary concern. Support was viewed as a requirement that could only be determined after a system was in physical operation and as such limited the consideration of support issues during the systems design and each subsequent stage of development phases (conception, preliminary and detailed design, production and/ or construction, customer use, and retirement and/or recycling). It then addressed that the supportability challenge facing every organization is to ensure that future support of a system and its cost of ownership receives the same importance during development and acquisition as performance. Because the production of a supportable system requires a joint effort by all organization members, working as a team; each team member having a stated role in the overall objectives of the group, QFD is becoming the preferable operational methodology used to ensure that all supportability elements are considered. A discussion of the customer's supportability aspirations is presented, along with how those aspirations can be measured and conducted. The chapter concludes with a discussion of how QFD can access key supportability elements and translate them into measurable requirements that serve as input into the systems development process starting in the system conception phase. This allows supportability characteristics to be included as requirements that can be measured as easily as performance characteristics.

Chapter 5

Supportability Characteristic Assessment

Supportability Characteristics Assessment

A system's supportability characteristics are expressed in terms of goals, objectives, thresholds, and constraints. All of these must be verifiable in the final design solution. Supportability element analysis provides a methodology to do such.

Support element analysis entails a series of steps that combine system design characteristics, systems use, support infrastructure, and support resources into a single optimized solution that achieves system performance requirements while simultaneously minimizing the total cost of ownership. The activities illustrated in Figure 5.1 encapsulate all these activities.[30,47]

To begin the process, there must first be a clear and unambiguous definition of supportability requirements for the system. These requirements are then translated into design supportability characteristics. They are then expressed in measurable goals, thresholds, and constraints. Whereas a "goal" is defined as an aim or desired outcome. A "threshold" is a minimum that must be attained. And a "constraint" is something that must be done or cannot be done. Supportability assessment results then provide the development team with measurable supportability characteristics that can be embedded into a final design solution.

DOI: 10.4324/9781003336044-7

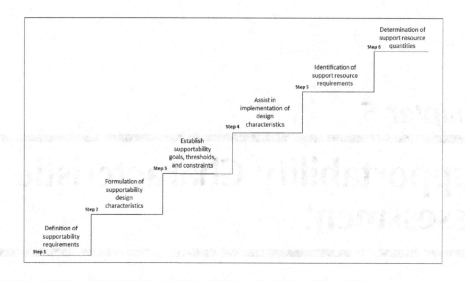

Figure 5.1   Supportability Assessment Steps.

First Functional, Then Physical

Within the system's design process, a functional set of requirements starts the development process by first addressing what the system must do and ends with a physical entity that will perform all those necessary functions. The process divides all activities surrounding the transformation into two distinct phases: Phase One, where analyses are performed on "What" are the functional capabilities of the proposed system, and Phase Two, "How" will the design solution be supported.[48–51]

Most, who have performed supportability analysis, are familiar with the latter rather than the former, functional requirements identification and implementation. However, it should be noted that ~70% of decisions affecting the cost of ownership are made during the functional stage of systems development. Therefore, functional supportability analyses must be considered an integral part of the decision-making process as the system is being planned and developed to ensure the final design solution achieves a balance between performance, supportability, and cost of ownership.

Functional Requirements Assessment

The application of supportability analyses to the functional requirements for a system creates a progressive sequence of events that starts with

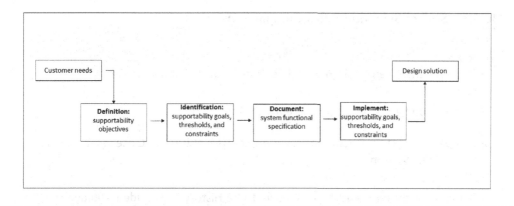

Figure 5.2   Supportability Analyses Steps.

the customer's need and ends with a system design solution of all requisite characteristics. These events and their sequence are illustrated in Figure 5.2.[30,47]

Determining the customer's specific issues surrounding need or want forms the necessary input into the supportability element analysis process. A system requirements study, in which supportability analysis plays a key role, is the vehicle for this determination. However, the systems requirements study is not an analysis; it is the gathering of existing information about the customer's needs and wants and is designed to present the information in an organized manner, thus providing a single starting point for the supportability element analysis.

Supportability Comparison Analysis

At the start of an acquisition process, the new system does not exist; only its functional requirements exist. It is through system assessment and planning during the conceptual stage of development that a functional description of the proposed system, identifying its supportability goals, thresholds, and constraints, is tabulated into a functional "block" diagram through which performance functions can be assessed on the basis of the current technology baseline. The functional description is the starting point for identifying possible support requirements for the proposed system. The next step in defining supportability requirements is comparing existing, similar systems.

Table 5.1   System Selection Rules Comparisons

System Selection Rules Comparison
➢Comparison System Performance Functions Must Be Similar To The New System.
➢Comparison System Must Be Currently In Operation.
➢Comparison System Operational Environment Must Be Very Close Operational Of The New System.
➢Comparison System Must Have Sufficient Use History To Provide Definitive Support Requirements.
➢Comparison System Support Environment Must Be Similar To Existing To Adaptable To New System.

Supportability assessment takes this block diagram and searches for an existing system with the same or similar performance functions. The rules for selecting a comparable system for analysis are provided in Table 5.1.[30,46,47,52]

The first system considered for selection is the system being replaced. It is the most appropriate and should be used unless its technology baseline is obsolete and does not provide a reasonable comparison of future requirements for the new system. If the system being replaced is unacceptable for comparison, then supportability engineering must identify a similar system with a comparable technology baseline.

After a system comparison candidate has been determined, a comparison analysis is performed on the candidate system. This analysis has two aspects: (1) defining support requirements for the comparison system, and (2) the identification of significant supportability issues. Note the definition of support requirements starts with determining how the comparison system is currently maintained. Figure 5.3 presents an example of a support philosophy.[30,46,47,52]

The diagram shows the overall approach used to support a system when it fails and the flow of materials between each location to support the process. It is a high-level depiction of the supported system but does not show the functions required to achieve this supportability philosophy. Actual functions to operationalize supportability are the next step in the process.

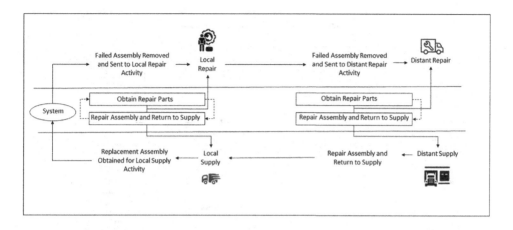

Figure 5.3   Philosophy of Supportability.

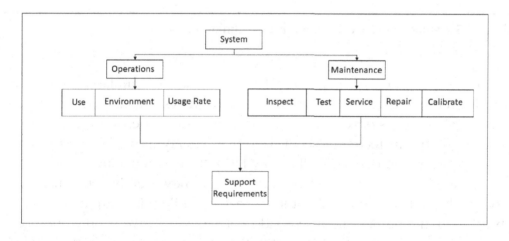

Figure 5.4   Identification of Support Functions.

Support requirements for a system are generated as that system is operated and needs to be maintained. Figure 5.4 illustrates an example of the support functions required to support a system with a specific technology baseline.[30,39,47]

The combination of all operations and maintenance activities drives requirements for support resources. If a new system is required, the first step in comparison analysis determines the necessary functions to support the new system. The second step is learning about the successes and potential failures of comparison systems through modeling techniques. Figure 5.5 illustrates performing a comparative analysis using operational availability and life-cycle cost.

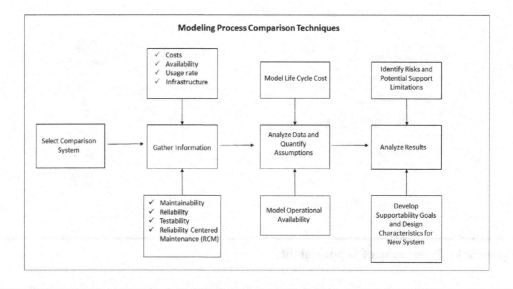

Figure 5.5   Modeling Process Comparison Techniques.

A comparison analysis compares the differences and similarities between two different options. One, what the comparison system was required to achieve when it was developed, and two, what is experienced when used. An example of this technique is measuring reliability using the comparison system's mean time between failures (MTBF). If the comparative system was required to achieve an MTBF of xxxx hour, however, in actual use, it only achieved 700 hours (about four weeks). While this is an interesting observation, the number themselves do not provide answers, only questions. The first is was the system used within the design constraints? If the system use exceeded its intended use profile or environment, then the difference between the required and actual MTBF may have been due to this, and reliability would not be an issue. On the other hand, if the comparison system was used within the conditions it was designed for, then it has a design problem, and reliability is an issue.

Every piece of information used by a comparison analysis requires this type of investigative logic applied to it. Statistics such as MTTR, fault detection and isolation rates, false alarm rates, MLH/OH, MLH/MA, operational availability, the average cost of spares, the average cost per maintenance action, and administrative and logistical delay time (ALDT) can provide insight into the successes and failures of support infrastructure for the comparison system. Table 5.2 provides a list of typical statistics that are subjected to comparative analysis.[30,39,46,47]

Table 5.2 Example of Comparative Statistics

	System Comparison Statistics
Systems	➤ Number of systems supported ➤ Number of operating locations ➤ Number of maintenance and support locations
System usage	➤ Operating time
Cost	➤ Unit price of system ➤ Average spare cost per repair
Reliability	➤ Mean time between failure (MTBF) ➤ Mean time between maintenance action (MTBMA)
Maintainability	➤ Mean time to repair
Testability	➤ Automatic fault detection and isolation % ➤ Manuel fault detection and isolation % ➤ Automatic test equipment requirements
Availability	➤ Measure availability Ai (inherent), Aa (achieved) and Ao (operational)
Supportability	➤ Administrative and logistics delay time ➤ Spares confidence level ➤ Maintenance proficiency level

The total range of statistics used to perform a comparative analysis depends on the evaluated system. Modeling is often used to determine a reasonable range of possible statistics along with sensitivity analysis. It is critical that all assumptions used in designing the modeling strategy be documented in the system requirements study so that all design/development teams within the organizations have the same base data for consistency across all outcomes of various system design disciplines.

Supportability Standardization Analysis

Standardization analysis is to identify potential options for system design development that minimize the requirements for support resources. Standardization means limiting the range of resources required to support the system under development. There are two sources of information used in a standardization analysis. One is the System Requirements Study, where they identify resources available to support the new system. And two, resources used by the current system that will become available when it is replaced.

Table 5.3   Categories for Standardization Analysis

	Categories for Standardization
Hardware	➢ Assemblies ➢ Materials ➢ Fit ➢ Access ➢ Left/right interchange
Software	➢ Language ➢ Modules ➢ Conventions ➢ Note coding
Resources	➢ Parts ➢ Tools ➢ Support equipment ➢ Facilities ➢ Personnel ➢ Training ➢ Packaging ➢ Transportation

Standardization analysis investigates each type of support resource to identify opportunities for their application to the new system design. Table 5.3 provides a list of typical resource categories that are analyzed.[47,52] Analysis categories include hardware, software, and support resources.

■ Various *hardware* options are investigated to identify standardization opportunities. Examples include the identification of a common power supply or pump with multiple applications. A standard grade of materials used throughout the system has the potential to lower production costs. Having a common fit of items such as circuit cards fit the same in the system can achieve a single repair procedure, thus lower removal and replacement time. Accessibility is another area where ease of access for all critical components is essential. Standard access covers and panels tend to make maintenance procedures shorter in duration.

■ Standardization of *software* design is extremely important. A single common language should be used for all application software in the system. Also, a single code functional flow should be rigorously maintained for all software modules. Finally, all system software should follow a standard method for note coding, and comments inserted in the code describing each function.

■ *Resource* standardization aims to limit the number of resources required to support the system in operations. These requirements originate via design engineering when a system design is created. Therefore, it is critical that supportability element analysis be conducted on these items before the final design solution is rendered.

o One of the most common applications of resource standardization analysis is *parts,* the basic building block of the system. The purpose of parts standardization is to produce a shopping list of parts that design engineering can use to select items for the system design. The standardization is not to establish a fixed limit but to require selected parts to be used wherever possible and to limit requirements for nonstandard parts.

o Requirements for *tooling* are typically created for the parts selected. There can, however, be another philosophical view taken to tools, which is to use existing tools as the basis for selecting parts. On radically modern designs, an even more creative requirement is to establish requirements for design engineering to produce a system that requires no disassembly or reassembly tools.

o A system's design technology baseline, operational concept, and support concept generate requirements for *support and test equipment.* Support and test equipment can be anything not part of a system necessary to operate or support it. A point to remember is supportability element analysis does not force a specific design attribute change; it identifies options for design engineers to pursue that will eventually result in a more supportable design. Some distinct categories of support equipment are provided in Table 5.4.

Table 5.4   Distinct Support and Test Equipment

Test And Support Equipment Categories
➢General Support Equipment
➢Peculiar Support Equipment
➢Maintenance Support Equipment
➢General Purpose Electronic Test Equipment
➢Special Purpose Electronic Test Equipment
➢Factory Test Equipment
➢Materials Handling Equipment

Table 5.5 Categories of Facilities

Facility Categories	
By Function or use	➤ Operation ➤ Maintenance ➤ Support ➤ Training ➤ Storage
By Type	➤ Permanent ➤ Mobile ➤ General purpose ➤ Special ➤ Shared ➤ Dedicated
By Feature or Construction	➤ Physical building, mobile shelter, dock, teenage, pier, ground, prepared pad, shipboard compartment, aircraft compartment 　➤ Basic 　➤ With specific capabilities 　➤ With specific installed equipment

Note that support and test equipment is divided into its use or technology. For example, the items required for maintenance, operations, and training. Standardization for support and test equipment is conducted similarly to tooling.[30,39,52]

o A *facility* is defined as a place that provides a capability. This means a facility could be a building, a confined space on board a ship, a runway, or a vacant piece of real estate. There is no such thing as a standard facility. How facilities can be described is illustrated in Table 5.5.

Since every facility is different, a standardization analysis investigates facility-use requirements. The two issues that must be analyzed are capacity utilization rate and physical limitations. Each available system must be studied via supportability element analysis to determine its capacity utilization rate and physical limitations to ensure that the new system does not exceed what is available.

o The personnel and training areas may not be commonly linked to standardization; however, they should always be part of a system standardization analysis performed via the supportability element analysis. The cost of personnel required to operate and support the system constitutes a major portion of through-life costs. The systems requirements study identifies the number of personnel and

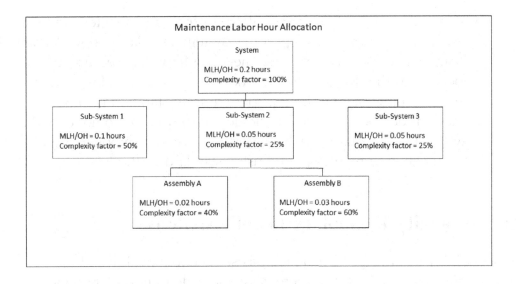

Figure 5.6   Maintenance Labor Hour Allocation.

the labor hours of each type that will be available to operate and support the new system. Using information on support personnel available, an estimate of available maintenance labor hours can be developed that becomes a design-to goal for design engineering. However, the derived statistic relates to the overall goal to allocate individual assemblies down into the sub-assembly levels. The way around this is by allocating available maintenance labor hours and allocating them down the system architecture like the allocation of MTBF and MTTR. MTBF can be used as a weighting factor in the apportionment, much like MTTR allocation. Figure 5.6 illustrates this technique using a complexity factor of each component to allocate labor hours.[46,52]

This technique works well overall; however, care must be taken because maintenance labor hour requirements will fluctuate with variations in system operating time. The allocation should be based on maximum usage during peak or surge conditions.

o Spares and support equipment require *packaging* for protection from damage during shipment, handling, and storage. Most industries have established standard packaging materials and containers and several sizes and shapes. There are also industry standards for cleaning, preserving, and packing items. Any spare or component should be capable of being packaged using standard containers and procedures; this should be a hard design-to goal.

o Many different methods are available to *transport* a system and the resources necessary to support that system. Standardization element analysis does not analyze these methods; however, because its focus is on the design characteristics of the system and resources that will allow them to be transported using standard methods, it has considerable influence in the design-to decision to not only the system but the spares. Each support equipment component should be designed to be transported using standard methods.

Supportability Technology Benefit Analysis

Supportability technology benefit analysis seeks commonality and use of existing resources; however, there is another side to new acquisition programs that is most common, the application of modern technologies. Technology improvements in system design typically provide opportunities to improve supportability as well. A technology benefits analysis looks for opportunities to apply state-of-the-art capabilities for support. Supportability element analysis searches for how modern technologies are applied to other acquisition programs with an eye to the future.

There is a continual improvement and evolution of technologies in reliability, maintainability, testability, transportation, support equipment, and computer-based training. A modern technology benefits analysis requires access to information on new and future technology innovations. There is no set method for performing this benefits analysis. Instead, it requires a vision of what the rest of the world is doing and where technology is headed. Forty years ago, the idea that a system could evaluate itself was considered a dream; today, BIT and BITE are standard.

A thorough analysis typically identifies many technologies that have the potential to provide benefit to a modern design; however, many of them may be in formative stages and not be sufficiently mature to apply to that modern design. The risk of using them may be too high to justify pursuing them. These are not eliminated from consideration; they are held in abeyance for future consideration. Each time a system is changed, these technologies should be revisited. A formal name for this is *Pre-Planned Product Improvement (P³I)*.[46]

P³I is a system acquisition strategy formulated in response to the high development costs of new systems, lengthening acquisition intervals, increasing the age of current inventories, constrained budgets, and various technology trends. It is founded on the assumption that quality enhancement modification of existing inventoried systems is a cheaper and quicker way to modernize than the development of entirely new systems. The P³I strategy aims to facilitate this process; its central element is the design of new systems from their origins to accommodate future quality upgrades.

Supportability Support Infrastructure Analysis

The customer has an existing infrastructure that supports all systems in their inventory. This infrastructure consists of maintenance capabilities, supply operations, facilities, transportation, and personnel. A support infrastructure analysis investigates two different issues: (1) the responsiveness of the infrastructure to demands for support and (2) any impact that the introduction of the new system will have on the infrastructure and other systems it supports.

The customer's support infrastructure must be analyzed to determine its responsiveness to requirements. When measuring responsiveness, one of the most significant factors that signal a degradation in system availability is Administration and Logistics Delay Time (ALDT). ALDT reflects the ability of the infrastructure to provide support on demand. Responsiveness is measured in both the response time and the quantities of resources held in awaiting a demand. This analysis focuses on identifying the bottlenecks that cause delays, time wasted for no valid reason, and how the infrastructure prioritizes its response to demand. Figure 5.7 provides an example that has been annotated with times for responsiveness of support infrastructure.[30,39,47,52]

Visibility of these times allows analysis and investigative work to determine ways to improve overall responsiveness, thus benefiting the new system and all other systems that share infrastructure.

Any infrastructure has maximum limits on its capacity to provide resources to all systems it supports. Supportability element analysis must have visibility of the existing system, the new system, other systems in operation, and other systems being acquired simultaneously to quantify the complete supportability issues so that steps can be taken to avoid capability shortfalls.

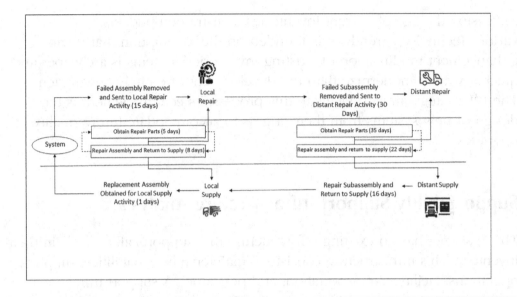

Figure 5.7   Response Times for Infrastructure.

Supportability Goals, Thresholds, and Constraints

Design criteria for supportability must eventually be expressed in measurable terms. While many supportability design characteristics are measurable when stated in terms of *no or must*, such as design where all on-equipment maintenance can be performed using *no* tools. However, other requirements must be stated in statistics. One of the significant areas that supportability element assessment is directly involved with is assessing the relationships between statistics developed by different disciplines (availability, reliability, maintainability, testability) and using statistics in the context of supporting the system and how the design solution optimizes support. Table 5.6 illustrates areas that these statistics may address.[30,46,47]

Statistics used by supportability element assessment are stated in terms of goals, thresholds, and constraints. The most common statistics used during acquisition are provided in Table 5.7.[46,52]

As functional supportability assessment goals, thresholds, and constraints are identified, it is necessary to test them for reasonableness, adequacy, and compatibility. At the time when these statistics must be determined, the new system does not physically exist. Only a functional description is available. The only viable method of assessing the statistics is to return to the comparative analysis presented and discussed earlier in this chapter.

Table 5.6   Supportability Objectives by Discipline

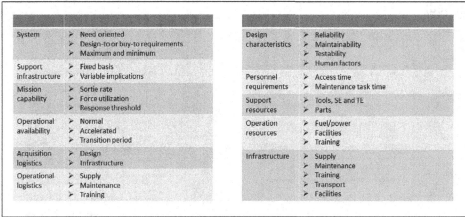

System	➤ Need oriented ➤ Design-to or buy-to requirements ➤ Maximum and minimum		Design characteristics	➤ Reliability ➤ Maintainability ➤ Testability ➤ Human factors
Support infrastructure	➤ Fixed basis ➤ Variable implications		Personnel requirements	➤ Access time ➤ Maintenance task time
Mission capability	➤ Sortie rate ➤ Force utilization ➤ Response threshold		Support resources	➤ Tools, SE and TE ➤ Parts
Operational availability	➤ Normal ➤ Accelerated ➤ Transition period		Operation resources	➤ Fuel/power ➤ Facilities ➤ Training
Acquisition logistics	➤ Design ➤ Infrastructure		Infrastructure	➤ Supply ➤ Maintenance ➤ Training ➤ Transport ➤ Facilities
Operational logistics	➤ Supply ➤ Maintenance ➤ Training			

Table 5.7   Goals, Thresholds, and Constraints Related to Supportability

Maintenance			Technical Data	
Mean Time To Repair	➤	Weighted average time required to return a system to an operable condition.	Technical document accuracy	➤ The percent of accuracy of technical documentation delivered with the system necessary for operations and support.
Mean Restoration Time	➤	Weighted average time required to return a soft-wear based system to an operable condition.	Percent embedded Technical Manuals (TMs)	➤ The percent of technical documentation that is embedded in a software-based system.
Maintenance Ratio	➤	The ratio of maintenance done at each level of support.	TM correction rate	➤ The percent of technical documentation that must be revised or corrected on an annual basis.
Max Time To Repair (MAX$_{TTR}$)	➤	The maximum time allowable for any single maintenance action performed on the system.		
Repair Cycle Time	➤	The amount of time from when a failed item is removed from the system until it is repaired and returned to supply for use again.	Supply Support	
Annual Maintenance Labor Hours	➤	The total number of labor hours required to support the system.	Waiting time – non-mission capable supply	➤ The annual amount of time a system is non-mission capable due to awaiting resources
Operation And Support (O&S) Cost Per Operating Hour	➤	The annual operation and support costs for a system divided by the number of annual operating hours.	Parts availability	➤ The percent of spares that are available when required.
Maintenance Downtime	➤	The total time a system is non-operational due to corrective and preventive maintenance.	Back-order rate	➤ The percent if spares that are not readily available for replenishment.
Waiting Time Non-mission Capable Maintenance (NMCM)	➤	The annual amount of time that a system is not mission capable due to corrective and preventive maintenance.	Back-order duration	➤ The average time required to receive a back-order spare.
			Failure factor accuracy	➤ The percent accuracy of predicted failure rates or MTBF.
Percent Organic Support	➤	The percent of total maintenance that is performed on the system by the operator/crew.	Order-ship time	➤ The average time from when an order for a spare are
Maintenance Hours To Operating/Flight Hours	➤	The ration of hours required for maintenance to the number of operating hours.	Spares cost to total cost of ownership (TCO)	➤ The ratio of cost of spares to overall cost of ownership.

This is the classic *What If?* scenario. Constructing additional versions of the comparison baseline, each statistic can be analyzed in terms of completeness and then be compared with the results of the system being replaced. This technique may reveal that some of the statistics do not affect changing the outcome of the analysis, while others may have a dramatic impact. Using the comparison analysis to match old and new provides a clear relationship between each statistic and its contribution to overall system supportability, operational availability, and cost of ownership.

Table 5.8 Goals, Thresholds, and Constraints Related to Supportability (continued)

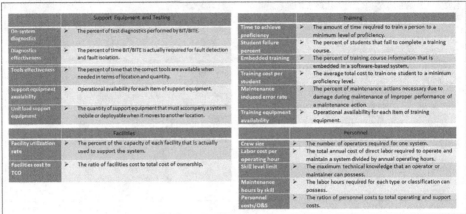

Support Equipment and Testing	
On-system diagnostics	➤ The percent of test diagnostics performed by BIT/BITE.
Diagnostics effectiveness	➤ The percent of time BIT/BITE is actually required for fault detection and fault isolation.
Tools effectiveness	➤ The percent of time that the correct tools are available when needed in terms of location and quantity.
Support equipment availability	➤ Operational availability for each item of support equipment.
Unit load support equipment	➤ The quantity of support equipment that must accompany a system mobile or deployable when it moves to another location.

Training	
Time to achieve proficiency	➤ The amount of time required to train a person to a minimum level of proficiency.
Student failure percent	➤ The percent of students that fail to complete a training course.
Embedded training	➤ The percent of training course information that is embedded in a software-based system.
Training cost per student	➤ The average total cost to train one student to a minimum proficiency level.
Maintenance induced error rate	➤ The percent of maintenance actions necessary due to damage during maintenance of improper performance of a maintenance action.
Training equipment availability	➤ Operational availability for each item of training equipment.

Facilities	
Facility utilization rate	➤ The percent of the capacity of each facility that is actually used to support the system.
Facilities cost to TCO	➤ The ratio of facilities cost to total cost of ownership.

Personnel	
Crew size	➤ The number of operators required for one system.
Labor cost per operating hour	➤ The total annual cost of direct labor required to operate and maintain a system divided by annual operating hours.
Skill level limit	➤ The maximum technical knowledge that an operator or maintainer can possess.
Maintenance hours by skill	➤ The labor hours required for each type or classification can possess.
Personnel costs/O&S	➤ The ration of personnel costs to total operating and support costs.

Using a QFD Modeling Methodology to Manage Functional Supportability

Another analysis tool used to assist system planners and developers is a QFD modeling methodology mentioned at the beginning of the chapter. Supportability characteristics described in this chapter would serve as "What" is needed. And the *Functional and Physical Attributes* that will be the subject of Chapter 6 would serve as "How" supportability characteristics can be measured and managed as they draw closer to entering the production life-cycle.

Summary

This chapter introduced the reader to supportability assessment for identifying the physical resources required to support a product and/ or service. It addressed how supportability assessments are performed as interrelated activities in building product and/or service systems. It discussed functional and physical sets of design process requirements, which accounted for over 70% of decisions affecting the cost of ownership. It also elaborated on the sequencing of those assessment activities used during the functional supportability assessment process to ensure the stated system meets custom specifications. A QFD modeling methodology that is currently being used by development teams to aid them in the supportability planning process was introduced by first structuring "What" is required about system design characteristics, system use, support infrastructure, and support resources and "How" a holistic solution can be attained that achieves system performance requirements, and then minimizing total cost of ownership.

Chapter 6

Functional Supportability Analysis

Physical Supportability Analysis

As was addressed in the previous chapter, *Supportability Characteristic Assessment* is responsible for the physical resources required to support a system being acquired. Physical supportability analysis is typically done much later in the acquisition process, and it is not usual for it to be done by a completely different organization. The system's design is in its final stages of completion when the physical supportability analysis is conducted. It follows the functional supportability analysis and, more commonly, may transpire several years afterward. The timing of performance depends on the design evolution's status. Since subsystems and assemblies contained in the design of a system evolve at different rates, some physical supportability analysis can begin while areas of the system are under development.

Physical supportability analysis is performed in three stages. Figure 6.1 illustrates these three stages.[30,39,47,53]

The first stage consists of activities that identify the resources required to support the new system in its pre-stated operational environment. These activities should always be done using a step-by-step process that provides visibility of decisions and an audit trail for future use in supporting the system throughout its operational life. The second stage is to determine the optimal support infrastructure and maintainability solution to achieve a balance between performance, support, and cost of ownership. This step is key to achieving the desired operational characteristics for the system by having

DOI: 10.4324/9781003336044-8

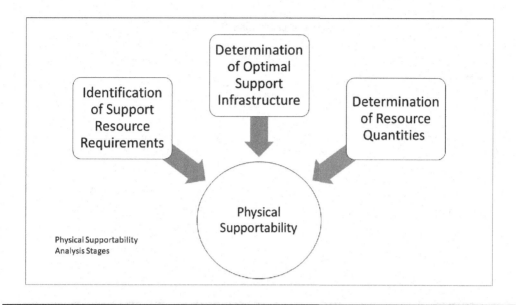

Figure 6.1   Physical Supportability Analysis Stages.

the right resources at the right place and time. The third stage focuses on determining the minimum quantity of each resource required to support the system at its pre-stated usage rate. The third stage of the process quantities the basis for procurement and deployment of the physical resources package required for through-life support when used within the specified conditions.

The identification of support resource requirements starts with the physical design and subjects it to a series of analyses that results in the definition of all resources needed. Figure 6.2 illustrates this entire process.[30,47,52]

Identification starts with a physical system design. Typically, this consists of engineering design and assembly drawings with appropriate parts list. Other source information is also required and is obtained from manufacturers, support organizations, and often prior users. However, the primary information source comes from previously described systems development efforts during the system's design.

The major activity within the process is identifying items that potentially require support. These items are called maintenance significant items (MSI), indicating that some type of maintenance support will be required. As shown in Figure 6.2, failure modes, effects, and critical analysis (FMECA) and variations of reliability-centered maintenance (RCM) provide valuable input into this identification activity. The FMECA indicates that an item will fail; therefore, support will be required. This gives a basis for ensuring that

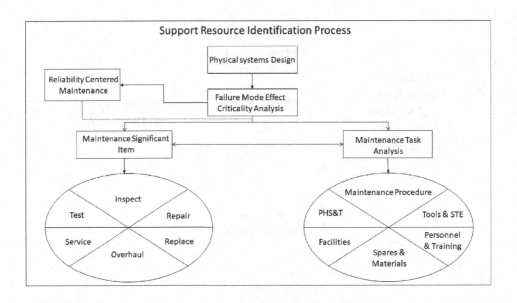

Figure 6.2   Support Resource Identification Process.

there is a method of restoring it to an operable condition in every way that a system can fail. Additionally, the RCM analysis identifies items that will require maintenance on schedule. Some others must also be applied to identify an MSI. These are illustrated in Figure 6.3.[30,47,52]

The first requirement for an item to be declared an MSI is that it must be possible to identify that the item requires maintenance for its support. Testing is how this is determined, which can be visual, manual, or automated; however, it must be reasonable to implement and cost-effective. All testing must be documented to ensure a solid audit trail. The next criterion for an MSI is that the item can be disassembled and reassembled and/or removed and replaced without destroying it. This goes back to the design criteria discussed in the previous chapter. Poor design techniques allow the production of items that inhibit proper access and replacement.

Finally, sufficient information must be available to identify and document all resources that may require repair. This information can be derived from assembly drawings, manufacturer source data, or other documentation produced during the design process. The system requirements study should be the source of existing support resources.

As reflected in Figure 6.2, the next step is to identify all tasks that will potentially be required to service each MSI. This includes all types of support, whether scheduled or unscheduled. Table 6.1 provides a list of service tasks normally associated with MSI support.[30,47,52]

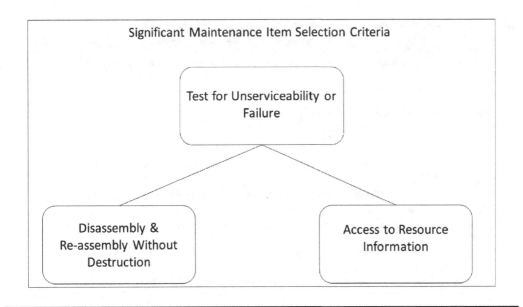

Figure 6.3   Significant Maintenance Item Selection Criteria.

Table 6.1   Description of Service Task

Description of Service Task	
Access	Operate
Adjust	Overhaul
Calibrate	Preserve
Clean	Process
Disassemble and Reassemble	Rebuild
Fault Location	Remove
Inspect	Remove and Repair
Install	Repair
Lubricate	Service
Mission Profile Change	Set Up
Monitor	Test

Identification of corrective servicing should be based on the technology baseline of the system, physical design features, and customer operational and support concepts. servicing tasks must be detailed enough so that an optimal support solution can be implemented.

Maintenance task analysis (MTA), as depicted in Figure 6.2, is a detailed step-by-step analysis of a maintenance action to determine how it should

Table 6.2 Task Analysis for Performing Servicing/Maintenance

Task Analysis for Performing Servicing/Maintenance
1. Person or persons participating in each step including s narrative description of what they are doing.
2. Time duration of each person's participation.
3. Tools and other support equipment needed.
4. Parts and materials required for the step.
After the completion of the above listed activities, the results are analyzed to determine the following issues about the total service/maintenance task.
Task Analysis **Follow-up** for Performing Servicing/Maintenance
1. The total elapsed time for the entire task from start to completion.
2. The type of person(s) that are required to perform the task based on their minimum technical capabilities and experience.
3. Any additional training that must be provided to the person to ensure proper task performance.
4. Any facility implementation such as space limitations, environmental controls, health hazards or minimum capability requirements.

be performed, who will perform it and all resources required to complete the task. MTA is a very laborious, time-consuming effort. However, its importance cannot be overstated. MTAs must be performed on all MSIs to ensure the complete identification of all resources to support the system. In addition, it is one of the most significant activities to be performed as it ensures an integrated physical support solution.

Performing an MTA starts with the identification of each step of the service/maintenance activity sequentially. Each step is analyzed to identify how the service/maintenance action would be performed. After a physical description of how the action will be performed is completed, each resource necessary to support the action is identified. Table 6.2 provides a listing of resources generally included.[46,52]

The MTA results must be analyzed to assess the item's compliance with all supportability issues, such as servicing/maintenance, accessibility, and standardization, established during earlier functional analyses. The source for comparison of the physical support requirements for acceptability must be the design instructions that created the item's design. This closes the loop between the requirements for the design and the actual results of the design process.

The results of the MTA are documented in a common source database that can be used to quantify the support requirements for the system. Typically, this is the logistics support analysis record (LSAR). This resource documentation then provides the information necessary to make decisions as to how, where, and when support will be provided for the system when it is operating.

After the completion of the above-listed activities, the results are analyzed to determine the following issues about the total service/maintenance task.

Level of Repair Analysis

The level of repair analysis (LORA) is the most important physical supportability decision made during the acquisition of a system. The LORA produces the final answer regarding how a system will be supported during its life-cycle. A LORA is performed in two steps:[46,54]

- Using non-economic decisions to make initial support decisions and
- Using an economic model to determine the most effective alternative when there is no reason to provide support by one method or another

The non-economic LORA decision criteria are a list of rules and guidelines used to determine if there is an overriding reason why service/maintenance should be performed. Table 6.3 lists some typical examples of these criteria.

Often organizations have policies that any item costing less than a predetermined price level will be arbitrarily discarded and replaced rather than repaired. Also, technical feasibility or limitations for performing service and/or repair may dictate a support solution. Typically, the buyer provides the non-economic LORA criteria to the seller. Results from the LORA form the

Table 6.3   Service and Maintenance Task Descriptions

Non-Economic Level of Repair Analysis Decision Criteria
➤Mission requirements
➤Safety
➤Human factors engineering
➤Constraints on existing support structure
➤Special transportation
➤Technical feasibility of repair
➤Security
➤Policy

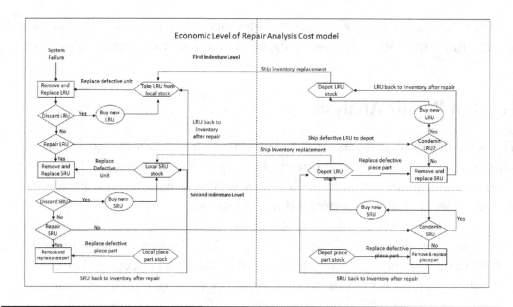

Figure 6.4   Economic Level of Repair Analysis Cost Model.

basis for eliminating items from the MSI list and elimination of tasks from the service/maintenance task list.

Decisions that cannot be made using LORA non-economic criteria are addressed using economic models that calculate the possible cost of all support options and then identifies the least cost solution. Figure 6.4 shows how viable options can be compared for the support of a system and modeled to determine each cost.[46,54]

The LORA process produces the final support solution for the system. It determines where each required service or maintenance action will be performed, the physical resources available to support those actions, and the infrastructure necessary to support activities throughout the system's life-cycle. Results of the LORA are documented in the LSAR and used as the basis for the development of the physical resources required for system support. LORA provides the final solution of what the minimum support arrangements must be for any system.

The Physical Product Support Resource Package

The physical product support resource process produces the identification and qualification of support resource elements required to support a

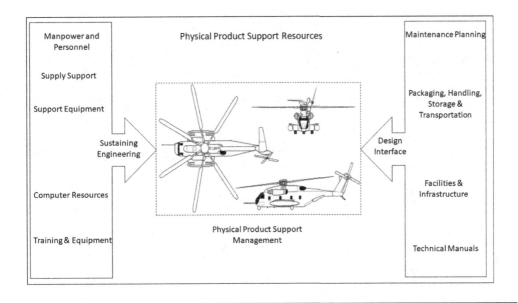

Manpower and Personnel	Physical Product Support Resources	Maintenance Planning
Supply Support		
Support Equipment		Packaging, Handling, Storage & Transportation
Sustaining Engineering		Design Interface
Computer Resources		Facilities & Infrastructure
Training & Equipment	Physical Product Support Management	Technical Manuals

Figure 6.5   Physical Product Support Resources.

system throughout its intended life-cycle. Each physical resource must be planned, procured if needed, and positioned so that when it is required, it will be available. These resource elements are provided in Figure 6.5.[39,46,52]

The physical product supportability analysis (PSA) process identifies each resource requirement as an activity. However, the procurement of sufficient quantities of each resource is a business decision that is made over the system life-cycle. Each resource requires analysis to determine the reasonable quantity to be procured on the basis of the cost of investment and the operational need at differing stages of the system's life-cycle. Figure 6.6 illustrates how the product physical supportability analysis process provides this identification of resources and serves as a common source for developing the final resource package to support a system over its life-cycle.[45,47,52]

After maintenance significant items and tasks are identified to support them, the execution of the associated task is assessed, and a LORA is conducted on each significant item. These assessments' results are then fed into the product support management logistics database. Before parsing information into each physical product supportability element, both the design interface and sustaining engineering elements are interrogated

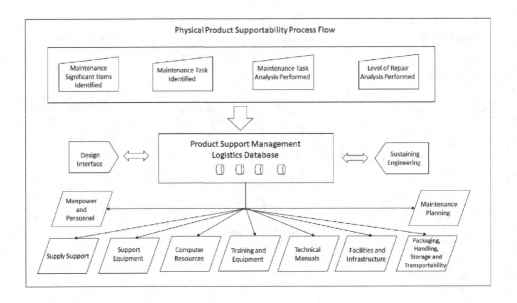

Figure 6.6   Physical Product Supportability Process Flow.

to ensure proper levels of supportability are distributed to each support element.

> *Design Interface*—It is the relationship of design to parameters and reliability/maintainability factors and support resource requirements. Figure 6.7 illustrates the supportability design-to parameters assessed.[30,47,52]

These physical product supportability design parameters are expressed in operational terms rather than inherent values and specifically relate to system readiness objectives and support costs. The design interface evaluates all facets of an acquisition, from design to support and operational concepts for supportability impact on the system and overall infrastructure.

> *Sustaining Engineering*—It spans those technical tasks (engineering and supportability (investigations and analyses) to ensure continued operation and maintenance of a system with managed risk. Sustaining engineering involves identifying, reviewing, assessing, and resolving deficiencies throughout system's life-cycle. Sustaining engineering returns a system to its baselined configuration and capability and

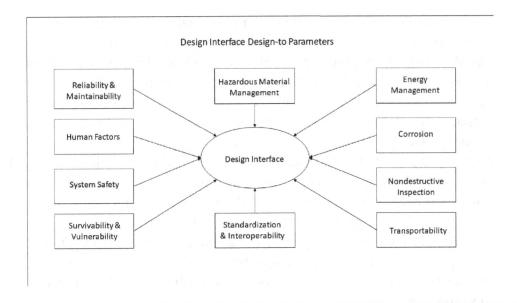

Figure 6.7   Design Interface Design-to Parameters.

identifies opportunities for performance and enhancement. It includes the measurement, identification, and verification of system technical and supportability deficiencies, associated root cause analyses, evaluation for deficiency correction, and the development of a range of corrective action options.

Once these two elements have been interrogated and program product supportability has been established, the information is then 11 support elements.

Computer Resources—These encompass the facilities, hardware, software, firmware, documentation, and personnel needed to operate and support critical system hardware and software systems. As a primary end item, support equipment and training devices increase in complexity, and more and more software is being used.

Facilities and Infrastructure—These consist of the permanent and semi-permanent real property assets required to support a system, including studies to define types of facilities or facility improvements, location, space needs, environmental requirements, and equipment. The lack of facilities can be as damaging to a system as a lock of spare parts, trained personnel, or support equipment.

Maintenance Planning—It establishes maintainability concepts and requirements for the system's life. It includes, but is not limited to, levels of repair, repair times, testability requirements, support equipment needs, manpower skills, facilities, interservice, organic and contractor mix of repair responsibility, and site activation. This element greatly impacts the planning, development, and acquisition of other supportability elements.

Manpower and Personnel—It involves identifying and acquiring personnel with the skills required to operate, maintain, and support systems over their lifetime. If the personnel needed are an additive requirement to existing staffing levels of an organization, a formalized process of identification and justification must be made. Add to this the necessity to train these personnel in their respective functions on the new system, the seriousness of any delays in the accomplishment of this element becomes apparent.

Packing, Handling, Storage, and Transportability—This is the combination of resources, processes, procedures, design, considerations, and methods to ensure that all system, equipment, and support items are preserved, packaged, handled, and transported properly including environmental considerations, equipment preservation, and transportability.

Supply Support—It consists of all management actions, procedures, and techniques necessary to determine requirements to acquire, catalog, receive, store, transfer, issue, and dispose of spares, repair parts, and supplies. This means having the right spares, repair parts, and supplies available, in the right quantities, at the right place, and at the right price. The process includes providing initial support and acquiring, distributing, and replenishing inventories.

Support Equipment—It is all equipment required to support the system throughout its intended life-cycle. This includes ground handling and maintenance equipment, tools, metrology calibration equipment, and manual and automatic test equipment (ATE). During the acquisition of systems, the supportability assessment team is expected to decrease the proliferation of support equipment and give more attention to the use of existing equipment.

Technical Manuals—These represent recorded information of scientific or technical nature, regardless of form or character, such as manuals or drawings. Computer programs and related software are not technical data; documentation of computer programs and related software are. However, technical manuals and engineering drawings are the most expensive and probably the most important data acquisitions to support a system.

Training and Equipment—It consists of the policy, processes, procedures, techniques, training devices, and equipment used to train personnel to acquire, operate, and support a system. This includes individual and crew training, new equipment, and initial, formal, and on-the-job training. Though the largest amount of training is accomplished before the fielding of a system, it must also be remembered that in most programs, a large number of personnel must also be trained during system development to support the system test and evaluation program.

Application of the Physical Product Supportability Analysis Process

Supportability analysis, both functional and physical, are critical processes in a system's design. Functional supportability analysis must be an integral part of the system development process to ensure the success of that system under development, and physical supportability analysis processes must validate this design-to success so the system can be supported adequately during its intended life-cycle.

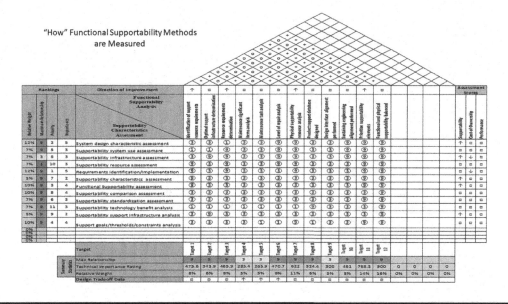

Figure 6.8 "How" Functional Supportability Methods are Measured.

The supportability analysis techniques presented in this chapter are proven methods to improve system supportability and lower the cost of ownership. Each step of the process described is interrelated and cannot be performed individually with any success. Their application is dependent upon the evolution of the system design. This said, I can tell you that these processes work! Having used them on numerous programs over the past 25 years, they have proven to be one of the most cost-effective methods available to develop reasonable supportability solutions for any system.

Developing the Functional Supportability Solution Using QFD

In Chapter 5, the supportability characteristic assessment criteria provided the "What" was required in our QFD HOQ model. In this chapter, the functional supportability analysis methods defined "How" those supportability characteristics could be measured. See Figure 6.9.

Characteristic assessment criteria were first assigned a level of importance by development team members based on a 5-point scale with 5 being the highest and 1 the lowest. Noted is that "system design characteristic assessment" and "requirements identification/implementation"

Characteristic Assessment Criteria Importance Level Assignment

Relative Weight	Maximum Relationship	Priority	Importance	Supportability Characteristics Assessment	Identification of support resource requirements	Optimal support infrastructure determination	Resource requirements determination	Maintenance significant items analysis	Maintenance task analysis	Level of repair analysis	Physical supportability resource analysis	Product support database designed	Design interface alignment performed	Sustaining engineering alignment performed	Prioritize supportability elements	Functional and physical supportability balanced
				Direction of Improvement	↑	□	↑	□	□	□	↑	□	□	□	↑	□
12%	9	2	5	System design characteristic assessment	③	③	①	③	③	⑨	⑨	③	③	⑨	⑨	⑨
7%	9	5	3	Supportability system use assessment	①	①	⑨	③	③	⑨	⑨	③	③	⑨	⑨	⑨
7%	3	8	3	Supportability infrastructure assessment	③	⑨	⑨	③	③	⑨	⑨	③	③	⑨	⑨	⑨
7%	1	10	3	Supportability resource assessment	⑨	③	⑨	③	③	⑨	⑨	③	③	③	⑨	⑨
12%	9	1	5	Requirements identification/implementation	⑨	③	⑨	③	③	③	⑨	③	③	③	⑨	⑨
5%	9	7	2	Supportability characteristics assessment	⑨	③	③	③	③	③	③	③	③	③	⑨	⑨
10%	9	3	4	Functional Supportability assessment	⑨	③	③	③	③	③	③	③	③	③	③	⑨
10%	9	8	4	Supportability comparison assessment	③	③	③	③	③	③	③	③	③	③	③	⑨
7%	9	6	3	Supportability standardization assessment	③	③	③	③	③	③	③	③	③	③	⑨	⑨
7%	9	11	3	Supportability technology benefit analysis	①	①	①	①	①	①	①	⑨	③	③	③	⑨
5%	9	9	2	Supportability support infrastructure analysis	③	⑨	③	③	③	③	③	③	③	③	③	⑨
10%	9	4	4	Support goals/thresholds/constraints analysis	③	③	③	③	①	①	⑨	①	③	③	⑨	⑨

Figure 6.9 "Hows" of the Supportability Characteristics.

were each ranked 5. This is not surprising since, at this planning stage of system development, many unknowns, and alternative design solutions are under consideration. Several four rankings were made. "functional supportability assessment," supportability comparison assessment" and, "support goals/thresholds/constraints." This implies that these assessment areas require equal supportability focus as the system is developed and ultimately fielded.

Team members then performed prioritization rank ordering. Note that priorities 1 and 2, "requirements identification/implementation" and "system design characteristic assessment," mirror the level of importance ranking with "functional supportability assessment" coming in at 3. This sends a clear message that the development team is focused on designing a system with supportabilities threaded through the build life-cycle note just tagged onto at the end of that cycle.

Assessing correlations among functional supportability analysis criteria (Figure 6.10) was then done in the model roof. Of interest here is the strong association of both "prioritize supportability elements" and, "functional and physical supportability balanced" criteria with all other functions. This supports the focus on post-deployment supportability. It should also be noted that there are no negative associations among the criteria. The absence of negative associations demonstrates that the development team's focus on building supportability into the system design is a priority.

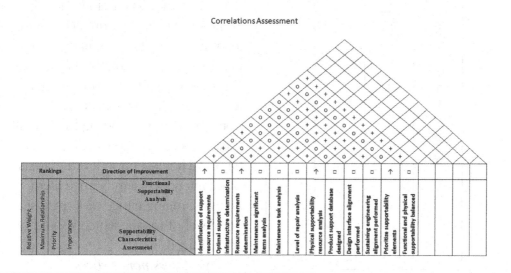

Figure 6.10   Correlation Matrix.

Summary Statistics

Summary Statistics																
Max Relationship	9	9	9	3	3	9	9	9	3	9	9	9				
Technical Importance Rating	475.6	343.9	465.9	285.4	265.9	470.7	622	324.4	300	461	768.3	900	0	0	0	0
Relative Weight	8%	6%	8%	5%	5%	8%	11%	6%	5%	8%	14%	16%	0%	0%	0%	0%
Design Tradeoff Data	□	□	□	↑	↑	↑	□	□	□	□	□	□				

Figure 6.11 Summary Statistics.

The *Summary Statistics* (Figure 6.11) provided next to the relationship matrix show a strong technical importance rating for "functional and physical supportability balanced" at 900 and "prioritize supportability elements" at 768 and "physical supportability resource analysis" at 622. The remainder of the functional supportability criteria averaging ~377 presents a picture of a balanced approach to system functional supportability during development and after deployment. Also serving as a visual queue to development team members is "design tradeoff data," provided just below the Summary Statistics room. This alerts team members to be vigilant to use design tradeoffs continuously as the system progresses through its development process. As can be noted, criteria supporting the overall build process are proceeding "on target." The exception are the areas of maintenance significance, item analysis, maintenance task analysis, and level of repair, which should be "maximized."

Importance Rating

Assessment Scores		
Supportability	Cost of Ownership	Performance
↑	□	□
□	□	□
↑	↓	□
□	□	□
□	↓	□
↑	□	□
↑	□	□
□	□	□
□	□	□
□	□	□
↑	□	□
□	□	□

Figure 6.12 Assessment Scores.

The *Assessment Scores* (Figure 6.12) room contains the three measurement criteria:

supportability, cost of ownership, and performance. These three metrics give a visual cue to development team members on where the emphasis needs to focus as the system development process proceeds. Noted the overall balance indicated by the 'on target" notation. There is a direct relationship between the initial importance and priority scoring for the supportability characteristic and the notation to "maximize" those characteristics called out.

Summary

This chapter began by ensuring the reader had grasped the concept that supportability assessment is responsible for the identification of the physical resources required to support the system during the development process and that this activity *Functional Supportability Analysis* is normally performed when the product and/or services system is nearing its final stages of completion just prior to customer deployment. Then, it introduced the reader to the three-stage processes of physical supportability analysis which are (1) identification of the complete range of resources required to support the product and/or service system; (2) the optimal support infrastructure and maintenance solution to achieve a balance between performance, support, and cost of ownership; and (3) determination of the minimum quantity of each resource identified to support the system at a pre-stated usage rate. The chapter concluded with a step-by-step build of a QFD Modeling methodology that linked those *Supportability Characteristic Assessment attributes* addressed in Chapter 5 to the *Functional Supportability Analysis* attributes addressed in this chapter, so a development team can better manage the integration of the two processes concurrently vice the current before and after sequential model currently followed and make decisions that focus squarely of balancing supportability, cost of ownership, and performance.

PART 3

Chapter 7

The Evolving Product and/ or Service Requirement

Systems Acquisition Case Study

Airline X, a major U.S. carrier, has a fleet of over 500 large aircraft. The carrier earns roughly half its revenue from the domestic market, with most of its fleet servicing it as the single-aisle B737 next generation (NG). The remainder of its one-aisle fleet are the types that are no longer produced by Boeing (MD90s and B737 classics). To improve the fleet's operating economy, X plans to launch an upgrading program to replace its aging and outdated aircraft with all B737 NGs.

X has determined the 737-700 as the main model in its upgrading program. These 737-700s are proposed to be put into service on U.S. domestic routes, with an average traffic capacity of 700 miles per route, six flights per day, and 360 available days per year. Based on these figures, the proposed aircraft traffic capacity can be calculated as ~207 million seat miles per year. Based on X's accounting policy, the airframe and engine have a depreciation period of ~25 years, with a residual value of ~5% of the initial purchase (book) value (trade price ~34 million per aircraft). X usually takes ~20 years as its aircraft's (economically) useful life in its acquisition decision and uses the figure between the book value and appraisal as the market value. Carrier X uses the current rate of the ten-year U.S. Treasury note @ 2% as risk-free and its current marginal income tax rate as 38.5%.

DOI: 10.4324/9781003336044-10

Carrier X has determined three main risk factors affecting the net present value (NPV) of the acquisition 737-800 upgrading program: yield, fuel prices, and residual value, which is directly affected by the aircraft's functional supportability assessment and packaging.

You have been selected to be a member of a team that has been formed to conduct a modeling evaluation of supportability factors for the proposed system versus potential alternatives over the projected life-cycle of the system. The task is to select and prioritize those supportability factors having the most potential impact on residual value over the system's useful life. Because of its ability to capture salient customer requirements and align their importance with technical and organizational requirements, QFD has been selected as the modeling methodology.

In preparation for executing the acquisition assessment, the QFD team began searching earnestly for examples of how a QFD modeling methodology had been used for *system acquisition evaluation along with functional supportability assessment and packaging.* Team members were disappointed when they found none. Team members in logistically supporting various aircraft systems in Airline X knew functional supportability planning was a life-cycle-oriented activity and that for the acquisition assessment to perform properly, an understanding of how functional supportability had been planned and aligned during the phases of systems development was necessary. In addition, those same team members were aware that a QFD modeling methodology that aligned functional supportability with the development phases of a system was under development. Hearing this, the QFD team lead immediately contacted the modeling developers and requested permission to review the methodology and use the results as a starting point for the *acquisition assessment.* Permission was granted, and an example of a *QFD Life-Cycle Modeling* methodology on a generic system was provided.

Before jumping into the instruction of how the *QFD Life-Cycle Modeling* methodology was designed and initiated, the acquisition team was given a review of the major steps in the system's design and development (see Figure 7.1).

Upon this review's completion, team members began reading the subject book chapter, starting with Defining the Need.

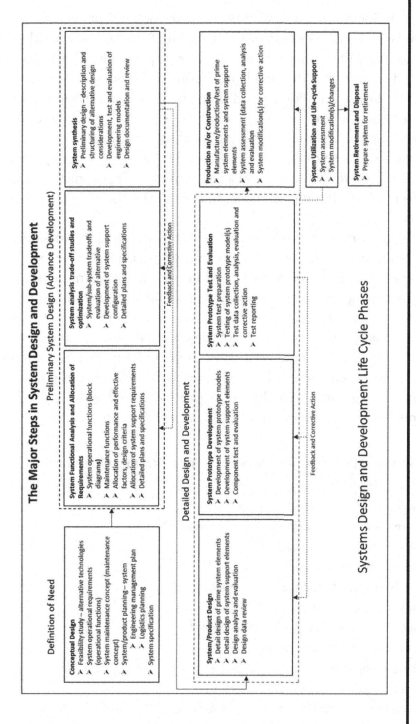

Figure 7.1   Systems Design and Development Life-Cycle Phases.

Defining the Need

The first step in identifying a new "System" (product and/or service) requirement is to define its need. Not what is the System, but what does it have to do to fulfill the customer's need? Several questions must be asked and answered as an initial step in clearly defining the need(s). These are called *critical starting questions*, which must be addressed because their answers constitute the final acceptability of the *system* to meet the customer's needs. Table 7.1 provides a list of these critical starting questions.[39,55]

The answers to these questions also form the basis for *System Functional Supportability Analysis*. They represent the minimum input information necessary to establish basic parameters that delineate the ultimate criteria for System success.

Answering the questions in Table 7.1 is not a simple task. No single system development team person or organization has all the correct answers. Experience has shown that most development team members and organizations have guesses or assumptions that they use as answers but seldom share or compare such with other team members. This, of course, results in confusion about system development goals and parameters. As a general quality tool in the context of TQM, QFD facilitates a strong correlation between customer needs and requirements and design requirements, along with the inclusion of product functional supportability requirements within the spectrum of those design requirements.

Table 7.1 System (Product and/or Service) Critical Starting Questions

System (Product and/or Service) Critical Starting Questions
➢ How will the customer actually use the system?
➢ What are the minimum performance requirements?
➢ Where will the system be used?
➢ How frequently will the system be used?
➢ Under what circumstances will the system be used?
➢ How will the customer measure the system success?
➢ How will the customer measure system failure?
➢ Are there any limitations of system use?
➢ Are there any limitations of system characteristics?
➢ Are there any economic issues or constraints?
➢ Are there any environmental issues or constraints?
➢ Are there any support limitations?

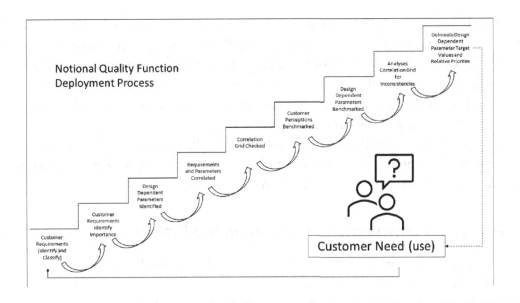

Figure 7.2   Notional Mapping of Customer Requirements into the QFD Process Sequence for the Systems Design Process.

Of course, answers to each question posed in Table 7.1 are important; however, the first question, addressing how the system will be used, is most important. The system's actual use (customer need) creates requirements for functional support and, therefore, is the initial focus of product supportability analysis (PSA). QFD, due to its logical process flow, can translate a prioritized set of subjective customer requirements into a set of system-level requirements during the system conceptual design stage. Figure 7.2 illustrates a notional mapping sequence of customer requirements and QFD activity methods and how they track into the system's design process.[3]

Let us now look at an example of how answering each critical starting question affects a system's (products and/or service) functional supportability profile. We start with "system use" because it creates support requirements. As these questions are addressed, we will also blend into our discussion how using a QFD modeling methodology can greatly enhance the life-cycle supportability planning of that system.

Environmental Impact on Systems Design

In assessing system use, the environment in which the system under development is to be used must be explicitly described. The specific conditions to which the system will be subjected significantly affect its operability. Furthermore, different environments pose different stresses on a system.

Environmental issues can be divided into two major categories: (1) The physical environmental effects on the system and (2) the system's effect on the environment. These two major categories are then measured via a range of acceptability and usage measurements.[56]

Using a QFD modeling process here effectively assesses the numerous system design impact elements and helps guide the QFD system acquisition team's decision-making about alternative design options.

The Physical Environmental Effects on the System

The physical environment where the system will be used can profoundly affect its ability to operate efficiently.

Six factors were selected for evaluation pressure, temperature, humidity, density, and supportability. The selection of these factors is based on their dominant effect on aircraft performance and availability and my firsthand exposure to each in operating aircraft systems in multiple environments. Either individually or together, pressure, temperature, and humidity have a pronounced effect on air density, which affects the performance element. Supportability, which is directly affected by each of these, can directly affect operational and overall readiness. Operating in the Middle East for any time certainly supports the notion. Figure 7.3 illustrates typical areas that must be considered when assessing the physical environment.[56]

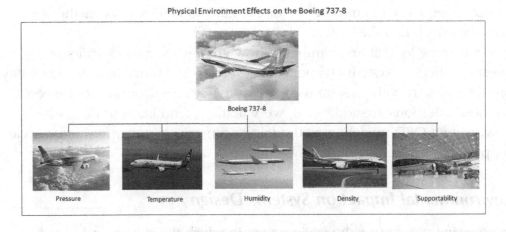

Figure 7.3   Physical Environmental Effects on the Boeing 737-8.

The temperature range of the location where the system will be operated directly impacts its success. If the location is very hot, the system will require some type of cooling. I experienced this directly while operating aircraft in the Middle East. If very cold, such as in Norway, some type of heating is required because metal structures become brittle. The humidity of the environment of operations must also be considered. High humidity levels lead to metal components' corrosion and interfere with electronic assemblies. Externally low levels of humidity cause accelerated deterioration of materials such as rubber gaskets or adhesives. Density additional is of concern for proper system operation. Lift and drag depend linearly on the density. Halving the density halves the lift, halving the density halves the drag. Some systems may be sensitive to shaking. I know from experience; this is very true in rotary-wing aircraft. Violent shaking or long-term movement degrades system performance and ultimately causes failure. Electronic systems can be adversely affected by all these environmental effects. Every possible influence within the environment should be identified and analyzed to ensure it will be successful by eliminating the effect through design characteristics or control measures.

As we build the initial HOQ model, we first evaluate the physical environmental effects on the system. They comprise the systems "What" in the HOQ matrix. Each environmental element is ranked by importance on

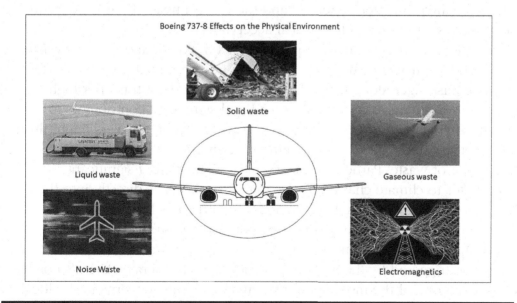

Figure 7.4   Boeing 737-MAX Effects on the Physical Environment.

a scale of 1 (lowest) to 5 (highest), and a relative weight is assigned. For example, pressure and density rare ranked at 5 and 4, respectively. While both profoundly affect aircraft design and material build, each affects the system's performance differently. Supportability is ranked five because regardless of operational profile, the environment in which the system operates dictates directly not only what it takes to support the system but how it is supported.

Priorities are then assigned to each environmental effect. Pressure has the highest ranking at number 5 because it directly relates to the altitude at which the system can efficiently operate and for the time it can do so. This directly affects operational efficiency and the cost of ownership. At number 4, temperature is an indicator of material design, reliability, and maintainability, which correlates with pressure. Coming in at number 3 is supportability, again, this points to where the system is to be operated and how it will be operated.

Relative weights are then assigned, which measure the importance factor percentage.

The Systems Effect on the Physical Environment

Just as the effect of the environment on the system requires assessment, so must the effect the system has on the environment be assessed. Examples of these are illustrated in Figure 7.4. Four types of waste have been selected to evaluate because of the direct influence on the physical environment in which the aircraft system operates and the direct impact it has on consumer perspectives and potentially political acceptance.

A system, such as an aircraft, produces solid, liquid, and gaseous waste, noise, and electromagnetic. *Solid waste* can be substantial. IATA estimates that one passenger alone leaves behind ~3.15 pounds of trash per flight. Gaseous waste emissions are substantial and significant contributors to climate change. *Liquid waste*, on a long-haul 747 flight, travelers might flush the toilets around 1,000 times, creating roughly 230 gallons of sewage— that's a lot of waste! Particle emissions from aircraft are *a* significant contributor to climate change. They emit *Gaseous waste* directly into the higher levels of the atmosphere. In addition, airplanes burn fossil fuel, which not only releases CO_2 emissions but also has strong warming non-CO_2 effects due to nitrogen oxides (NO_x), vapor trails, and cloud formation triggered by the altitude at which aircraft operate. Aircraft noise is considered one of the most significant environmental concerns in the local communities of modern cities, affecting people living near airports. *Aircraft*

Figure 7.5 Hazardous Waste System Effect on the Environment.

Relative Weight	Maximum Relationship	Priority	Importance	Direction of Improvement / System Effect on the Environment / Environmental Effect on the System	Solid Waste	Liquid Waste	Particle Emission	Electromagnetic	Gasous Waste	Noise Pollution	Hazardous Waste
25%	9	5	5	Pressure	1	3	1	3	3	9	9
15%	3	4	3	Temperature	1	3	1	1	3	1	3
15%	3	2	3	Humidity	1	3	1	1	3	1	1
20%	1	1	4	Density	1	3	1	1	1	1	1
25%	9	3	5	Supportability	9	9	9	9	9	9	9

noise is intermittent, and exposure to it during the night may result in sleep disturbance. Noise-induced sleep disturbance refers to awakenings, changes to sleep structure such as changes to sleep stages, arousals in heart rate, and body movements.

These types of waste require control, storage, and disposal. Storage and disposal of environmentally hazardous waste increases the cost of a system operation and support, which generally increases the cost of ownership significantly. Many systems, such as aircraft, produce emissions like fumes, smoke, dust, or noxious odors that negatively affect the environment. Often, electronic systems produce *Electromagnetic Emissions* that interfere with other systems and are sometimes physically harmful. Limiting the environmental impact must be a central consideration in a system's design characteristics and QFD provided an excellent methodology to do so.

The system's effects on the environment are depicted as the "hows" in Life-Cycle model. Each environmental element is evaluated and assigned a direction of improvement annotation indicating it should be maximized, considered on target (balanced), or minimized.

In the HOQ matrix roof, each environmental attribute is correlated with each other as either strong positive ++, positive +, negative -, strong negative— or 0 no correlation. For example, hazardous waste, which can be defined as any of those listed in Figure 7.5, is correlated strong positive with each of the other system's physical effects on the environment. Gaseous waste is not surprisingly positively correlated with solid, liquid, and particle, a by-product of all three.

Performance, Quality, Support, and the Cost of Ownership

The goal of identifying system supportability requirements is to create a range of acceptability that will be used throughout the systems life-cycle starting with the conceptualization stage. The range of acceptability establishes a set of objectives, goals, thresholds, and constraints applied to all stages of systems development. In addition, the concept of attaining a balance between performance, supportability, and ownership cost is critical, along with the measurability of system characteristics via Technical Performance Measurements (TPMs) to provide the highest functional supportability at the lowest cost of ownership.

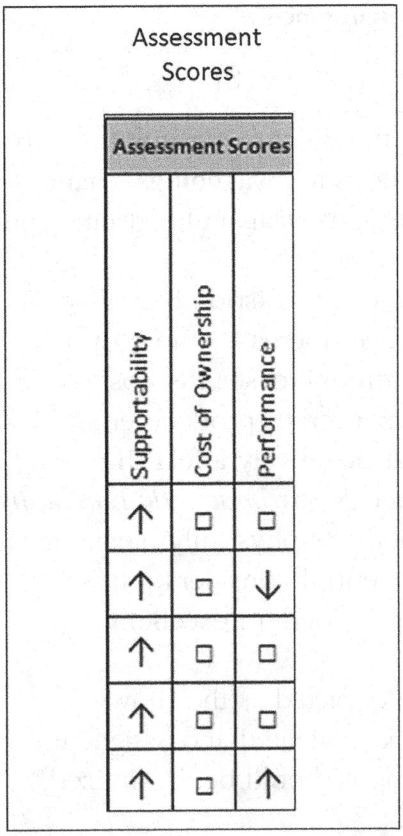

These are depicted as assessment scores in the HOQ matrix. These elements are evaluated on the basis of the influence each has on the operational requirements and the environmental impact assessment elements previously assessed. While they are not quantitatively linked. Each element, supportability, cost of ownership, and performance is assessed as needing either to maximize, on target, or to minimize and act as a cue to development team members to stay on target. Note that supportability is annotated with consistent maximize on each environmental effect. This is expected given that the system is in the conceptual stage. Also note that the cost of ownership is on target. To the financial folks in the crowd, you should be giving the development team high fives! Performance is expected to be split

Figure 7.6   Assessment Scores for Systems Effect on the Environment.

here. As we move into the preliminary and detailed design stages, we will witness changes in this measurement.

System Rate of Use

The rate of frequency of system use being developed must be determined to establish a baseline in the conceptual stage of development. It subsequently will serve as the analyses bases for decisions throughout its life-cycle. Two main statistics are measured when determining the rate or frequency of use:

■ Measurement base and
■ Number increments of the measurement base

Table 7.2 illustrates a general set of usage measurement bases.

As illustrated in the table, the use of a system can be measured in time, distance, volume, or events. Most electronic systems are measured in operating time, and usually, the number of hours the system is operated. The usage rate of a pump is usually measured in volumes such as gallons or liters pumped per minute or hour. More complex systems have more than one usage measurement base. For example, the usage of an aircraft is measured in several different ways: flying hours for the complete aircraft, operating hours for the engine, and number of landings (cycles) for the landing gear.

Usage measurement bases are correlated with the assessment scoring characteristics. Serving the same purpose as the assessment scoring,

Table 7.2 Usage Measurement Bases

Time	Distance	Volume	Events
Years	Miles	Barrels	Units Produced
Months	Meters	Gallons	Production Strokes
Weeks	Kilometers	Liters	Transmission
Days	Yards	Milliliters	Mission Count Per Time Unit
Hours	Feet	Centimeters	Event Measurement Accuracy
Minutes	Inches	Cubic inches	Cycles

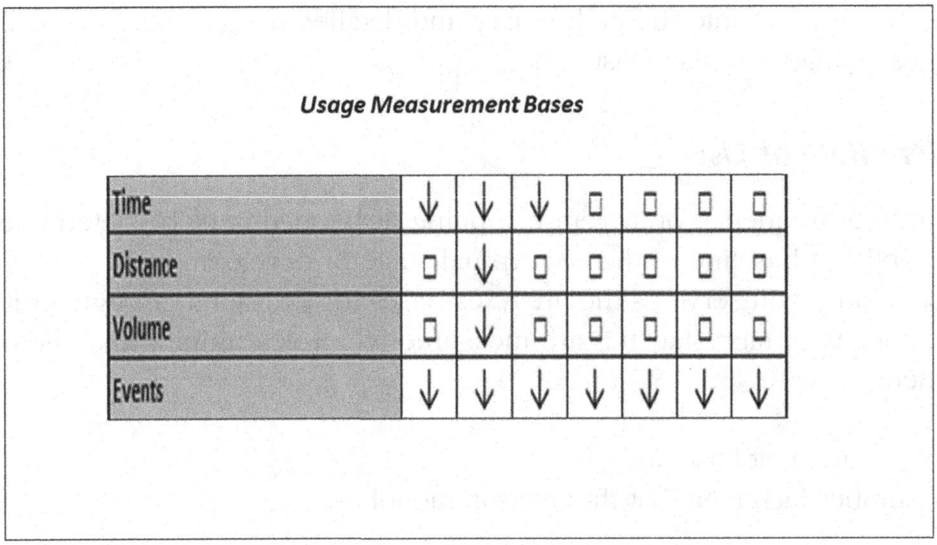

Usage Measurement Bases

Time	↓	↓	↓	☐	☐	☐	☐
Distance	☐	↓	☐	☐	☐	☐	☐
Volume	☐	↓	☐	☐	☐	☐	☐
Events	↓	↓	↓	↓	↓	↓	↓

Figure 7.7   Usage Measurement for System Effect on the Environment.

Table 7.3   System Use Rate Examples

Automobile	Computer system	Transfer process	Aircraft
12,000 miles driven yearly	18 hours operated daily	1000 strokes per hour	-1200 operating hours yearly -1500 engine hours yearly -600 landings yearly

they help team members visibly discern the relationship with customer requirements and specification characteristics to ensure systems alignment and balance.

Once the appropriate measurement base, or bases, has been defined, the number of increments of each measurement basis is determined. The number of increments combined with the measurement base results in the system usage rate. Table 7.3 lists examples of system usage rates.

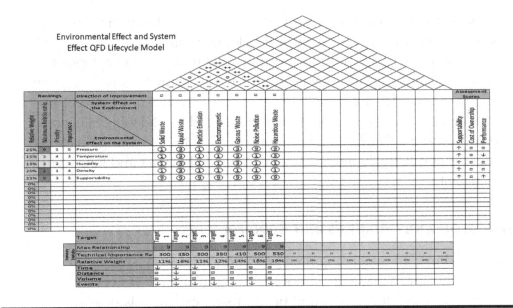

Figure 7.8   Environmental Effect and System Effect QFD Life-Cycle Model.

System usage is an extremely significant statistic that must be determined and agreed to by all development team members before making any development or procurement decisions. Lack of a complete definition of system use can result in inappropriate system characteristics, loss or degradation of capability, or the system being overdesigned. Any of these unwanted events will result in an undesirable and unnecessary increase in the cost of ownership.

The final step in constructing the initial QFD Life-Cycle model HOQ matrix is to link all the rooms into a unified model in the relationship matrix. Figure 7.8 illustrates these finished matrices. The QFD team now has a framework from which they can evaluate the system's design ideas and alternative technologies.

The relationship matrix presents relationship scoring of "Why" and "How" criteria on 1, 3, and 9 scales. One the lowest association with nine the highest. Column scores are summarized in the summary statistics room below the relationship matrix. Two important statistics are presented here. *The Technical Importance Rating and Relative Weight.* Examination of the technical performance ratings shows that initially hazardous waste, noise pollution, and liquid waste are focus areas when considering design solutions. While not all that surprising, this is interesting that all three are very political and may point to the use of environmentally friendly alternate technologies early in the development cycle. This said, our initial analysis tells us that the technology bases of development may be more oriented towards the modernization of an existing system than the development of a totally new system. This may mean that trade-off analysis will be pretty active during the development cycle. Provides us with knowledge of how they may want to evaluate criteria when engaged in tradeoff evaluations. A look at *Relative Weight* and the even spread of the percentage data tells us there is considerable interest in environmental impact and long-term sustainability.

System Support Analysis and Requirements

The importance of expending time and effort to identify specific requirements for the system cannot be overemphasized. However, the benefits of producing a sound product support analysis plan and identifying functional support requirements can only be realized when the requirements are communicated to all development team members and to all organizations involved in the development or procurement of the system. Figures 7.9 and 7.10 provide illustrations of supportability analysis elements and supportability requirements, respectively.

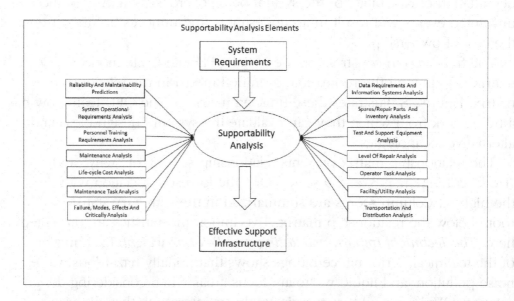

Figure 7.9   Supportability Analysis Elements.

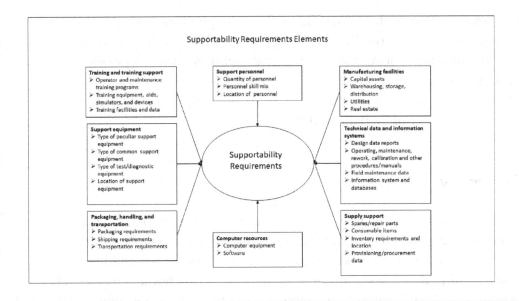

Figure 7.10 Supportability Requirements Elements.

System Support Infrastructure

A system must also be adequately supported to operate efficiently. Adequate support starts with an infrastructure that can provide resources to operate and maintain the system. Then the resources required to be delivered by the infrastructure must be identified and obtained in sufficient quantities. The actual support resources required to support a system can only be identified after the design solution has been achieved. However, at the start of the procurement process, it is important to define the system's need, where and how it is intended to be operated and how it will be supported throughout its life. Employing a QFD methodology to link all developmental and supportability factors together throughout all phases of a system life-cycle is becoming the method of choice because of its ability to link all aspects of system requirements into one holistic model flow. It also acts as a central organizational station where all skills involved in building the system can plan, share ideas, and evaluate all necessary tradeoffs to ensure that supportability, performance, and cost of ownership are equally assessed during the development process.

By using the QFD process to help define operational requirements and measurements for a system, related factors can be readily identified and applied to the systems development process, ensuring it will be designed to satisfy the customer's needs (specifications). This will lead to the development of the TPMs that are then applied to design-to criteria for all Functional Supportability Elements and marked as Critical to Quality (CTQ) attributes. Those critical TPMs will subsequently be prioritized and allocated across each phase of the system life-cycle based on the range of acceptability where performance, functional supportability, and cost of ownership are equally balanced.[47]

Summary

This chapter acted as a pivot for the reader. They were placed in the realm of the systems development life-cycle process, which is the basis for new or redesigned products and/or services, and presented with how defining those system requirements drives functional supportability elements and packaging. The chapter presented the reader with a real-world *Systems Acquisition case study*, which would serve as a thread throughout Chapters 7, 8, and 9. It required the reader to assess a chosen system by selected functional supportability elements and how they should be prioritized and packaged during its forecasted operational life-cycle. Because the prioritizing and packaging of those elements required an understanding of how they were initially conceptualized and architected during each of the systems life-cycle phases, a structured process by which all functional supportability elements are planned, assessed, and measured during each life-cycle phase starting with conception and ending in retirement was conducted using a *QFD Life-Cycle Modeling* methodology. Understanding the *need* for the system was initially addressed. It then led the reader through a discussion of *critical starting questions* that required addressing as an initial step in defining requirements. The chapter then illustrated to the reader, through a QFD Life-Cycle Modeling methodology, how environmental development criteria affected the conceptualization of the overall system. It then addressed how this same *QFD Life-Cycle Modeling* methodology was used to aid in the evaluation of the rate of use and support infrastructure and as a basis for the product and/or services supportability requirements study. The chapter referred to the assessment criteria of *performance, support, and cost of ownership*. It reiterated that the overarching goal during all phases of system development was attaining a balance between each criterion.

Next Steps

Once the selected *System Acquisition QFD team* members finished reading the *QFD Life-Cycle Modeling* initialization steps, the team lead solicited their thoughts on understanding the overall methodology. Most team members stated that while most were not familiar with the QFD methodology, they did grasp its structured approach and logical sequencing. However, as more discussion ensued, it was evident many were perplexed about its application processes for the system as it moved through its development life-cycle. Hearing this, the team asked the model developers, "could you walk us through an application process." The developers responded, "Absolutely!"

Chapter 8 will present the application of the *QFD Life-Cycle Modeling* methodology, starting with the Conceptual Design stage of development and ending with Systems Retirement and Disposal, and illustrate how it is used to assess "Why" and "How" required functional supportability elements are planned, measured, and ranked during each life-cycle phase. The results from this analysis will aid the *Systems Acquisition QFD team* formed by Airline X in their acquisition evaluation.

Chapter 9 will present the *QFD Acquisition Modeling* methodology used by team members for the tasking described in the case study as, "Carrier X has determined there are three main risk factors affecting the NPV of the 737-800 acquisition program, yield, fuel prices and residual value which is directly affected by the aircraft's functional support packaging."[57–60]

Chapter 8

Using a Quality Function Deployment Life-Cycle Methodology to Create and Design a System

Systems Architecting, Methodologies, and Results

The design of a system (product or service) evolves through a series of activities that start with identifying a need and result in a final physical design. Figure 8.1,

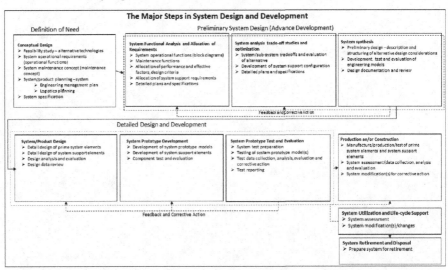

Figure 8.1 The Major Steps in System Design and Development.

DOI: 10.4324/9781003336044-11

initially presented in Chapter 7, where the Conceptualization of the system was addressed, is restated. Our discussion will begin with the Preliminary System Design stage, where *system functional analysis and allocation* are conducted, *tradeoff studies and optimization* are executed, and *system synthesis* is performed. Participation in the evolutionary process of creating the design offers significant opportunities for supportability analysis to interject requirements for improving the supportability of offering of the system and limiting the overall cost of ownership.[30,61–66] We start with systems architecting.

Systems Architecting

The first step in creating a system is identifying the limits of acceptability for the system delivered to the customer. The role of system architecting in the design process is to establish a creditable range of acceptability within which the design must reside. Systems architecting is an art, not a scientific process. It is an inductive, non-analytical approach to creating complex systems. It requires development team members to use insight, vision, intuition, judgment, and feelings or taste to guide design activities. It has proven to be the most appropriate method of creating new and unprecedented systems marked by complexity. Figure 8.2 illustrates some of the reasons system architecting is applied to acquire a new system.[39,46,47,52]

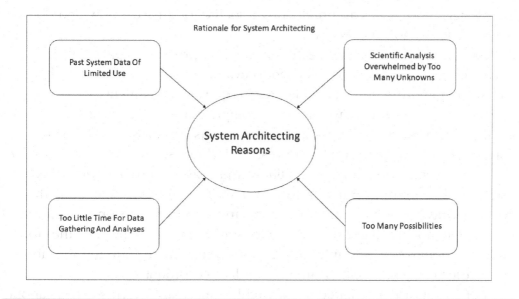

Figure 8.2 Rationale for System Architecting.

Most new systems are developed to replace those that are aging and possibly obsolete or that the changing market dynamics. Such may be the case with the system being considered in the case study presented in Chapter 6. Electronic systems may also be a classic example of this. The old system may have been in use for many years and a tremendous amount of usage and support data is available for analysis. However, the technology baseline is usually obsolete, the environment of use may have changed, and the new system may be more advanced. All these situations make the historical data on the old system useless in developing the new system.[67]

To be effective, any scientific analysis must investigate facts. Any attempt to perform this task with no boundaries or limits is overwhelming. There are just too many unknowns of what the future holds. Therefore, at the beginning of systems development, assumptions must be made, decisions about the future unknowns must be defined, and limits set for the new system. This is the purpose of systems architecting.

Starting a system design process with little or no direction is akin to wandering aimlessly in a desert with no water. First, there must be some initial definition of goals to be reached. The same is true for the system development effort. There are just too many possibilities; without a clear understanding of the final goals coupled with limitations and boundaries, it will not be successful.

Finally, the design of a system is time-dependent; a fast and furious process creates it. There is normally little time for gathering and analyzing. The design process has an unrelenting appetite for answers now and does not settle for tomorrow very well.

To begin the systems architecting evaluation process, a QFD Life-Cycle Modeling methodology is used to evaluate the reasons for systems architecting and the unmeasurable areas requiring assessment.

Systems architecting reasons would comprise the "What" for the architecting process. An importance ranking has been assigned to each reason criterion ranging from 1 (lowest) to 5 (highest). Note that at this stage of development, "too many possibilities" and "past system data of limited use" have been ranked 5 and 4, respectively. This indicates that while the system being developed might be a new and improved version of a current system, technology might pose limitations to its use of such. Also, the "too many possibilities" would indicate that the development team must establish boundaries because of either time or funding constraints.

Priorities are then assigned to the architecting reasons. This tells us about the order in which the reasons are assessed. In this case, the assessment

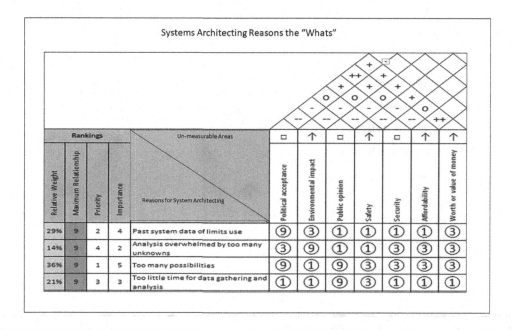

Figure 8.3   Systems Architecting Reasons the "Whats."

order is "too many possibilities" and "past system data of limits use." This priority order tells us that the team formed to guide the development process is squarely focused a process-driven development.

Unmeasurable Areas

There are many issues that the design process must address when considering architecting the system and planning its supportability. Unfortunately, many prominent issues that guide the system's development cannot be readily measured. Figure 8.4 illustrates some of the more significant unmeasurable areas that must be considered before starting the system architecting process.[39,46,47,52]

Public opinion must be considered. If the public has concerns at the start of a product development process or acquisition, their concerns must be addressed. Market surveys, opinion polls, and consumer research provide valuable insight into identifying and resolving these issues. Here QFD is specifically designed to capture these attributes and provide the visibility necessary for prompt action.

Along with public opinion, there may be a requirement for *political backing* or funding. A system characteristic or technology that is not

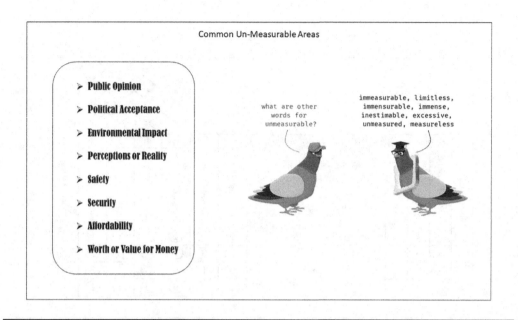

Figure 8.4 Common Unmeasurable Areas.

politically acceptable has little chance of success. This has been a consistent issue with designing systems with a military application.

Any final design solution must conform to some perceived *environmental acceptance.* An assessment of how the system will affect the environment must be conducted, and questions must be answered as to what resources it will take from the environment and what byproducts or emissions will be placed into the environment by the proposed system.

Differences in the *customer's perception and reality* are another challenge that systems architecting must address. The customer may have a need perception of a requirement is a requirement and how it must be designed to meet that requirement. However, meeting that need may be impossible based on design restrictions. I am reminded of a quote from an unnamed politician, "truth is what people believe, and that is not necessarily the real truth." It is worth mentioning that QFD, because of its design around the "VOC," is the tool of choice for minimizing the perception gaps.

Safety and Security are always a concern when architecting a system. A system's safety is often dictated by three issues: its technology bases, environmental bases, and *usage profile.* Systems architecting must consider these three issues when developing the range of acceptability of any design aspect. In addition, some systems have an inherent requirement for security. For example, data systems must have security features to protect their content from unauthorized access or modification. Military systems must consider national security implications as well.

System architecting of a new system must consider *affordability*, not cost of ownership. Affordability looks at the larger scale to determine the range of expenditures caused by any potential system design. For example, if one needs transportation normally, they do not immediately rush out and purchase a vehicle. The wise consumer first considers the affordability of any means of transportation. It may be more practical to use an alternate means of transport such as public transport.

In addition to affordability, systems architecting must consider the *worth or value of money* that the customer places on the systems being designed. The customer has a sense of value from the expenditure of possessing the system. The higher the value placed on the system, the more consideration must be given to performance and supportability characteristics.

Unmeasurable elements serve as the "How" criteria in Figure 8.5. These criteria are assessed as needing either to maximize, considered on target, or to minimize. Criteria at the stage of development are

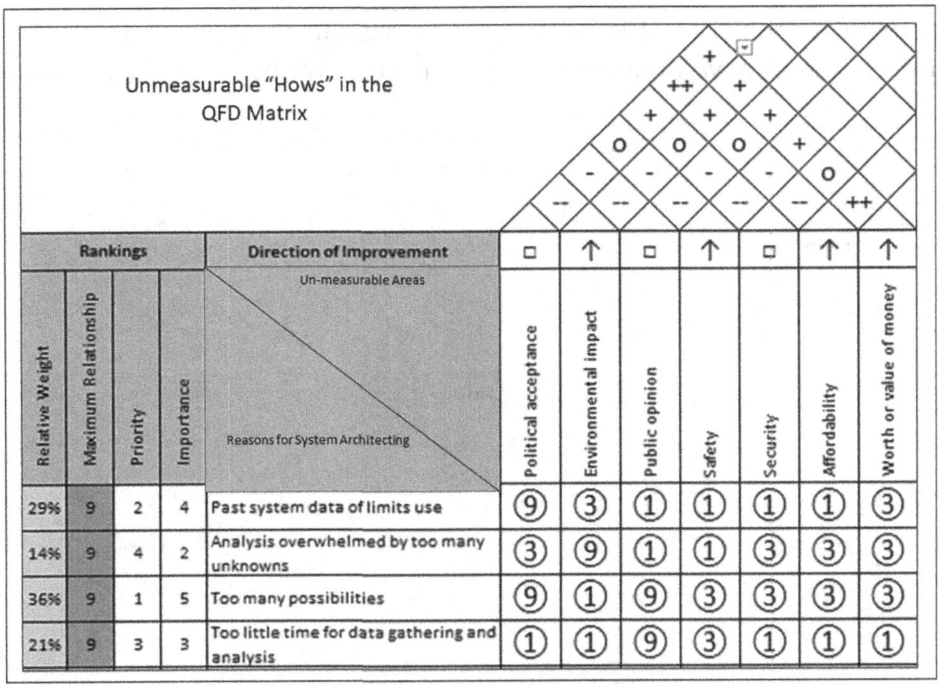

Rankings				Direction of Improvement		□	↑	□	↑	□	↑	↑
Relative Weight	Maximum Relationship	Priority	Importance	Un-measurable Areas Reasons for System Architecting		Political acceptance	Environmental impact	Public opinion	Safety	Security	Affordability	Worth or value of money
29%	9	2	4	Past system data of limits use		⑨	③	①	①	①	①	③
14%	9	4	2	Analysis overwhelmed by too many unknowns		③	⑨	①	①	③	③	③
36%	9	1	5	Too many possibilities		⑨	①	⑨	③	③	③	③
21%	9	3	3	Too little time for data gathering and analysis		①	①	⑨	③	①	①	①

Figure 8.5   Unmeasurable "Hows" in the QFD Matrix.

expected to change as the system build progresses through its life-cycle; however, even at this early stage, it is clear there is an emphasis on the environmental impact, safety, affordability, and worth or value of money. In the matrix, roof correlations are housed between the unmeasurable criteria. Since these are qualitatively discerned, they provide a visual to team members of the interdependences of the criteria. As an example, there is a very strong association (double pluses ++), between "worth or value of money" and "affordability." There are also some negative associations (notated by the —) between affordability and security. The more security you build into the system, the more costs are incurred, which negatively affects affordability.

Methodologies

As applied system architecting to define system parameters, four methods can be applied. These methods, which can be either qualitative or quantitative, are illustrated in Figure 8.6. When used together, these methods can provide the basis for determining the range of acceptability for potentially any design solution.[47]

The normative method of system architecting identifies established parameters for the type of system codes or regulatory agencies. For example, authoritative organizations may have published standards to which

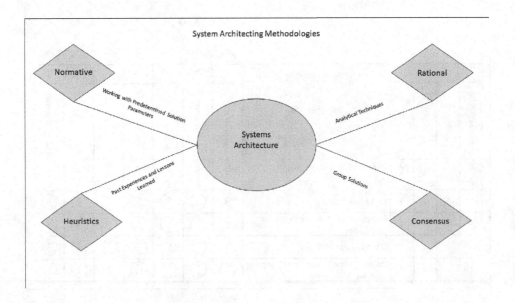

Figure 8.6 System Architecting Methodologies.

the organization must conform (e.g., IEEE standards or ISO specifications, military standards, or trade handbooks). Systems architecting identifies the applicable established parameters and then expresses them in terms appropriate for the new system.

The next step of system architecting is to apply analytical techniques to rationalize parameters for the system. This analysis is performed for system-level characteristics to determine any measurable points for the parameters. Conceptual modeling using appropriate assumptions and usage projections is most beneficial for this step. The modeling results can be used to determine minimum and maximum limits for the system that point toward achieving necessary levels of operational effectiveness O_E, operational availability A_O, and cost of ownership. This modeling determines what the system needs to attain, not what it will achieve.

The third step of the system architecting process is to obtain input from all the groups participating and associated with the system. This group includes the customer, all engineering specialists, manufacturing, quality, finance, and especially, supportability assessment. Systems architecting takes the inputs from each group and attempts to develop a set of system parameters, which each group agrees meet their specific concerns. The focus is then to define the qualitative and quantitative parameters further so that the final design foundation will produce a system that each group will accept as a reasonable solution.

Table 8.1 Common Heuristic Examples

Common Heuristic Examples
➤ Keep it simple (the KISS principle).
➤ If it can go wrong, it will (Murphy's law).
➤ Do not assume that the original statement of the problem is the best, or even the right one.
➤ If you cannot explain it in five minutes, either you do not understand it or it does not work.
➤ All the serious mistakes are made on the first day of a project.
➤ A model is not reality.

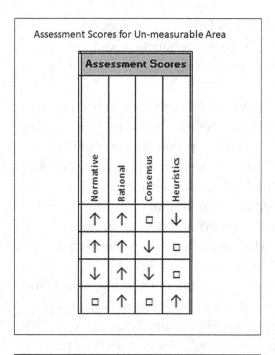

Figure 8.7 shows a table titled "Assessment Scores for Un-measurable Area" with columns Normative, Rational, Consensus, Heuristics.

Figure 8.7   Assessment Scores for Unmeasurable Areas.

The last step of this process is to apply common sense. The formal name for this method is an application of heuristics. A heuristic is a lesson, or truth, learned in a previous specific situation that is proven to apply to all future situations. Table 8.1 lists some common heuristics, each of which is common sense and self-explanatory. However, they apply to any system development project.

From my experience, the most applicable is the challenge of simplicity. The second is always to expect the unexpected, what could go wrong. Finally, it is always best to research the basic premises upon which the project is established because the original problem statement may not be the real problem. Anytime a modeling technique is applied to a project, especially in its formative stage, all development team members must understand that modeling results are not the final truth; they are only projections of reality.

System architecting methods comprise our HOQ in the "Assessment Scores" room. These scores serve as a notional cue to team members that a desired methodology is preferred over another. In this case, the relational methodology is preferred with the normative as acceptable if there is a comparative system to aid in assessment.

The final step in our QFD Model build is to populate the relationship matrix that links the reasons for system architecture with the unmeasurable criteria. This model is reflected in Figure 8.8.

Below the relationship matrix, summary statistics are provided. The Technical Importance Rating is important. This uses the column ratings of relationship strength of 9, 3 and 1 reflected in the matrix along with relative weight percentages in the Rankings column to give an importance rating of the strength of the relationship between the "whys" and "hows." Political acceptance and public opinion, with technical importance ratings of 643 and 557, respectively, and relative weight

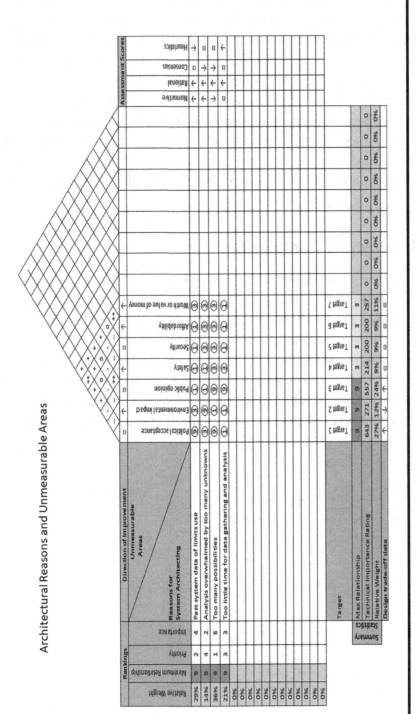

Figure 8.8   Architectural Reasons and Unmeasurable Areas.

percentages of 27% and 24% are by far the most important statistics at the stage of development which is not surprising. At this early stage of development, considerable pressure is on the development team to market and sell the conceptual idea for system development to assure continued support and, more importantly, funding.

An additional attribute captured and annotated in the matrix is Design Tradeoff Data. It is just below the summary statistics. I have found that while this data point is not quantitatively linked to other matrix elements, it serves as a visual cue to development team members to be conscious of where tradeoff decisions should be considered during the development process, especially the early stages of development.

System Architecting Complexity

One of the central challenges for system architecting is understanding the interrelationships of all the system functions and producing a set of parameters that guide all design and development activities. As each additional function is integrated into the system, its complexity increases exponentially. Therefore, system architecting must understand the interrelationships of all the system functions. A "function" in this context refers to a specific or discrete action, or a series of actions, necessary to achieve a given level of performance. The methodology by which

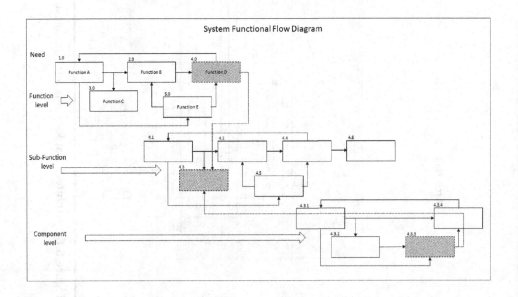

Figure 8.9 System Functional Flow Diagram.

Table 8.2   Functional Diagram Approach Outcomes

Functional Diagram Approach Outcomes
➤That all facets of system design and development, operations, support, and retirement /disposal are covered; that is, all significant activities within the system life cycle.
➤That all elements of the system are fully recognized and defined to include: prime equipment, spare/repair parts, test and support equipment, facilities, personnel, data, and software.
➤That a means is provided for relating system packaging concepts and support requirements to specific system functions.
➤That all proper sequences of activity and design relationships are established along with critical design interfaces.

these functions are aligned and assessed is called a "functional analysis." Functional analysis is "an iterative process of breaking requirements down from the system level to the subsystem, and as far down in a hierarchical structure as necessary to identify input design criteria and/or constraints for the various elements of the system."

Functional analysis is facilitated through a functional flow diagram. As illustrated in Figure 8.9, diagrams are developed primarily to structure system requirements into functional terms.[30]

They are developed to illustrate basic system organization and to identify functional interfaces. The functional analysis and the generation of functional flow diagrams are intended to enable the completion of the design, development, and system definition process comprehensively and logically. Top-level requirements are identified, partitioned to a second level, and down to the depth required for "definition." More specifically, as illustrated in Table 8.2, functional flow approach helps ensure systems architecting reflects the following:

Systems Architecting Results

The systems architecting process defines the parameters to which the system design must adhere. The parameters are best described as issues and considerations expressed in quantitative terms, where possible, limitations,

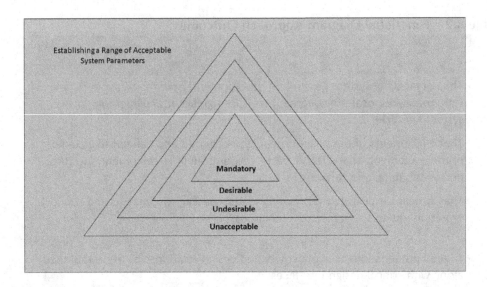

Figure 8.10   Establishing a Range of Acceptable System Parameters.

and boundaries. They form the goals, thresholds, and constraints of the system supportability process. The concept presented in Figure 8.10 shows that parameters are identified as being mandatory, desirable, undesirable, and unacceptable.[30]

A mandatory parameter must be achieved. An aircraft capable of reaching a speed of Mach 2.2 would be an example of a mandatory parameter. A desirable parameter should be achieved if possible. Such as the aircraft going Mach 2.2 should not suffer from excise vibration during speed runs. An undesirable parameter should not occur but may be acceptable if no alternative is possible. An unacceptable parameter is an outcome that will not be accepted. For example, the aircraft will not reach Mach 2.2.

The system architecting process clearly defines the range of acceptability for performance, supportability, and cost of ownership parameters for the new system. These parameters are then passed as TPMs into the overall systems development process for scientific implementation into the design solution. Here the QFD Life-Cycle Modeling technique of assessing the "Whats" and "Hows" is superior as the systems development moves further throughout its life-cycle.[46,68]

Systems Engineering Process and Development Cycle

It requires scientific analysis, engineering techniques, and methods to create a system that meets a specified need. This occurs via a systems engineering

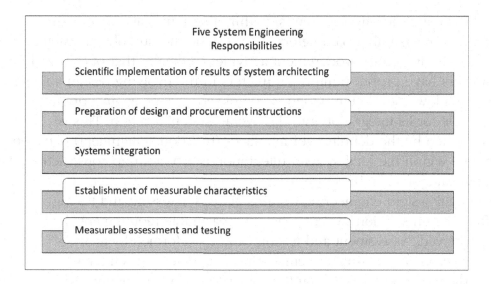

Figure 8.11   Five System Engineering Responsibilities.

(SE) process where the definition of that need gives primary direction for all activities associated with the SE process.

Systems Engineering as defined by International Council of Systems Engineering (INCOSE) is a "transdisciplinary and integrative approach to enable the successful realization, use, and retirement of engineered systems, using systems principles and concepts, and scientific, technological and management methods." The responsibilities of system engineering range from a few to more than a dozen, depending on what you are reading. That said, from my perspective, five over-arching responsibilities of system engineering warrant address. Figure 8.11 illustrates these five responsibilities.

While there is no specific order of these responsibilities, all are built around systems integration. First, the range of acceptable system parameters is analyzed to determine the most appropriate system engineering activities. Each parameter is analyzed to determine the most appropriate method of describing its measurable characteristics. Where a specific parameter cannot be translated into a measurable requirement, system engineering investigates alternatives for expressing the requirement, or investigates sub-elements of the parameters that can be measured. The measurability of each parameter is mandatory. If a requirement cannot be measured, its achievement cannot be verified.

System engineering is then responsible for ensuring instructions are issued to design engineering for creation off, or ensuring instructions are issued to create the physical item(s) within a system that contains the appropriate measurable parameters. These same measurable parameters must also be issued to procurement activities to ensure that outsourced parameters have proper built-in parameters in the evolving design solution.

As each lower-level item design is completed, system engineering is responsible for its integration into the overall system solution. This is accomplished by the definition of interfaces (functional alignment) between each item within the total system. Integration is a bottom-up construction of the physical system architecture.

The final system engineering responsibility is assessing and testing the final design solution to verify that all measurable requirements have been achieved. Assessment and testing can be performed by analysis, demonstration, and testing. System engineering determines the most appropriate method for verifying the achievement of each parameter.

System Development Cycle

Every decision made during the system architecting process must consider the effect of that decision on performance, supportability, and cost of ownership. The areas of supportability and cost of ownership are, of course, the focus of supportability management. As the system moves through each stage of its life-cycle, differing types and amounts of support are required. An illustration of a typical system development cycle for a system was provided in Figure 8.1.[30]

As illustrated in Figure 8.1, a system begins with the definition of a need. Once that need has been completely defined, the process moves into the conceptual design stage. This stage starts with system architecting and then moves to systems engineering. The next stage is the development of a preliminary design solution. A detailed design activity next produces a product baseline, which is then passed to manufacturing for the system's production. The final system is then delivered to the customer, placed into service, and sustained throughout its intended life-cycle. In the final stage, retirement and/or disposal, the system is again assessed by system engineering to discern whether it warrants consideration for either a life extension or retirement/recycling. Supportability assessment and management participate in all these phases of a system life-cycle.

In the paragraphs to follow using the same QFD Life-Cycle Modeling methodology introduced in Chapter 4 when the need for the system was assessed and introduced in this chapter to assess measurable and unmeasurable criteria, this same modeling methodology will be used

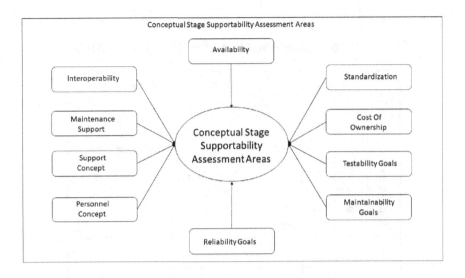

Figure 8.12   Conceptual Stage Supportability Assessment Areas.

to illustrate how supportability requirements can be measured in the consecutive phase of the systems life-cycle. Starting with the Conceptual phase, the "Whats" from one phase will become the "Hows" to the next phase as the system progresses through its life-cycle. At the end of this process, we will again visit the acquisition case presented in Chapter 4 and work through the systems acquisition process using QFD.

Conceptual Stage Supportability Planning

Supportability management focus during the *conceptual design stage* centers on the development of requirements that will eventually produce a supportable design. Requirements are stated in terms of objectives, goals, thresholds, and constraints. Each requirement must be determined according to the overall goals of availability and cost of ownership. Targets for inherent, achieved, and operational availability are established. The ability to analyze various design and technology alternatives is mandatory at this stage.

Typically, several design approaches are developed to meet the stated customer need(s). Each design approach is assessed via the supportability process to determine the preferred supportability element design concept. Figure 8.12 indicates the areas that supportability assessment addresses during the conceptual design stage.[30,39,52]

Conceptual Stage Ranking of Assessment Criteria

Relative Weight	Maximum Relationship	Priority	Importance	Direction of Improvement
14%	9	1	5	Availability
14%	9	2	5	Reliability
9%	9	8	3	Standardization
11%	3	3	4	Cost of Ownership
9%	9	9	3	Testability
11%	9	4	4	Maintainability
6%	9	7	2	Personnel Concept
9%	9	5	3	Support Concept
9%	9	6	3	Maintenance Concept
9%	9	10	3	Interoperability

Rankings / Direction of Improvement: Preliminary Stage Supportability Assessment — Conceptual Stage Supportability Assessment

Figure 8.13   Conceptual Stage Ranking of Assessment Criteria.

All supportability elements, including reliability, maintainability, and testability, are developed with specific targets that can be assessed as to how they support the overall system availability targets.

These supportability elements would comprise "What" requirements in our QFD Life-Cycle model.

Supportability assessment during the conceptual design stage identifies potential standardization interoperability for inclusion into system design requirements. Initially, assessment criteria are ranked by level of importance by the development team on a scale of 1 to 5, with one being the least and five being the most important. Noted here is that both availability and reliability are the most important during this stage of system development. And the cost of ownership and maintainability as the next most important. Of interest is that with the exception of personnel concept, ranked at 2, all other assessment criteria are ranked mid-range 3 for importance. This reflects a focused development effort that understands that supportability, performance, and cost of ownership must be focused on from the start of development.

Each supportability assessment criterion then received a priority ranking. The top priorities of significance, were availability, reliability, cost of ownership, and maintainability. Not surprisingly, the priorities and importance rankings mirror each other. The difference is that the priorities give the order in which tradeoffs are considered as the system progresses through the development stages.

Preliminary Design Supportability Planning

In the preliminary design stage, the system functional block diagram (see Figure 8.14) is an important tool used to understand dependencies. Because this diagram starts with the top-level system functions, then divides them into sub-systems/assemblies, and finally into the lowest

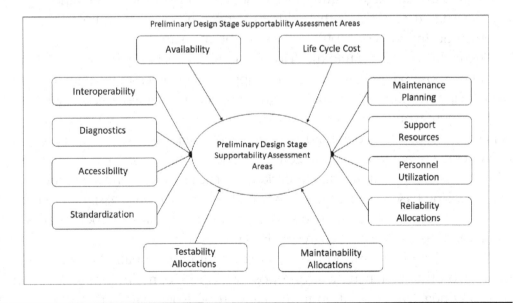

Figure 8.14   Preliminary Design Stage Supportability Assessment Areas.

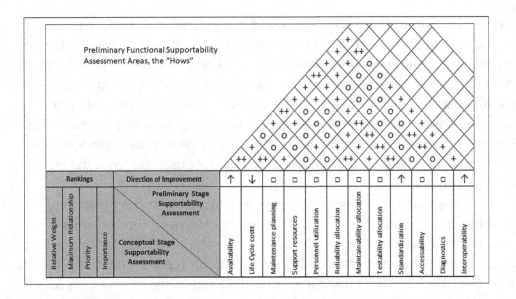

Figure 8.15   Preliminary Design Stage Supportability Assessment Areas.

level (component) or procurable items, it is also used for overall system reliability and maintainability planning thus forming the bases for system availability.

Supportability planning and assessment during the Preliminary Design Stage is a refinement, amplification, and expansion of all activities started in the conceptual stage. Figure 8.15 illustrates some of the significant engineering characteristics that address "How" the system requirements assessed during the conceptual stage can be measured.

These elements constitute the "Hows" in our QFD Life-Cycle model. They would be those preliminary functional supportability assessment elements that would support those conceptual design supportability assessment elements. Each element would be assessed as either maximized (up arrow) kept on target (square) or minimized (down arrow). As noted, availability, standardization, and interoperability are to be maximized during sequential stages of development while focusing on minimizing life-cycle cost. These recommendations are not surprising based on the importance and priority rankings assigned to the conceptual supportability elements. The one outlier is that interoperability is emphasized as the system progresses into preliminary design.

These preliminary supportability areas would additionally be correlated with each other as having a strong positive, positive, neutral, negative, or strong negative correlation in the HOQ roof. Note that there are strong correlations among those preliminary functional assessment areas thus supporting the supportability maximization recommendation. The evidence of the strong positive of standardization, life-cycle cost, and availability illustrates all TPMs are aligning with the central themes. In addition, the positive trend illustrated by interoperability with the "How" assessment attributes indicates that a "design for producibility" is being adapted.

Adjunct to this Life-Cycle Model HOQ would be assessment scoring that contains the architecting methodologies. These would be assessed similarly to the preliminary assessment areas, maximize, minimize, or keep on target. Its purpose is to express to team members the necessary orientation during this architecting methodology focus. From the scoring, it can be interpreted that the rational methodology would be chosen during the development process. This is not surprising since a solid analytical approach is highly desirable even if the developed system has a solid normative type available.

Before proceeding into the Detailed Design stage, the development team would populate the relationship matrix linking the conceptual system requirements and preliminary design attributes. These would be scored as a strong, medium, or weak relationship with a numerical score of 9, 3, and 1, respectively. An importance rating sum and relative weight are then provided.

Architecting Methodologies

Normative	Rational	Consensus	Heuristics
↑	↑	□	↓
↑	↑	□	↓
□	↑	□	□
↑	↑	↑	↑
↑	↑	□	□
↑	↑	□	□
□	↑	□	□
□	□	□	□
□	↑	□	□

Figure 8.16 Architecting Methodologies.

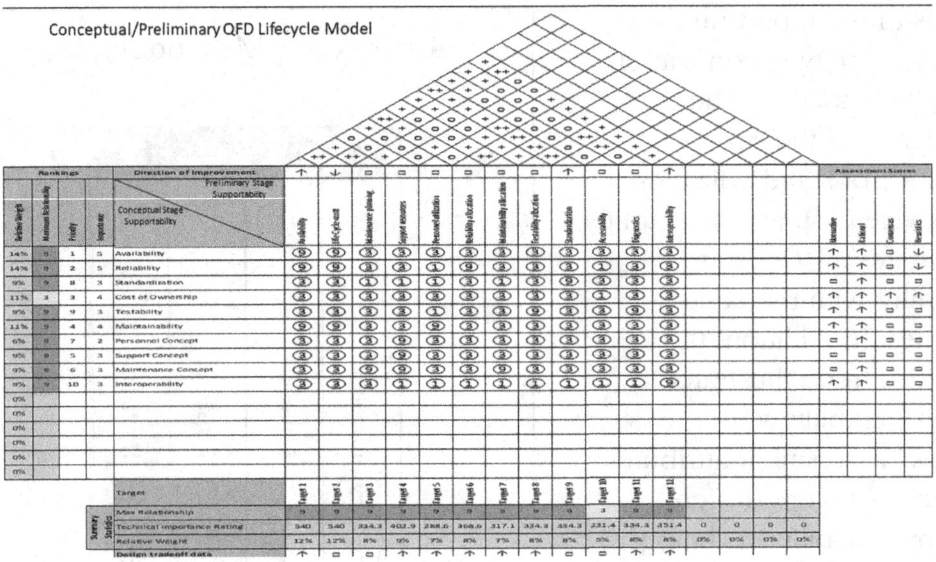

Conceptual/Preliminary QFD Lifecycle Model

Figure 8.17 Conceptual/Preliminary QFD Life-Cycle Model.

Examining the Technical Importance Ratings shows that "availability" and "life-cycle cost" are tied with an importance rating of 540 and a relative weight of 12%. Support Resources rounds out the top three with a rating of 403, thus indicating there is considerable interest in the overall supportability of the system before engaging in the detailed design process. The relatively balanced average of the remainder of the assessment criteria indicates equal interest in transitioning into the detailed design stage with a broad focus on supportability.

The additional statistic of "Design Tradeoff Data" has been added in the summary statistics room just as it was in the architecting HOQ so that team members would be reminded that tradeoff analysis must continue to be a top priority so that cost saving can be maximized during the development process.

Detailed Design and Build Functional Supportability Planning

Functional requirements are transformed into physical entities during the detailed design and build stages. Instructions are issued to design engineers for an item's form, fit, and function. The physical item designed must possess the proper supportability characteristics to be supportable. Supportability assessment and planning work directly with design engineering to

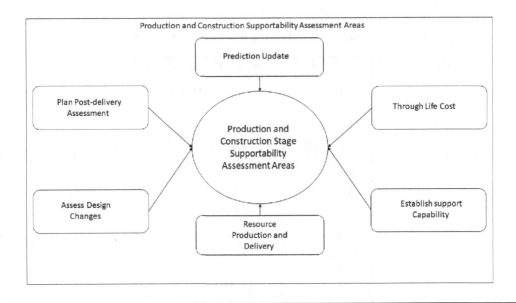

Figure 8.18   Production and Construction Supportability Assessment Areas.

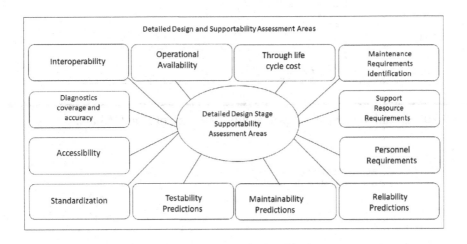

Figure 8.19   Detailed Design and Supportability Assessment Areas.

ensure these characteristics are embedded into the final design solution. Figures 8.18 and 8.19 illustrate some important areas continually analyzed during these phases of systems development.[30,39,52]

This detailed design and build stage should produce a system that attains a reasonable balance between performance, supportability, and cost of ownership. It is important to note here the engineering members of the development team generally do not have a vision of how all these pieces

Detailed Design Supportability Assessment, the "Whats"

	Rankings			Direction of Improvement
Relative Weight	Maximum Relationship	Priority	Importance	Production and Delivery Supportability / Detailed Design and Build Supportability
13%	9	1	5	Operational Availability
8%	9	5	3	Reliability prediction
8%	3	9	3	Standardization
10%	1	4	4	Through life cycle cost
13%	9	8	5	Testability prediction
8%	9	2	3	Maintenance requirements identification
10%	3	3	4	Personnel requirements
8%	9	7	3	Support resource requirements
8%	3	6	3	Maintainability prediction
8%	3	10	3	Interopability
8%	3	11	3	Diagonistics coverage and accuracy
0%	9	12		Accessability

Figure 8.20   Detailed Design Supportability Assessment, the "Whats."

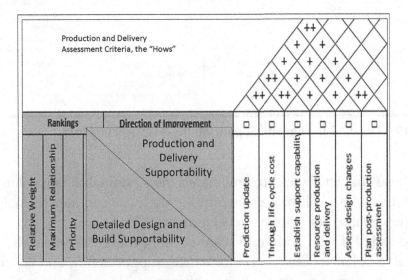

Figure 8.21   Production and Delivery Assessment Criteria, the "Hows."

of the system fit together to form a whole holistic system. It is the supportability teams' responsibility to provide such as vision.

This QFD Life-Cycle model uses the defined detailed design supportability assessment areas as the "What" is required. Just as in the conceptual and preliminary HOQ model, each assessment area level of importance is ranked and assigned a numerical factor. We see that operational availability is ranked 5 and is tied with testability prediction with a score of 5. This is not surprising during this stage of development since the emphasis was squarely on reliability and maintainability during the detailed design stage. The ranking of personnel requirements with a score of 4 indicates that the emphasis is on the personnel needed to support the system after deployed. The priority rating shows a similar pattern of focus with operational availability ranked as number 1, maintenance requirements identification as number 2, and personnel requirements as number 3. This clearly shows that KPIs are focused on these areas as the system moves closer to In-Service sustainment stage. Relative weights follow this same pattern: operational availability at 13%, testability prediction at 13%, and personnel requirements coming in at 10%. Clearly, the team is focused on functional supportability during its next phase.

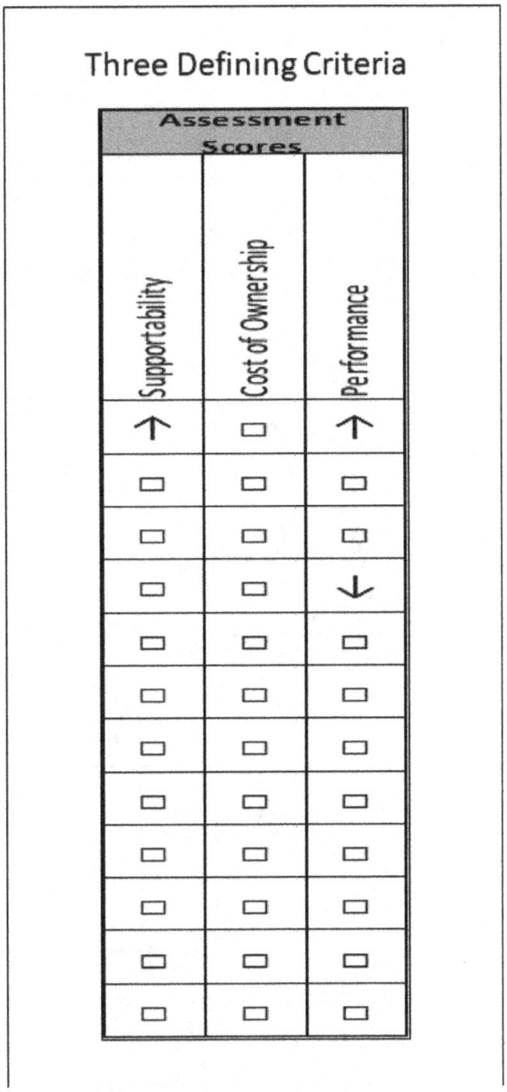

Production and Delivery Assessment criteria for the detailed design stage supportability assessment areas comprise the "How" in the QFD Life-Cycle model. Each of these elements is assessed as to the direction

Figure 8.22 Three Defining Criteria.

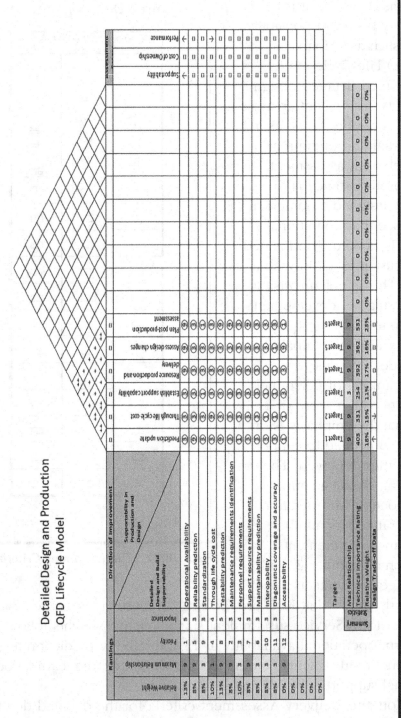

Figure 8.23   Detailed Design and Production QFD Life-Cycle Model.

of improvement, either needing to be maximized, considered on target, or held to a minimum. They are them correlated to each other, positive, negative, or on target in the HOQ roof. The scoring of all criteria is annotated as "on target" this indicated that the system build is proceeding as intended in a balanced fashion.

In the roof of the matrix, each "How" criteria correlation is assessed using the same scaling as used in the QFD preceding Life-Cycle Models. Note that there is either a strong positive or positive association among each supportability criteria. This confirms that the development team is driving the program in the right direction with a clear vision of what is necessary to field a cost-effective supportable system.

In the adjunct room of the Life-Cycle Model HOQ are the three defining criteria of performance, supportability, and cost of ownership with directional improvement indicators. Principally the theme of "considered on target" is also reflected here. This should not be surprising since we are approaching the In-service phase, where the system will become fully operational. Again, these metrics serve as visual cues that help alert and guide the development team members' decision process.

The QFD Life-Cycle Model reflected in Figure 8.23 summary statistics indicates the strength of the relationship between detailed design supportability and production and delivery. Note that the Technical Importance Rating "plan post-production assessment" with a high score of 531 firmly establishes that the development teams focus on producing a system ready for in-service supportability. A score of 403 for "prediction update" reinforces this focused support planning and indicates that appropriate funding has been earmarked for this purpose.

The final statistic annotated "design tradeoff data," just as it has in the previous Life-Cycle Planning QFD models remind team members to keep an open mind as they approach In-Service sustainment supportability planning for tradeoff opportunities.

In-Service Sustainment and Functional Supportability Planning

In-service sustainment and functional Supportability planning are blended with the final life-cycle phase of System Retirement and Disposal to ensure that all planning, decision-making, and subsequent execution strategies have been properly executed and completed.

There should be minimal design activities, assuming the final system design achieves the required supportability characteristics. However, there

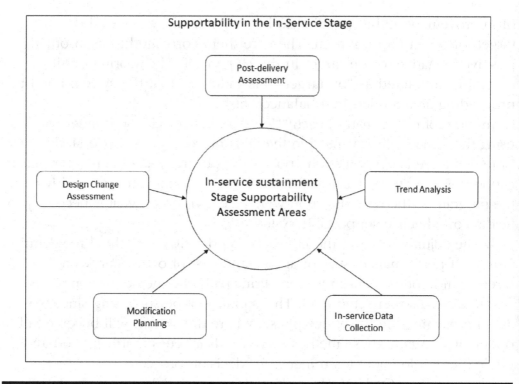

Figure 8.24   Supportability in the In-Service Stage.

can be design changes necessary for production improvements. Each design change must be assessed to determine any effect on supportability or the support resource package. Where a design change affects supportability or the support resource package, supportability assessment and planning must ensure that appropriate actions are taken to limit or avoid the impact of the change.

Introduction of the system to the market and end customer presents a different set of challenges for supportability assessment and planning. This stage of the development cycle has two significant activities: first, assessing the achievement of supportability and second, formulation of modifications and upgrades to either resolve shortfalls in the original design or modifications and improvements that increase the supportability potential of the system. Figure 8.24 illustrates some of the activities that occur during this stage.[30,39,52]

The basis of activity comes from the post-delivery assessment. The customer performs this assessment. It provides specific feedback on the supportability characteristics of the design and the adequacy of the support resource package delivered to the end customer. Supportability assessment and planning continually review and improve the system design and support

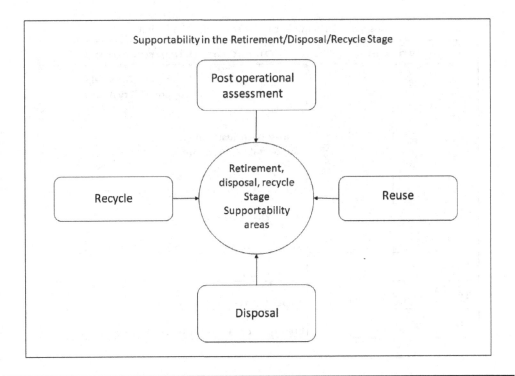

Figure 8.25   Supportability in the Retirement/Disposal/Recycle Stage.

infrastructure throughout the system's life. This activity also constitutes the start of planning for the replacement and/or retirement/disposal/recycling of the system.

System disposal, retirement, and potential recycling are all important parts of the supportability assessment and planning process as the system moves through its life-cycle. At some point, any system will become one of the following: uneconomical to maintain, obsolete, or unrepairable. Therefore, a comprehensive supportability plan to include anticipated equipment phase-out and disposal to include potential recycling is critical and necessary. Figure 8.25 illustrates some of the activities associated with the stage of the product life-cycle.

Another area that must be considered in this life-cycle phase is sustainability. The post-operational supportability assessment and plan must address this because of the environmental impact the system may have had on the environment. Any hazardous or toxic materials or waste products must be dealt with per applicable guidance, policy, regulation, and statutes and ultimately address system design for the environment in terms of ecological, political, and social considerations.

Relative Weight	Maximum Relationship	Priority	Importance	In-service Sustainment and Assessment, the "Whats"
	Rankings			Direction of Improvement
				Retirement, Disposal, recycle Supportability Assessment
				In-service Sustainment Supportability Assessment
26%	9	5	5	Post delivery assessment
21%	9	4	4	Trend analysis
21%	3	2	4	In-service data collection
16%	1	1	3	Modification planning
16%	9	3	3	Design change assessment

Figure 8.26 In-service Sustainment and Assessment, the "Whats."

Relative Weight	Maximum Relationship	Priority	Importance	Retirement, Disposal, and Recycling, the "Hows"	Post operational assessment	Reuse	Disposal	Recycle
	Rankings							
				Retirement, Disposal, Recycle Supportability Assessment / In-service Sustainment Supportability Assessment				
26%	9	5	5	Post delivery assessment	⑨	③	③	①
21%	9	4	4	Trend analysis	⑨	③	③	③
21%	3	2	4	In-service data collection	⑨	⑨	③	⑨
16%	1	1	3	Modification planning	③	③	③	③
16%	9	3	3	Design change assessment	③	③	③	③

Figure 8.27 Retirement, Disposal, and Recycling, the "Hows."

Once these last formal life-cycle development phases have identified all necessary activity criteria for a final QFD Life-Cycle Model, HOQ will be constructed to help the development team.

Criteria for in-service sustainment and supportability constitute the "What" QFD Life-Cycle model. As performed in the previous HOQ builds, each assessment criteria's level of importance is assigned a value ranging from 1 least important to 5 most important. We can ascertain from the scoring that post-delivery assessment with a score of 5 is considered critical, followed by trend analysis and in-service data collection with scores of 4, respectively. This would support the previous planning for support personnel and data collection in earlier development stages. Priority rankings principally mirror the importance rankings except for "design change assessment," which is not surprising since considerable planning for in-service delivery of what critical change modifications to the system would be necessary as it natures in-service.

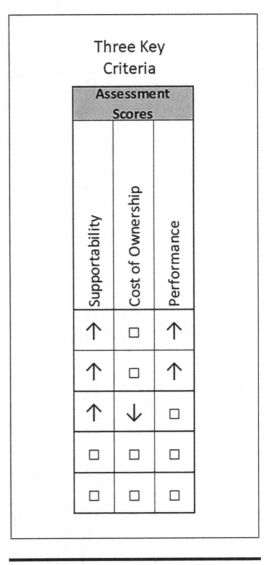

Figure 8.28   Threew Key Criteria.

Retirement, disposal, retirement, and recycling assessment criteria constitute the "How" for in-service sustainment and supportability criteria. As has been done on previous development models scoring for these criteria would be based on whether the need for the criteria to be maximized, considered on target, or held to a minimum. Reflected in the model, all criteria are considered on target. This should be considered no surprise at the development stage where deployment is imminent.

The matrix roof reflects that each criterion is strongly positive related, which is to be expected based on where the system is in the life-cycle phase.

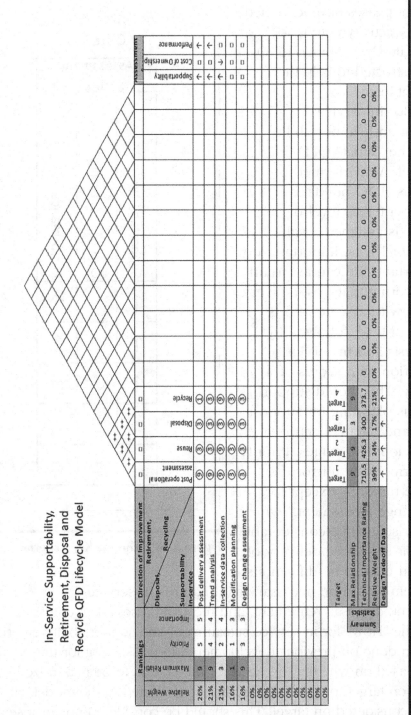

Figure 8.29   In-Service Supportability and Retirement, Disposal, and Recycle QFD Life-Cycle Model.

The adjunct room to the relationship matrix houses the three criteria of performance, supportability, and cost of ownership. Recommending that the supportability criteria be maximized along with performance is not surprising at the stage of development. What does stand out is that "in-service" data collection is flagged as a potential cost of ownership item that should be monitored as the system enters operation. Again, these criteria are provided as visual cues to the support team to maintain balance in their approach to support the system in-service and retirement.

The final matrix to be constructed for this development phase is the overall model containing the relationship matrix that assesses in-service sustainment and retires, disposal, and recycle supportability assessment.

Examination of the Technical Importance Rating included in the Summary Statistics, the score of 711 clearly indicates that "post-operational assessment" is central to the development team's minds. Following with a score of 426 is that of "Reuse," which sends a clear message that the aspects of maintainability and reliability are being emphasized so that the system can experience a potentially longer life during its intended operational life.

The final statistic annotated "design trade-off data," just as it has in the previous Life-Cycle Planning QFD models; its purpose is to remind team members to keep an open mind as they approach In-Service sustainment supportability planning. This is especially critical that these directional annotations be illustrated to be maximized during this stage of development because the in-field alterations to the system configuration are expected; they are exceedingly expensive.

Summary QFD Life-Cycle Model

The final QFD Life-Cycle Model is a summary matrix that presents an order by which system-build functional supportability criteria would be considered during the system's life-cycle, starting in conception and ending in retirement.

Summary supportability criteria the "Whats" were selected from each QFD Life-Cycle Model starting with chapter seven's environmental effects model. Based on "importance level" two criteria were selected from each model for 14 supportability criteria. The "importance" criteria were then ranked using the same scale (1–5) as on all other life-cycle models. Supportability, with a score of 5, tops the list of priorities, with six of the

Summary Supportability Criteria, the "Whats"

Rankings				Direction of Improvement	
Relative Weight	Maximum Relationship	Priority	Importance	Summary Supportability Criteria the "What's"	Summary Supportability Criteria the "How's"
8%	9	9	4	Pressure	
10%	9	3	5	Supportability	
6%	3	14	3	Too many possibilites	
8%	1	13	4	Past system data of limits use	
8%	9	2	4	Overall Availability	
8%	9	5	4	Reliability	
6%	9	1	3	Operational availability	
6%	9	11	3	Testability prediction	
6%	9	12	3	Post delivery assessment	
6%	9	10	3	Trend analysis	
8%	9	6	4	Be easy to maintain	
6%	9	4	3	Be cost effective to maintain	
6%	9	8	3	System design characteristic assessment	
8%	9	7	4	Requirements identification/implementation	

Figure 8.30   Summary Supportability Criteria, the "Whats."

remainder scored as 4. The remaining scores were 3s. The high score on supportability and the 4 and 3 consistencies clearly indicate a well-disciplined development strategy and life-cycle supportability focus.

Priorities of 1–14 were then assigned to each "What" criteria in the same manner as on all preceding life-cycle models. These priorities

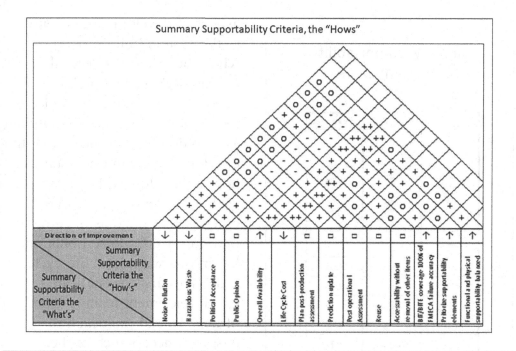

Figure 8.31   Summary Supportability Criteria, the "Hows."

illustrate the order in which the listed "What" criteria would be considered as the system moves through its development process. For example, operational availability (fully mission capable of performing) and overall availability (partially capable of performing) are listed as the first and second priorities, followed by supportability at number 3 and cost of ownership at 4. The prioritization profile provides evidence that the development team is well versed in building a superior system that is customer centric with an evaluated supportable throughout is intended life-cycle.

Summary supportability criteria for the "Hows" were selected from each life-cycle model's "technical importance ratings." The two highest importance ratings from each model were selected to form 14 criteria. Each criterion was evaluated just as all preceding model "How" criteria had either needing to be "maximized, considered on target or minimized." Four of these criteria were rated as needing to be maximized during the build process, "overall availability, BIT/BITE coverage 100% of FMECA (Failure Modes, Effects, and Critical Analysis) failure accuracy, prioritize supportability elements and, functional and physical supportability balanced." This clearly shows that a "trade-off"

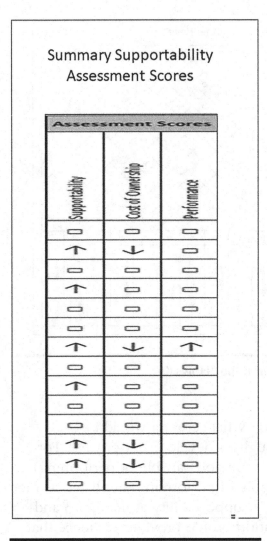

Figure 8.32 Summary Supportability Assessment Scores.

aspect of development is central to the system build process when the criteria of "overall availability" is identified as needing to be maximized vice the "What" criteria of "operational availability." It also shows that the development team understands how critical testing is during each life-cycle phase. Three criteria were rated as needing to be minimized, "noise pollution, hazardous waste and life-cycle cost." The first two indicate the development team is aware of how critical political and customer acceptance of the system is under development, with the third providing the overall mindset of cost control. The remainder of the criteria were rated as "to be held constant," which means that a balanced approach must be observed when applying all technical solutions, and the cost of ownership must be observed consistently.

The summary model roof provides correlation associations between the "How" supportability criteria. Each criterion was evaluated in the same manner as all preceding model criteria: "strong positive, positive, neutral, negative or strong negative." Standing out in this analysis is the strong positive associations of "overall availability and life-cycle cost" as well as the negative association of "political acceptance and public opinion." The strong positive of overall and life-cycle cost shows that the selection of criteria across all life-cycle model is focused on developing a system that could serve multiple operational scenarios with the ability to operate within established cost parameters. On the other hand, the

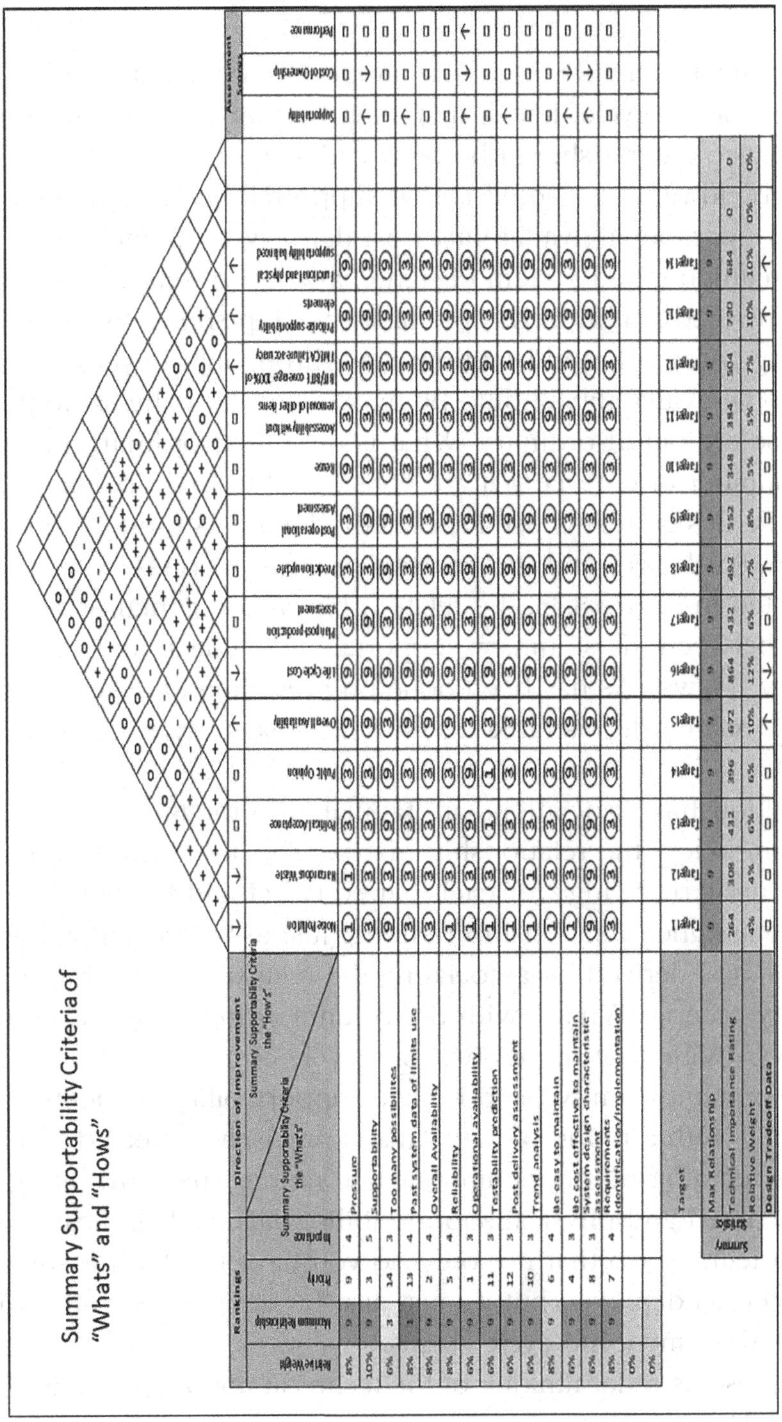

Figure 8.33 Summary Supportability Criteria of "Whats" and "Hows."

negative association of political acceptance and public opinion shows that the development is well aware of the importance of each to market success.

The assessment scores look at how supportability is managed through the development life-cycle. Recall that supportability, cost of ownership, and performance criteria should be balanced as the system progresses through the build process. Noted is that supportability, past system data of limits use, operational availability, post-delivery assessment, cost-effective to maintain, and system design characteristics assessment are each recommended maximized. Cost of ownership shows that the same supportability criteria should be minimized throughout development. And operational availability should be maximized over the same period. None of these are out-of-ordinary. What is out-of-the-ordinary in a good way is the number of criteria that are considered to be in balance. This shows that the design teams used the methodology as the QFD life-cycle models were developed, and the analysis process is on target.

As illustrated in Figure 8.33, the relationship matrix contains the associations between the summary supportability "Whats" and summary supportability "Hows." As has been done on preceding life-cycle models, each criteria's relationship is ranked as a 1 (least significant), 3 (moderate), or 9 (strong).

These relationship associations are tabulated in the Summary Statistics room below the relationship matrix. The Technical Importance Ratings give numeric ratings for each paired (what and how) association based on the assigned relationship ranking. Just as in preceding life-cycle models, it is derived by associating the relative weight in the supportability criteria "Whats" with the column rating of the relationship matrix "Hows." With a rating of 864, "Life-cycle costing" is center stage for the development team with "prioritize supportability elements" coming second with a rating of 720. This is precisely expected from a development team based on its number one rating. The third rating of 684 for "functional and physical supportability balanced" indicates the development team grasp that not only do you have to plan for support after the system is deployed but it must also be designed into it during each of its development life-cycle stages.

Table 8.3 presents order ranking of the technical importance ratings by score magnitude.

Table 8.3 Order Ranking of the Technical Importance Ratings by Score Magnitude

Technical Importance Rating by Category	Score
1. Life Cycle Cost	864
2. Prioritizes Supportability Elements	720
3. Functional and Physical Supportability Balance	684
4. Overall Availability	672
5. Post Operational Assessment	552
6. BIT/BITE Coverage 100% of FMECA Failure Accuracy	504
7. Prediction Update	492
8. Plan Post-Production Assessment	432
9. Political Acceptance	432
10. Public Opinion	396
11. Accessibility Without Removal of Other Items	384
12. Reuse	348
13. Hazardous Waste	308
14. Noise Pollution	264

Summary

Chapter 8 built on the discussion points presented in Chapter 4 and walked the reader through product and/or service system creation and systems architecting in the design process. It began by defining that the role of system architecting was to establish a creditable range of acceptability within which the design must reside, and that systems architecting was an art and not a scientific process. It then detailed that because systems architecting uses insights, vision, intuition, judgment, and feelings or taste as primary means of guiding its activities, QFD has proven to be a tool of choice to create new and unprecedented products and/or services systems. The discussion then focused on defining four methods commonly applied through systems architecting to define the system support parameters. It showed by example how QFD could be used to rationalize parameters for the product and/or service system because of its analytical mapping techniques. It then stressed that the range of acceptable system parameters produced by systems architecting is the basis for all systems life-cycle management, the TPMS. And, because the measurability of each parameter was mandatory, QFD, with its ability to compare and cross-correlate those parameters, was the analysis tool of choice to ensure parameters are "built in" to the evolving design solution. The chapter concluded with a discussion of how supportability functions act as an active participant in each stage of the system development process and that QFD again was the tool of choice to ensure that every decision made during the product and/or service system design process considers performance, supportability, and cost of ownership.

Chapter 9

Quality Function Deployment Acquisition Modeling Case Study

Case Restatement:

Airline X, a major U.S. carrier, has a fleet of over 500 large aircraft. The carrier earns roughly half its revenue from the domestic market, with most of its fleet servicing the domestic market being the single-aisle B737 next generation (NG). The remainder of its one-aisle fleet are the types that are no longer produced by Boeing (MD90s and B737 classics). To improve the fleet's operating economy, X plans to launch an upgrading program to replace its aging and outdated aircraft with all B737 NGs.

X has determined the 737-8 MAX as the main model in its upgrading program. These 737-MAX are proposed to be put into service on U.S. domestic routes, with an average traffic capacity of 700 miles per route, six flights per day, and 360 available days per year. Based on these figures, the proposed aircraft traffic capacity can be calculated as ~207 million seat miles per year. Based on X's accounting policy, the airframe and engine have a depreciation period of ~25 years, with a residual value of ~5% of the initial purchase (book) value (trade price ~34 million per aircraft). Airline X usually takes ~20 years as its aircraft (economically) useful life in its acquisition decision and uses the figure between the book value and appraisal as the market value. Carrier X uses the current rate of the ten-year U.S. Treasury note @ 2% as risk-free and its current marginal income tax rate as 38.5%.

DOI: 10.4324/9781003336044-12

Airline X has determined three main risk factors affecting the NPV of the acquisition 737-8 MAX upgrading program: yield, fuel prices, and residual value, which is directly affected by the aircraft's functional supportability packaging.

Monday Morning, Starting the QFD Acquisition Modeling Project; 0830 in a Large Airline X Conference Room

Angela, Airline X QFD team lead, walked to the back of a podium positioned on a corner of a large oval table surrounded by wall-attached whiteboards and started to speak. "Hope all had a restful weekend." "Think we can agree that last week was pretty intense." Heads nodded in agreement. "I hope you all get a chance to review the chapter materials that were presented on the QFD Life-Cycle Modeling methodology?" "Not sure if I understand everything that was presented and discussed but I do know we have our work cut out for us." Heads nodded in agreement again! Angela continued, "I need to ensure everyone is here that is required to be here so allow me to go through the list." "Just say 'yes' if I call out your discipline, O.K.?" "Finance, Accounting, Marketing, Maintenance, Operations, Network planning, Passenger services, Cargo operations, Supply chain, Logistics, Support equipment, Flight operations, Personnel, Information systems, Data analytics, Systems engineering, Maintenance control, Ground operations." "Did I miss anyone?" Angela then stated, "Because our timeline to get the evaluation completed is very tight, I have requested that one of the developers of the life-cycle modeling methodology, John, help us to set up the acquisition model to ensure we all understand what we are doing and why we are doing it." With this, Angela introduced John to the team.

John rose from his seat, thanked Angela, and then spoke, "Good morning, everyone. I am excited to be able to work with you on this QFD acquisition modeling project." John continued, "I think you are all aware of my background and feelings about QFD's applications, right? I am a strong advocate of its use and have experienced firsthand its power when used to its fullest." "It is a very versatile planning and analysis tool that can be applied to multiple situations in many ways." "We have work to do, and it is going to take every skillset we have in this room to produce an assessment of the 737-8 acquisition that gives leadership the ability to make an informed decision."

With this, John stated, "I think we are all aware of what the tasking is for the project, but for clarity, I want to reiterate to ensure we are all on the same page." "We have been formed to conduct a modeling evaluation of supportability factors for the proposed 787-8 MAX versus potential alternatives over the projected life of the aircraft and to select and prioritize those having the most potential impact over the aircraft's useful life-cycle. Because of its ability to capture salient customer requirements and align their importance with technical and organizational requirements, QFD was selected as the modeling tool." John paused momentarily and then stated, "any questions?" All was quiet!

Monday, 1000—Airline X Conference Room—Organizing the Process

John was encouraged that all the 18 organization disciplines he had suggested were in attendance. He was also impressed that they had brought alternate backup staff members as suggested. The oval table would accommodate the 18 primary discipline representatives; alternates would be located behind close to the white boards where each discipline had an assigned section of the board upon which to take notes. The room had four monitors, allowing all attendees to have a line of sight. The conference room layout had four breakout rooms for sub-teams to meet.

Team members were then briefed on the daily procedures, meeting times, and delivery schedules.

John then activated the projector and began to speak, "Before starting the analysis, let us review the differences between the QFD Life-Cycle Model that each of you just finished studying and the QFD Acquisition Model that we will build."

John continued, "The basic structure of both models is identical; the rooms where the information resides, and the way information that is housed in those rooms differs." "Let's start with the QFD Life-Cycle Model." Room #3 contains "assessment scores" in the life-cycle model. You probably noticed in your recent review of the QFD Life-Cycle Modeling methodology (Figure 9.1), all models except for one assessed three critical criteria: performance, cost of ownership, and supportability. The one exception assessed methods by which data could be analyzed during the formative stage of system design specification(s) planning. Room #8 contains "design tradeoff data" only. Both sets of annotations made in these two rooms in the life-cycle model are "notional" only. Neither quantitatively measure. They are used by development team members as a visual cue and serve as discussion points for each "systems development drive" meeting. Both use scoring notations as either needing to be "maximized," "hold on target," or "minimized."

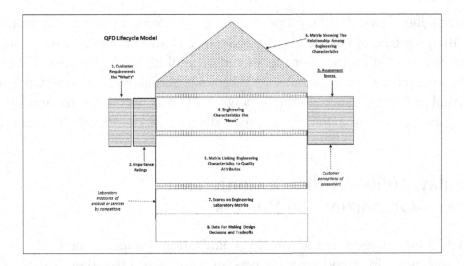

Figure 9.1   The QFD Life-Cycle Model Components.

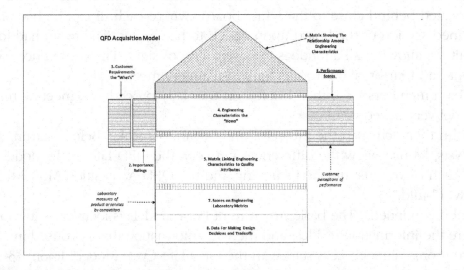

Figure 9.2   The QFD Acquisition Model Components.

John continued, "the QFD Acquisition Model (Figure 9.2) has assessment of competition" annotated in room #3. Data reflected here quantitatively compares the primary system under consideration with potential alternatives based on the criteria established by the acquisition team. Room #8 contains a "technical competitive assessment" that reflects how the primary system under consideration ranks amongst its principal competitors' systems.

Having completed all primary discussions, John began to walk the team through the acquisition assessment process.

Methodology

Step 1: Capturing Customer Requirements

A benefit of QFD is the ability to capture salient customer requirements and align them with technical and organizational requirements. To capture customer requirements, create customer sets to participate in the process. Stakeholders form a customer set with first- and second-degree connections to the situation.

In considering the acquisition of a new aircraft such as the 737-8, Airline X identified a customer set(s) to identify aircraft requirements and align them with Carrier's technical and organizational requirements. As a result, the customer team listed the following (see Table 9.1).

Selected members from both primary and secondary customer sets would be engaged as team members of the QFD Acquisition Modeling, providing direct input into the development process.

Step 2. Identify Operational Support Criteria

In this step, the customer team identified the operational support criteria to focus on during the evaluation period. The identified operational support criteria form the basis for the "why" attributes that express the VOC. The team's initial step was to review the final QFD model output from the Life-Cycle Assessment. The ranking of the technical importance ratings would provide team members with how Airline X customer evaluation criteria could be finalized (see Table 9.2).

Following a review of the QFD Life-Cycle Modeling ranking of technical importance rankings, the team identified Airline X's operational customer evaluation criteria. First, organizational team members, including customer set representatives, evaluated the importance of each criterion.

Table 9.1 Customer Sets

Primary Customer Set	*Secondary Customer Set*
Ramp Agents	Public Customer Base
Pilots/Co-Pilots	Second/Third-Level Maintenance Personnel
First-Line Maintenance Personnel	Logistics Support Organization and Staff
Aircraft Service Crew	Support Personnel

on a scale of 1 to 5 (where 1 is the lowest importance and 5 is the highest). Next, the individual team member assessments were averaged to obtain an overall score for each evaluation criterion. Finally, the customer evaluation criteria were ranked on the basis of the average score for each criterion.

The acquisition assessment team considered the operational support criteria for introducing a new aircraft into Airline X's fleet. The team members individually scored the evaluation criteria from which the criterion average was determined. The team then ranked and presented their recommended evaluation criteria in Table 9.3.

Table 9.2   Chapter 8 Summary QFD Life-Cycle Modeling Ranking of Technical Importance Ratings

Technical Importance Rating by Category	Score
1. Life-Cycle Cost	864
2. Prioritizes Supportability Elements	720
3. Functional and Physical Supportability Balance	684
4. Overall Availability	672
5. Post-operational Assessment	552
6. BIT/BITE Coverage 100% of FMECA Failure Accuracy	504
7. Prediction Update	492
8. Plan Post-Production Assessment	432
9. Political Acceptance	432
10. Public Opinion	396
11. Accessibility Without Removal of Other Items	384
12. Reuse	348
13. Hazardous Waste	308
14. Noise Pollution	264

Table 9.3   Score and Rank of Customer Evaluation Criteria

Customer Evaluation Criteria*	Overall Score Average	Rank
Maintenance Ownership Costs	4.6	1
OEM Modification Support Costs	3.9	2
Mission Capabilities	3.7	3
Avionics Systems Support	3.3	4
Propulsion Systems Support Costs	3.1	5
Other Categories	2.3	6

Table 9.4   Customer Evaluation Criteria and Life-Cycle Model Technical Importance Rating Association

Rating	Technical Importance by Category	Score	Customer Evaluation Criteria
1	Life-Cycle Cost	864	Maintenance ownership cost
2	Prioritizes Supportability Elements	720	Maintenance ownership cost
3	Functional and Physical Supportability Balance	684	Maintenance ownership cost
4	Overall Availability	672	Maintenance ownership cost Mission capabilities
5	Post-operational Assessment	552	Maintenance ownership cost
6	BIT/BITE Coverage 100% of FMECA Failure Accuracy	504	Mission capabilities Avionics system support Propulsion systems support costs
7	Prediction Update	492	Mission capabilities Propulsion systems support costs
8	Plan Post-Production Assessment	432	Maintenance ownership cost OEM modification support cost
9	Political Acceptance	432	Other categories
10	Public Opinion	396	Other categories
11	Accessibility Without Removal of Other Items	384	Mission capabilities Avionics system support Propulsion systems support costs OEM modification Support cost
12	Reuse	348	Other categories
13	Hazardous Waste	308	Other categories
14	Noise Pollution	264	Other categories

With the identification of the customer evaluation criteria, the acquisition assessment team could associate them with the QFD Life-Cycle Modeling importance rating ranking (see Table 9.4).

Step 3. Selecting Customer Evaluation Criteria for Analysis

To down-select customer evaluation criteria for further analysis, the acquisition assessment team used the customer evaluation criteria and technical importance rating association output from Table 9.4 and ranked each evaluation criteria by the scoring average used in Table 9.3 (see Figure 9.3).

Three order customer evaluation criteria were then down-selected to the top three for further analysis based on time and available resources. Ideally, all evaluation criteria would be considered. However, limited resources often dictate a more focused or reduced analysis. Therefore, the process of scoring and ranking evaluation criteria in step 2 provides an objective decision criterion to down-select the evaluation criteria. The top three evaluation criteria to be used in the QFD Acquisition assessment are provided in Table 9.5.

Rank Ordering Customer Evaluation Criteria by QFD Lifecycle Technical Performance Rating								
Technical Improtance Rating by category from Lifecycle Model	Rating Score from Lifecycle model	Maintenance ownershhip Cost	OEM modification support cost	Mission capabilities	Avionics systems support cost	Propulsion systems support cost	Other caegories	
1. Life Cycle Cost	864	4.6						
2. Prioritizes Supportability Elements	720	4.6						
3. Functional and Physical Supportability Balance	684	4.6						
4. Overall Availability	672	4.6	3.9	3.7				12.2
5. Post Operational Assessment	552	4.6	3.9	3.7	3.3	3.1	2.3	20.9
6. BIT/BITE Coverage 100% of FMECA Failure Accuracy	504	4.6	3.9	3.7	3.3	3.1		18.6
7. Prediction Update	492	4.6	3.9	3.7	3.3	3.1		18.6
8. Plan Post-Production Assessment	432	4.6	3.9	3.7	3.3	3.1	2.3	20.9
9. Political Acceptance	432	4.6	3.9	3.7			2.3	14.5
10. Public Opinion	396						2.3	2.3
11. Accessibility Without Removal of Other Items	384	4.6	3.9	3.7	3.3	3.1		18.6
12. Reuse	348	4.6	3.9	3.7				12.2
13. Hazardous Waste	308	4.6	3.9	3.7			2.3	14.5
14. Noise Pollution	264	4.6	3.9	3.7			2.3	14.5
Sum Rankings Customer Evaluation Criteria		59.8	39	37	16.5	15.5	13.8	

Figure 9.3 Rank Ordering Customer Evaluation Criteria by QFD Life-Cycle Technical Performance Rating.

Table 9.5 Down-Selected Customer Evaluation Criteria

Evaluation Criteria	Abbr[1]	Avg Customer Score	Rank
Maintenance ownership cost	MX	4.6	1
OEM modification support costs	MS	3.9	2
Mission Capabilities	MC	3.7	3

[1]The abbreviations will be used when constructing the house of quality to identify root customer evaluation criteria.

Customer Requirements: Selecting the "Whats"

Step 4. Assessing the Importance and Prioritization of the Integrated Product Support Elements Influencing Customer Criteria Over the Expected System Life-Cycle

All acquisition assessment team members reviewed the definitive *Integrated Logistics Support Guide* that detailed all 12 IPS elements and criteria by which they should be measured for systems life-cycle support. Each focused on identifying and understanding functional supportability requirements. The IPS elements define the support requirements best related to system design and each other, develop and acquire the required support, provide required operational support at the lowest cost, and seek readiness and Life-Cycle Cost improvements in the materiel system and support systems during the operational life-cycle. They additionally ensure a process is in place that repeatedly examines functional support requirements throughout the service life of the system.[47]

The acquisition assessment team then ranked and prioritized all 12 IPS elements based on Airline X current and anticipated operational scenarios (see Table 9.6).

Table 9.6   IPS Element Importance and Priority Rank

Integrated Product Support Elements	IPS Importance Rank*	IPS Priority Rank**
Design interface	5	3
Sustaining engineer	4	4
Supply support	5	5
Maintenance planning and management	5	2
Packaging, handling, storage, and transportation	2	7
Technical data	3	9
Support equipment	3	6
Training and training support	4	8
Manpower and personnel	5	1
Facilities and infrastructure	1	10
Computer resources	1	11
Product support management	3	8

* Rate importance from 1 to 5, with 5 the highest importance.
** Rate the priority from 1 to 12, with 1 the highest priority.

Step 5. Select the Top-Five IPS Functional Supportability Elements by Order of Importance and Priority

The acquisition assessment team then selected the top-five supportability elements based on assigned importance and priority (see Table 9.7).

Step 6. Select Functional Supportability Sub-Elements for Selected IPS Elements. These Will Be Ranked by Importance and Priority to Form the Customer Evaluation Criteria or "Whats"

The customer team completed an IPS evaluation leading to a down-select of five IPS elements and ten associated sub-IPS elements (see Table 9.8). The identified sub-elements would form the explicit and implicit customer requirements. The customer requirements are a basis for the "How" attributes in the QFD model development.

Table 9.7   Top-Five Prioritized IPS Elements

Selected IPS Element	Priority Order
Manpower and personnel	1
Maintenance planning and management	2
Design interface	3
Sustaining engineering	4
Supply support	5

Table 9.8   Prioritized IPS Elements and Sub-elements

IPS Element	IPS Sub-elements*
Manpower and personnel	Level of personnel attrition rates by maintenance/ support echelon
	Training program compatibility with staffing mix
Maintenance planning and management	Level of repair policy
	Test and support equipment levels
Design interface	Utilization parameters
	Expected system, availability, dependability, and readiness criteria
Sustaining engineering	Reliability, maintainability, and supportability for units and assemblies/sub-assemblies
	Trade-off evaluations
Supply Support	Inventory safety stock needed
	Provisioning and procurement cycle needed

* See IPS Rank Test element example tab.

Table 9.9 Functional Requirements for Airline X

Evaluation Criteria	Functional Requirements
Maintenance Ownership Cost	Cost per Available Seat Mile ($/seat nm)
	Support Equipment Required ($k per a/c)
	Personnel Training Cost ($M per a/c)
	Parts Inventory Required (Safety Stock %)
OEM Modification support costs	Cabin Reconfiguration (hr. per a/c)
	Fuel Systems Modification ($M per a/c)
	Onsite Technical Support (Y/N)
	OEM sole source part distributor (Y/N)
Mission Capabilities	Range (nm)
	Life-Cycle (hrs.)
	Operating Cost ($/hr.)
	Availability (%)
	Passenger Seats *Dual Cabin Configuration

Functional Requirements: Selecting the "Hows"

Step 7. Identifying Functional Requirements to Assess Customer Requirements

The acquisition assessment team then focused on identifying the functional requirements associated with customer evaluation criteria (see Table 9.9). In conjunction with the customer sets, participants, the acquisition assessment team identified functional requirements to capture "How" the customer requirements should be evaluated. Thirteen measurable functional requirements were identified as evaluation criteria (see Table 9.9).

Targets for Functional Requirement: Selecting the "Targets"

Step 8. Identifying Target Values for the Functional Requirements

The acquisition assessment team then sets appropriate *Technical Performance Measure (TPM)* target values for the selected functional requirements. The TPM target values established the benchmark performance by which alternatives would be evaluated relative to the target and to each other. The acquisition assessment team established the target value for each functional requirement (see Table 9.10).

Table 9.10   Functional Requirement Targets for Airline X

Functional Requirements	Target
Cost per Available Seat Mile ($/seat nm)	$0.122
Support Equipment Required ($k per a/c)	$25k
Personnel Training Cost ($M per a/c)	$0
Parts Inventory Required (Safety Stock %)	95%
Cabin Reconfiguration (hr. per a/c)	70
Fuel Systems Modification ($M per a/c)	$0
Onsite Technical Support (Y/N)	Y
OEM Sole Source Part Distributor (Y/N)	N
Range (nm)	3,500
Life-Cycle (hrs.)	60,000
Operating Cost ($/hr.)	7,900
Availability (%)	95%
Passenger Seats *Dual Cabin Configuration	120

Table 9.11   The Direction of Improvement Assessment

Direction	Symbology
Maximize	↑
On Target	◊
Minimize	↓

Direction of Improvement

Step 9. Assessing the Direction of Improvement

The team then assessed each proposed alternative relative to the established target values. The direction of improvement assessment provided the acquisition assessment team an indication of how the proposed alternative's engineering characteristics must change to align with the targets. The direction of improvement symbology is qualitatively assigned on the basis of team consensus (see Table 9.11).

Competition Performance

Step 10. Research the Competition's Performance

The acquisition assessment team then analyzed potential alternatives. Utilizing the functional requirements criteria derived for the system under consideration and gathering comparable data for each viable alternative based on system requirements. Data sources for each alternative include but are not limited to open-source reporting and internal/external analyses (see Table 9.12).

Step 11. Correlation Associations

The team then assessed relationships between the functional requirement "Hows." The product support elements are assessed by assigning correlations between them. These were assigned by assessment qualitatively by team members. Correlation associations are reflected in the roof of the HOQ and are based on the following scale (see Table 9.13).

Table 9.12 Customer and Competitor Functional Requirement Information

Functional Requirements Criteria	A220	A319	737-8	E195
Cabin Reconfiguration (hr per a/c)	65	80	95	50
Personnel Training Cost ($M per a/c)	$0.4M	$0.8M	$0	$0.5M
Onsite Technical Support (Y/N)	Y	N	N	N
OEM sole source part distributor (Y/N)	N	Y	Y	N
Support Equipment Required ($k per a/c)	$19k	$27k	$20k	$17k
Range (nm)	3,100	4,100	4,200	3,300
Passenger seats *dual cabin configuration	124	143	154	110
Fuel Systems Modification ($M per a/c)	$1.1M	$0	$0	$1.5M
Availability (%)	99%	95%	96%	99%
Cost per Available Seat Mile ($/seat nm)	$0.118	$0.120	$0.123	$0.119
Operating Cost ($/hr)	6,200	8,200	8,100	5,900
Parts Inventory Required (Safety Stock %)	97%	98%	97%	96%
Life-Cycle (hrs)	65,000	55,000	60,000	70,000

Table 9.13 Functional Requirement Correlations

Correlation Assessment	Value
Strongly correlated	++
Correlated	+
No correlation	0
Negative	-
Strongly negative	–

Technical Assessment

Step 12. Benchmarking Technical Performance

The acquisition assessment team then performed a technical competitive benchmarking of potential alternative systems. The potential alternatives are individually assessed relative to the target values. The technical competitive assessment includes all internal and external alternatives. Benchmarking alternative performance is based on the relative technical competitive assessment scores described in Table 9.14.

The benchmarking technical competitive assessment results are presented in Table 9.15 and reflected in the lower room of the HOQ (Table 9.16).

Table 9.14   Relative Technical Competitive Assessment

Competitive Assessment	Value
Poor	1
Fair	2
Average	3
Good	4
Excellent	5

Table 9.15   Technical Competitive Assessment of Alternatives

Functional Requirements	A220	A319	737-8	E195
Cost per Available Seat Mile ($/seat nm)	5	4	3	5
Support Equipment Required ($k per a/c)	4	2	4	5
Personnel Training Cost ($M per a/c)	2	1	3	2
Parts Inventory Required (Safety Stock %)	1	1	1	3
Cabin Reconfiguration (hr per a/c)	4	2	1	5
Fuel Systems Modification ($M per a/c)	2	3	3	2
Onsite Technical Support (Y/N)	5	1	1	1
OEM sole source part distributor (Y/N)	5	1	1	5
Range (nm)	2	4	5	2
Life-Cycle (hrs)	4	2	3	5
Operating Cost ($/hr)	4	1	2	5
Availability (%)	5	3	4	5
Passenger Seats *Dual Cabin Configuration	3	4	5	2

Table 9.16   Relationship Matrix Symbology

Strength of Relationship	Symbology
Strong	⑨
Medium	③
Weak	①

Relationships

Step 13. Forming the Relationship Matrix

The acquisition assessment team then developed the relationship matrix, the central core of the HOQ. This would demonstrate whether the functional characteristics have adequately addressed the critical to customer (CTQ) customer requirements previously established in Step 3. The strength of the relationships is depicted as presented in Table 9.16.

Step 14. Integration of Benchmarking and Importance Ratings

The acquisition assessment then integrated benchmarking and importance ratings to compare them with selected IPS and supportability elements. This comparison would indicate where a change in the selected IPS element is warranted.

Competitive Comparative Assessment

Based on the relationship matrix analyses and the scoring of relative importance rating and importance weight, the team can view the analyses of competitive comparative assessment more objectively than subjectively. For example, after ranking the functional support criteria by importance rating and weight, the team could decompose each SQC into "sub-SQCs" and compare them to a competitor's design. Then, key sub-functions can be compared to the competitor's sub-functions, providing that a functional support criterion has been chosen and its sub-functions detailed.

Step 15. Building the House of Quality

The basis for the HOQ is the customer requirements (the Whys), identified in Step 2 (Table 9.8). Each IPS sub-element requirement

Customer and Functional Requirements

Row #	Relative Weight	Maximum Relationship	Priority (ordered from 1 to X)	Importance (1 = Low, 5 = High)	Customer Requirements (Explicit and Implicit) (the "Whats") Customer Evaluation Criteria
1	10%	9	9	5	Level of Personnel Attrition Rates by Maintenance/Support Echelon
2	10%	9	10	5	Training Program Compatability with Staffing Mix
3	10%	9	5	5	Level of Repair Policy
4	10%	9	6	5	Test and Suppot Equipment Levels
5	10%	9	3	5	Utilization Parameters
6	10%	9	1	5	Expected system Availability, Dependability and Readiness Criteria
7	8%	9	2	4	Reliability, Maintainability and Supportability factors for Units, Assemblies and Sub-assemblies
8	8%	9	8	4	Tradeoff Evaluations
9	10%	9	4	5	Inventory Safety Stock Needed
10	10%	9	7	5	Provisioning and Procuremet Cycle Needed

Figure 9.4   Customer and Functional Requirements.

Functional Requirements

Column #	1	2	3	4	5	6	7	8	9	10	11	12	13
Direction of Improvement	◊	↑	◊	↓	↓	◊	↑	↓	◊	◊	↓	↑	◊
Customer Evaluation Criteria	MX	MX	MX	MX	MS	MS	MS	MS	MC	MC	MC	MC	MC
Functional Requirements (the "Hows") Product Support Elements / Customer Requirements (Explicit and Implicit) (the "Whats") Customer Evaluation Criteria	Cost per Available Seat Mile ($/seat nm)	Support Equipment Required ($k per a/c)	Personnel Training Cost ($M per a/c)	Parts Inventory Required (Safety Stock %)	Cabin Reconfiguration (hr per a/c)	Fuel Systems Modification ($M per a/c)	Onsite Technical Support (Y/N)	OEM sole source part distributor (Y/N)	Range (nm)	Life Cycle (hrs)	Operating Cost ($/hr)	Availability (%)	Passenger seats "dual cabin configuration

Figure 9.5   Functional Requirements.

is listed vertically in the HOQ. IPA sub-elements were first rated by importance on a scale of 1 to 5, with the 1 being the lowest and 5 the highest. Sub-elements could receive the same level of importance. We see in the ratings except for two (reliability, maintainability, supportability factors for units, assemblies, and sub-assemblies and tradeoff evaluations)

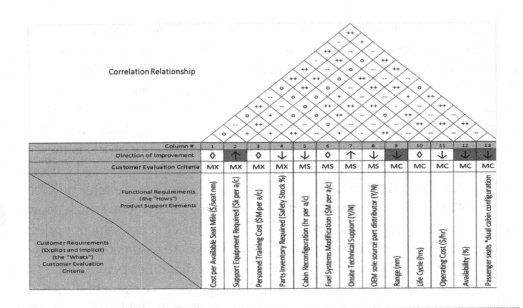

Figure 9.6 Correlation Relationships.

all received a rating of 5. The two that received a rating of 4 were identified as having been assessed during the build phases of system development.

The acquisition assessment team then prioritized the IPS sub-elements on a scale of 1–10. Unsurprisingly, the top three priorities are expected system availability, dependability, and readiness criteria; reliability, maintainability, and supportability factors for units, assemblies, and sub-assemblies; and utilization parameters 1, 2, and 3, respectively. All of these are components of a package for sustaining system performance during its operational life-cycle.

Relative weight assigned to each IPA sub-element is a measure of the balance among the sub-element criteria and is derived via the importance factors assigned to each criterion. The ~10% balance among each evaluation criterion provides the acquisition assessment team with a high level of confidence that the selection methodology used for customer evaluation criteria is on target.

The basis for the functional requirements (the Hows) is identified in Table 9.9, under Step 7. Each functional requirement identified is listed horizontally in HOQ. Atop each functional requirement is the evaluation criteria abbreviation presented in Table 9.10. By rank order, functional requirements are grouped, and a Direction of Improvement, as explained in Step 9 (Table 9.11), marking used as a visual cue that alerts team members of what is needed to ensure alignment with Technical Targets identified in Step 8 (Table 9.10).

The next step in building the HOQ is to populate the roof by establishing correlation relationships between each functional requirement. As Step 11 Table 9.13 explains, correlations range from strongly correlated to strongly negative. Correlations are qualitatively assigned and are used by the acquisition assessment team to gauge initial associations and aid in the modification decision-making process during the operational life-cycle of the system. What should be noted in these correlation associations is the strongly positive relationships (++) between the three down-selected customer-evaluated criteria (MX, MS, and MC). These same criteria were rank ordered by the QFD life-cycle technical performance rating assessment, which shows the measurement criteria are on target for the acquisition assessment project.

The next room on the house to construct is the "Assessment of Competition." Recall this is one of the two rooms that differ between the QFD Life-Cycle Modeling construct and the QFD acquisition assessment model.

Data used to construct this room came from Step 10 Table 9.12. Potential competitors were selected on the basis of their comparable classification to the base system under consideration, the Boeing 737-8. Each was assessed on a 6-point scale from 0 to 5, with 0 being "does not meet" and 5 being "completely satisfies." Each selected competitor was assessed using the functional requirements data presented in Table 9.9. Note the 737-8 system consistently ranks above the median of ~3.13. It also ranks second only to the A319, which would require retraining of personnel increasing the cost by ~$.08 million lacks the seating capacity of the 737-8 by ~11 seats. Revenue per seat mile ranks high when it comes to determining overall yield.

The next room to construct is the "Technical Competitive Benchmarking" of alternative systems. Data used to construct this room is derived from Step 12 Table 9.15. Each system assessed in the competitive analysis based on target values of functional requirements is now subjected to a competitive technical assessment on those criteria as well. Each is ranked on a scale of 1 to 5, with 1 being "poor," and 5 being "excellent." Average scores for all the assessed systems run ~3.04 out of 5, indicating that each could potentially be suited for Airline x's mission profile. However, as should be noted by the graphic portrayal of the data, the 737-8 is well within the range of acceptability.

One of the last rooms constructed in the HOQ is the one that houses the relationships between the customer requirements and the functional requirements, the central core of the HOQ. Each "What" requirement is linked to each "How" requirement, and the relationship is measured on a 9 (strong), 3 (medium), and 1 (weak) scale (see Step 13 Table 9.16).

Directly below the relationship matrix are assigned "Target Values." Recall earlier in our discussion of assessing the direction of improvement

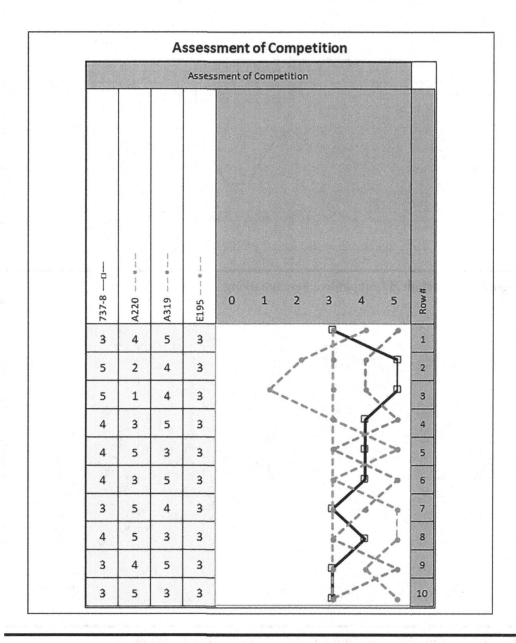

Figure 9.7   Assessment of Competition.

(see Step 9 Table 9.11) that target values directly influence the direction and amount of movement of each functional requirement, ensuring continuous alignment between them.

Directly below the target values are "Maximum Relationship" numerical annotations. These relationships tell the highest rating between each "What" and "How" criteria. Just below these statistics are "Relative Importance Ratings." These numerical values are derived by summing each value

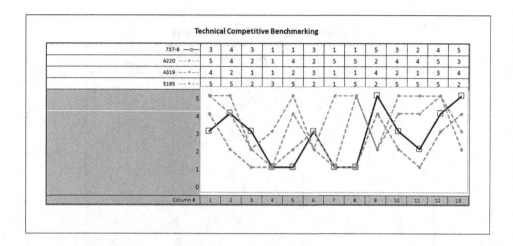

Figure 9.8   Technical Competitive Benchmarking.

Customer and Functional Requirement Relationships

Customer Requirements (Explicit and Implicit) (the "Whats") Customer Evaluation Criteria \ Functional Requirements (the "Hows") Product Support Elements	Cost per Available Seat Mile ($/seat nm)	Support Equipment Required ($K per a/c)	Personnel Training Cost ($M per a/c)	Parts Inventory Required (Safety Stock %)	Cabin Reconfiguration (hr per a/c)	Fuel Systems Modification ($M per a/c)	Onsite Technical Support (Y/N)	OEM sole source part distributor (Y/N)	Range (nm)	Life Cycle (hrs)	Operating Cost ($/hr)	Availability (%)	Passenger seats "dual cabin configuration"
Level of Personnel Attrition Rates by Maintenance/Support Echelon	1	1	9	1	1	3	9	1	1	1	3	9	1
Training Program Compatability with Staffing Mix	1	1	9	1	1	1	9	3	1	1	3	3	1
Level of Repair Policy	3	1	3	1	1	1	9	3	1	1	3	9	1
Test and Suppot Equipment Levels	3	9	3	3	1	1	3	1	1	1	3	3	1
Utilization Parameters	1	1	3	1	1	1	1	1	9	3	9	9	9
Expected system Availability, Dependability and Readiness Criteria	1	1	3	9	1	1	9	3	3	1	9	9	1
Relaibility, Maintainability and Supportability factors for Units, Assemblies and Sub-assemblies	1	1	3	3	3	3	3	1	1	3	9	9	1
Tradeoff Evaluations	9	1	1	1	1	1	1	3	3	3	9	9	3
Inventory Safety Stock Needed	1	1	3	9	1	1	3	3	1	3	3	3	1
Provisioning and Procuremet Cycle Needed	1	1	1	9	1	1	1	1	1	3	3	3	1
Target	$0.12	$25K	50	95%	70	50	Y	N	3,500	60,000	$7,500	95%	120
Max Relationship	9	9	9	9	3	3	9	3	9	3	9	9	9
Relative Importance Rating	100.0	88.0	186.0	186.0	56.0	66.0	236.0	96.0	106.0	94.0	252.0	312.0	96.0
Importance Weight	5%	5%	10%	10%	3%	4%	13%	5%	6%	5%	13%	17%	5%

Figure 9.9   Customer and Functional Requirement Relationships.

(1,3,9), then multiplying them. Finally, the "Importance Weight" tells us what percentage of each "What and How" relationship makes up the total requirement associations assessed.

When all rooms were defined and populated, the acquisition assessment team, then put the entire model together, forming an HOQ (see Figure 9.10). The next step for the assessment team was interrupting the QFD Acquisition Modeling process results.

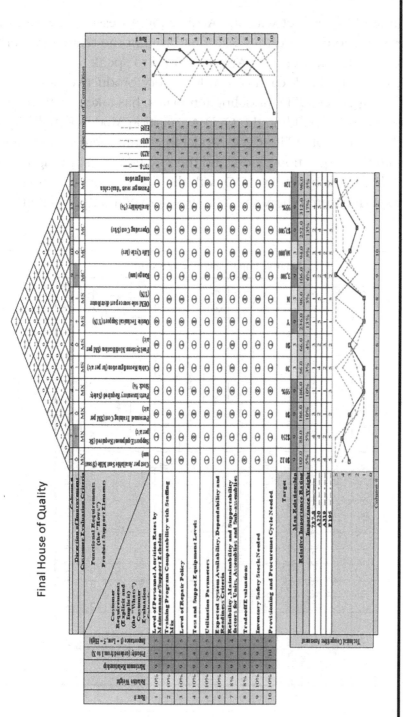

Figure 9.10 Final HOQ for Acquisition Assessment QFD Model.

Step 16: Interrupting the Results

Angela, John, and James met with the Acquisition Assessment team in the same conference room where they had first brought the team together. There was complete silence; then Angela started to speak.

"First off, I want to thank each of you for a very productive two weeks of work. John, using James QFD Modeling templates, has taken us through a step-by-step process of building the QFD Acquisition Model. Initially by using data derived from the QFD Life-Cycle Model to ensure there was linkage and alignment with the acquisition model and then by taking us through a room-by-room build of the acquisition HOQ with the explanation provided as to what each room measured, how the data was derived that populated that

Relative Importance Rating Scores

1	2	3	4	5	6	7	8	9	10	11	12	13
◊	↑	◊	↓	↓	◊	↑	↓	◊	◊	↓	↑	◊
MX	MX	MX	MX	MS	MS	MS	MS	MC	MC	MC	MC	MC
Cost per Available Seat Mile [$/seat n mi]	Support Equipment Required [$k per a/c]	Personnel Training Cost [$M per a/c]	Parts Inventory Required [Safety Stock %]	Cabin Reconfiguration [hr per a/c]	Fuel Systems Modification [$M per a/c]	Onsite Technical Support [Y/N]	OEM sole source part distributor [Y/N]	Range [nm]	Life Cycle [hrs]	Operating Cost [$/hr]	Availability [%]	Passenger seats *dual cabin configuration
1	1	9	1	1	3	9	1	1	1	3	9	1
1	1	9	1	1	1	9	3	1	1	3	3	1
3	1	3	1	1	1	9	3	1	1	3	9	1
3	9	3	3	1	1	3	1	1	1	3	3	1
1	1	3	1	1	1	1	1	9	3	9	9	9
1	1	3	9	1	1	9	3	3	1	9	9	1
1	1	3	3	3	3	3	1	1	3	9	9	1
9	1	1	1	1	1	1	3	3	3	9	9	3
1	1	3	9	1	1	3	3	1	3	3	3	1
1	1	1	9	1	1	1	1	1	3	3	3	1
$0.12	$25k	$0	95%	70	$0	Y	N	3,500	60,000	$7,900	95%	120
9	9	9	9	3	3	9	3	9	3	9	9	9
100.0	88.0	186.0	186.0	56.0	66.0	236.0	96.0	106.0	94.0	252.0	312.0	96.0
5%	5%	10%	10%	3%	4%	13%	5%	6%	5%	13%	17%	5%

Figure 9.11 Relative Importance Rating Scores.

Table 9.17   Customer Down-Selected Evaluation Criteria

Evaluation Criteria	Abbr	Avg Customer Score	Rank
Maintenance ownership cost	MX	4.6	1
OEM modification support costs	MS	3.9	2
Mission Capabilities	MC	3.7	3

Functional Requirements Support Elements Ranking

Functional Requirements Product Support Elements Ranking	Maintenace ownership cost (MX)	OEM modification support cost (MS)	Mission capabilities (MC)
1. Availability %			312
2. Operating cost ($/hr.)	252		
3. Onsite technical support - Yes		236	
4. Parts Inventory Required (Safety Stock %)	186		
5. Personnel training cost ($M per a/c)	186		
6. Range (nm)			106
7. Cost per Available Seat Mile ($/seat nm)	100		
8. Passenger seats *dual cabin configuration		96	
9. OEM sole source part distributor (Y/N)		96	
10. Life Cycle (hrs.)			94
11. Support Equipment Required ($k per a/c)			88
12. Fuel Systems Modification ($M per a/c)		66	
13. Cabin Reconfiguration (hr. per a/c)		56	
	724	550	600

Figure 9.12   Functional Requirements Support Elements Ranking.

room and, how the data was used. We now want to interpret what the HOQ provides us, how decisions can be derived from its use, and understand what our two weeks of work mean. We then need to provide our management team with information so it can move forward with the 737-8 system acquisition process. John, I would ask you for your help is doing this."

John stood and reached over the projector console, switched on the overhead projector, and spoke. "Folks, you all saw this yesterday when we finished the 'Relationship Matrix' structuring process." This is where we will start examining what the HOQ is telling us.

We start with the "Relative Importance Rating" scores annotated in the lower portion of the matrix. Recall these show the relationships between the customer requirements and the functional requirements. The relative importance scores reflect the strength of that relationship.

Customer Criteria and Customer Requirements Matrix

Customer Requirements Evaluation Criteria Prioritized	Maintenace ownership cost (MX)*	OEM modification support cost (MS)**	Mission capabilities (MC)***
1. Expected system, availability, dependability, and readiness criteria			3.7
2. Reliability, maintainability and supportability for units, assemblies/sub-assemblies			3.7
3. Utilization parameters	4.6		
4. Tradeoff evaluations	4.6		
5. Inventory safety stock needed	4.6		
6. Test and support equipment levels	4.6		
7. Provisioning and procurement cycle needed		3.9	
8. Tradeoff evaluations		3.9	
9. Level of personnel attrition rates by maintenance/support echelon	4.6		3.7
10. Training program compatibility with staffing mix			3.7
	23	7.8	14.8

*Average customer rating score 4.6
**Average customer rating score 3.9
***Average customer rating score 3.7

Figure 9.13   Customer Criteria and Customer Requirements Matrix.

The first step in assessing what the HOQ model is telling us is to assess the relative importance rating scores. The standard by which they should be assessed is the "Customer Down-Selected Evaluation Criteria" initially presented in Step 3 (Table 9.5). However, it is provided again because of their critical importance to understanding how a QFD Acquisition Model is interrupted.

Each "Functional Requirement Product Support Element" used in the HOQ is ranked and prioritized by "Relative Importance Rating" and matched to the "Customer Down-Selected Criteria" contained in Table 9.5. The numerical ratings are then summed. Note that based on the QFD Acquisition Model scoring, the customer down-selected evaluation criteria rank order sequencing presented in Table 9.5 has changed from MX, MS, MC, to MX, MC, MS. While the change may seem modest (only a 50-point spread), what it does signal is the "mission capabilities" criteria might better serve as an indicator of functional supportability requirements over the life-cycle of the 737-8.

The other aspect to consider in shifting rank order priorities is that those functional requirements aligned with each customer down-selected criteria would be reprioritized on the basis of this shift in ranking. As an example, those functional requirements such as availability, range, life-cycle, support equipment would shift in priority before onsite technical support, passenger seats dual cabin configuration, OEM sole source part distribution, fuel systems modification, and cabin reconfiguration.

The second step in interpreting what the QFD model tells us is to map the customer down-selected criteria to the customer requirements presented in step 1. Recall that when we started constructing the Acquisition HOQ, we went through a process of assigning priorities to the "customer requirements evaluation criteria." By taking that prioritized list of evaluation criteria and mapping them to the "down-selected customer requirements" with the respective scoring presented in Table 9.5, we can confirm that the prioritization shift of MX, MC, and MC, witnessed in the functional requirements product support elements criteria is confirmed. This shift would indicate to the Airline X management team that reprioritization is warranted that shifts emphasis from provisioning and procurement cycle needed and tradeoff evaluation to the expected system, availability, dependability, and readiness criteria; reliability, maintainability, and supportability for units, assemblies/sub-assemblies; level of personnel attrition rates by maintenance/support echelon, and training program compatibility with staffing mix.

After John finished providing the team with the interpretations of QFD Acquisition Assessment results, Angela rose from her seat. "Thank you, John, for leading us through an interpretation of the model, and thank you, James, for developing the model. I believe I can speak for the entire team when I say we had no idea you could pack so much information into such a compact model. Nor did I fully realize the inter-relationship each piece of information has when performing an acquisition analysis. I am sold on using the QFD methodology. I am sure our management team will be as well." Angela continued, "Our next step is to schedule a meeting with the management team and provide them with our findings and recommendations. When I learn the date, John and James, would you be available to attend?"

Summary

The supportability assessment process illustrated in the above case illustrates how the use of a QFD-based life-cycle methodology can augment the decision-making process by clearly evaluating and prioritizing supportability requirements to facilitate system acquisition decisions. It also illustrates the benefits derived through the mobilizing of cross-functional team to participate in the evaluation process.

Appendix

Table 9A.1   Integrated Product Support Element Importance and Priority Ranking

Management Category	Integrated Product Support (IPS) element	This IPS Element Addresses the Following Sub-elements	Rank Importance (1 to 5)	Rank Priority (1 to X)
Life-Cycle Sustainment Management	Product Support Management	Comprehensive Configuration Control Plan		
		Establishment of Comprehensive Continuous Process Improvement Plan		
		Postproduction Support Planning		
		Reverse Logistics and Retrograde Movement		
		Life-Cycle Management Systems Development		
		Average:		
	Supply Support	Quantity of Spares/Repair Parts		
		Logistics Pipeline Needed		
		Inventory Safety Stock Needed		
		Provisioning and Procurement Cycle Needed		
		Expected Supply Availability Requirement		
		Average:		
	Packaging, Handling, Storage, and Transportation	Expected Transportation and Handling Requirements for Maintenance-Defined Levels		
		Transportation and Handling Environments by System Category		
		Modes of Transportation Defined		
		Requirements for Reusable Containers		
		Special Packaging Requirements		
		Average:		
	Maintenance Planning and Management	Echelons or Levels of Maintenance Needed		
		Basic Maintenance Functions Needed by Level		
		Level of Repair Policy		
		Test and Support Equipment Levels		
		Logistic pipeline between proposed levels		
		Average:		

Table 9A.1 *(Continued)*

Technical Management	Design Interface	Mission Profile		
		Basic Performance Parameters		
		Forecasted Life-Cycle		
		Utilization Parameters		
		Expected system Availability, Dependability, and Readiness Criteria		
		Average:		
	Sustaining Engineering	Operational and Maintenance Function to Support		
		Reliability, Maintainability, and Supportability factors for Units, Assemblies, and Sub-assemblies		
		Tradeoff Evaluations		
		Allocation Coast Factors		
		Average:		
	Technical Data	Operating and Maintenance Procedures		
		Identification of Procedures for Test and Support in Intended System		
		Average:		
	Computer Resources	Types of Computer Support Systems Needed		
		Level of Scalability		
		Level of Modular Replacement Criteria		
		Level of Integration		
		Types of Operating Systems		
		Average:		
Infrastructure Management	Facilities and Infrastructure	Facility Requirements to Support the Intended Systems Selected		
		Environmental System Requirements		
		Spare/Repair Parts Storage		
		Warehousing Requirements		
		Average:		
	Manpower and Personnel	Operational and Maintenance Personnel Requirements		
		Level of Personnel Attrition Rates by Maintenance/Support Echelon		
		Training Program Compatibility with Staffing Mix		
		Average:		

(Continued)

Table 9A.1 *(Continued)*

	Support Equipment	Life-Cycle Spares/Repair Parts for Support Requirements		
		Logistics Pipeline		
		Test and Acceptance Procedures		
		Supply Availability Requirements		
		Average:		
	Training and Training Support	Operational and Maintenance Personnel Requirements		
		Skill Levels Needed by Maintenance Echelon		
		Personnel Effective Factors		
		Training Equipment Requirements		
		Specific Training Programs		
		Average:		

Supporting Material for Case Study Instructions

Table 9A.2 Customer Requirements ("Whats") Assessment of Competition Comparison of IPS to Target Functional Requirements

IPS Element	IPS Sub-Elements	Functional Requirements	Target	A220	A319	737-8	E195
Manpower and personnel	Level of personnel attrition rates by maintenance/ support echelon	Cabin Reconfiguration (hr per a/c)	70	65	80	95	50
	Training program compatibility with staffing mix	Personnel Training Cost ($M per a/c)	$0	$0.4M	$0.8M	$0	$0.5M
Maintenance planning and management	Level of repair policy	Onsite Technical Support (Y/N)	Y	Y	N	N	N
		OEM sole source part distributor (Y/N)	N	N	Y	Y	N
	Test and support equipment levels	Support Equipment Required ($k per a/c)	$25k	$19k	$27k	$20k	$17k

Table 9A.2 *(Continued)*

Design interface	Utilization parameters	Range (nm)	3,500	3,100	4,100	4,200	3,300
		Passenger seats *dual cabin configuration	120	124	143	154	110
	Expected system, availability, dependability, and readiness criteria	Fuel Systems Modification ($M per a/c)	$0	$1.1M	$0	$0	$1.5M
Sustaining engineering	Reliability, maintainability, and supportability for units and assemblies/ sub-assemblies	Availability (%)	95%	99%	95%	96%	99%
	Tradeoff evaluations	Cost per Available Seat Mile ($/seat nm)	$0.122	$0.118	$0.120	$0.123	$0.119
		Operating Cost ($/hr)	7,900	6,200	8,200	8,100	5,900
Supply Support	Inventory safety stock needed	Parts Inventory Required (Safety Stock %)	95%	97%	98%	97%	96%
	Provisioning and procurement cycle needed	Life-Cycle (hrs)	60,000	65,000	55,000	60,000	70,000

Table 9A.3 Customer Requirements ("Whats") Assessment of Competition

IPS Element	IPS Sub-elements	Functional Requirements	Target	A220	A319	737-8	E195
Manpower and personnel	Level of personnel attrition rates by maintenance/ support echelon	Cabin Reconfiguration (hr per a/c)	70	4	2	1	5
	Training program compatibility with staffing mix	Personnel Training Cost ($M per a/c)	$0	2	1	3	2
Maintenance planning and management	Level of repair policy	Onsite Technical Support (Y/N)	Y	5	1	1	1
		OEM sole source part distributor (Y/N)	N	5	1	1	5
	Test and support equipment levels	Support Equipment Required ($k per a/c)	$25k	4	2	4	5

(Continued)

Table 9A.3 *(Continued)*

Design interface	Utilization parameters	Range (nm)	3,500	2	4	5	2
		Passenger Seats *Dual Cabin Configuration	120	3	4	5	2
	Expected system, availability, dependability, and readiness criteria	Fuel Systems Modification ($M per a/c)	$0	2	3	3	2
Sustaining engineering	Reliability, maintainability, and supportability for units, assemblies/ sub-assemblies	Availability (%)	95%	5	3	4	5
	Tradeoff evaluations	Cost per Available Seat Mile ($/seat nm)	$0.122	5	4	3	5
		Operating Cost ($/hr)	7,900	4	1	2	5
Supply Support	Inventory safety stock needed	Parts Inventory Required (Safety Stock %)	95%	1	1	1	3
	Provisioning and procurement cycle needed	Life-Cycle (hrs)	60,000	4	2	3	5

Table 9A.4   Comparative Assessment of Functional Requirements ("Hows") to Target

Evaluation Criteria	Functional Requirements	Target	A220	A319	737-8	E195
Maintenance ownership cost	Cost per Available Seat Mile ($/seat nm)	$0.122	$0.118	$0.120	$0.123	$0.119
	Support Equipment Required ($k per a/c)	$25k	$19k	$27k	$20k	$17k
	Personnel Training Cost ($M per a/c)	$0	$0.4M	$0.8M	$0	$0.5M
	Parts Inventory Required (Safety Stock %)	95%	97%	98%	97%	96%
OEM modification support costs	Cabin Reconfiguration (hr per a/c)	70	65	80	95	50
	Fuel Systems Modification ($M per a/c)	$0	$1.1M	$0	$0	$1.5M
	Onsite Technical Support (Y/N)	Y	Y	N	N	N
	OEM sole source part distributor (Y/N)	N	N	Y	Y	N

Table 9A.4 *(Continued)*

Mission Capabilities	Range (nm)	3,500	3,100	4,100	4,200	3,300
	Life-Cycle (hrs)	60,000	65,000	55,000	60,000	70,000
	Operating Cost ($/hr)	7,900	6,200	8,200	8,100	5,900
	Availability (%)	95%	99%	95%	96%	99%
	Passenger Seats *Dual Cabin Configuration	120	124	143	154	110

Table 9A.5 Functional Requirements ("Hows") Technical Competitive Assessment

Evaluation Criteria	Functional Requirements	Target	A220	A319	737-8	E195
Maintenance ownership cost	Cost per Available Seat Mile ($/seat nm)	$0.122	5	4	3	5
	Support Equipment Required ($k per a/c)	$25k	4	2	4	5
	Personnel Training Cost ($M per a/c)	$0	2	1	3	2
	Parts Inventory Required (Safety Stock %)	95%	1	1	1	3
OEM modification support costs	Cabin Reconfiguration (hr per a/c)	70	4	2	1	5
	Fuel Systems Modification ($M per a/c)	$0	2	3	3	2
	Onsite Technical Support (Y/N)	Y	5	1	1	1
	OEM sole source part distributor (Y/N)	N	5	1	1	5
Mission Capabilities	Range (nm)	3,500	2	4	5	2
	Life-Cycle (hrs)	60,000	4	2	3	5
	Operating Cost ($/hr)	7,900	4	1	2	5
	Availability (%)	95%	5	3	4	5
	Passenger Seats *Dual Cabin Configuration	120	3	4	5	2

PART 4

Chapter 10

Managing the Quality Function Deployment Process

Management's Influence on QFD

A well-executed QFD project can coordinate resources throughout the organization, can add expertise continuously from suppliers and customers, and can ensure that the product and/or service is exactly what is expected by the buyer. Many of the challenges for a specific QFD effort generally are unknown until encountered. However, as illustrated in Figure 10.1, some

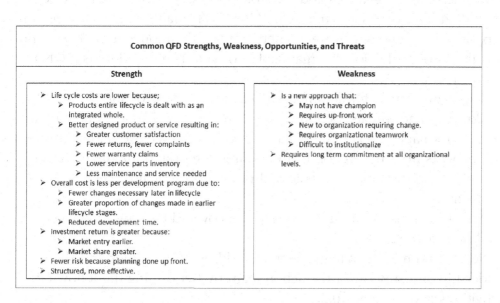

Common QFD Strengths, Weakness, Opportunities, and Threats

Strength	Weakness

➤ Life cycle costs are lower because;
  ➤ Products entire lifecycle is dealt with as an integrated whole.
  ➤ Better designed product or service resulting in:
    ➤ Greater customer satisfaction
    ➤ Fewer returns, fewer complaints
    ➤ Fewer warranty claims
    ➤ Lower service parts inventory
    ➤ Less maintenance and service needed
➤ Overall cost is less per development program due to:
  ➤ Fewer changes necessary later in lifecycle
  ➤ Greater proportion of changes made in earlier lifecycle stages.
  ➤ Reduced development time.
➤ Investment return is greater because:
  ➤ Market entry earlier.
  ➤ Market share greater.
➤ Fewer risk because planning done up front.
➤ Structured, more effective.
	➤ Is a new approach that:
	  ➤ May not have champion
	  ➤ Requires up-front work
	  ➤ New to organization requiring change.
	  ➤ Requires organizational teamwork
	  ➤ Difficult to institutionalize
	➤ Requires long term commitment at all organizational levels.

Figure 10.1 Common QFD Strengths, Weaknesses, Opportunities, and Threats.

DOI: 10.4324/9781003336044-14

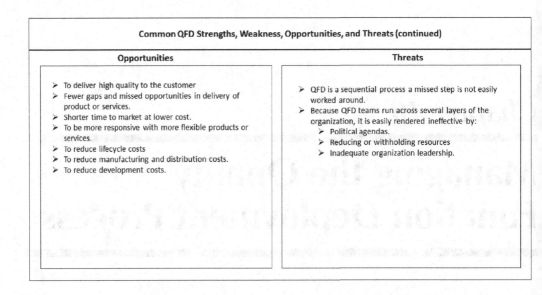

Figure 10.2 QFD Strengths, Weaknesses, Opportunities, and Threats (continued).

common strengths, weaknesses, opportunities, and threats (SWOT) are common to all QFD projects.[1,69–72]

To increase the chances and level of success, management must be aware of, and address issues identified via this SWOT analysis. By providing timely support, management can significantly impact the morale and effectiveness of a group of professionals organized into what is referred to as a QFD Action Team.

The main vehicle for attaining QFD benefits and avoiding many of the weaknesses and threats identified in Figures 10.1 and 10.2 is investing in a high-performance QFD Action Team. However, to achieve maximum results and benefits from that action team requires senior and middle managers to understand the tasks and potential problems the team faces upon deployment.

The three most important issues to the covered by senior management are listed in Table 10.1.[1,69]

Senior and middle management can address these issues and show leadership and support of the action team by performing the following activities listed in Table 10.2.

Table 10.1   Three Most Important Issues for Senior Management

Three Most Important Issues for Senior Management
Getting started: Important Issues to be Covered
➢ First, senior management leadership must be visible and engaged. All functional units within the organization must understand the strategic worth of the QFD effort and buy-in to its success.
➢ Second, if team members are removed from the action team during engagement, there will be a reduction in the effectiveness and thus reduces the chances of success.
➢ Third, timely action is essential when an impediment exists to the QFD process.

Table 10.2   Senior and Middle Management Support Activities for the QFD Action Team

Senior and Middle Management Support Activities for the QFD Action Team
Senior Management Actions
➢ Attending and overview session for senior management. Typically, these last around 4 hours and walk the executive through the QFD implementation process.
➢ Have a senior executive address the first action team "kick off" meeting.
➢ Attend the process review "de-brief" session.
➢ Be active in communicating with the action team.
Middle Management Actions
➢ Carefully consider which subordinates are assigned to the action team.
➢ Actively engage in receiving and acting on communications from action team members.
➢ Attend management meeting. Typically, these last around 4 hours.
➢ Actively participate in process review "de-briefing" sessions.

First Issue

To successfully implement a QFD approach to design, leadership, vision, and, most of all, commitment to the process at both the senior and middle management levels is crucial. If an action team senses a lack of stakeholder

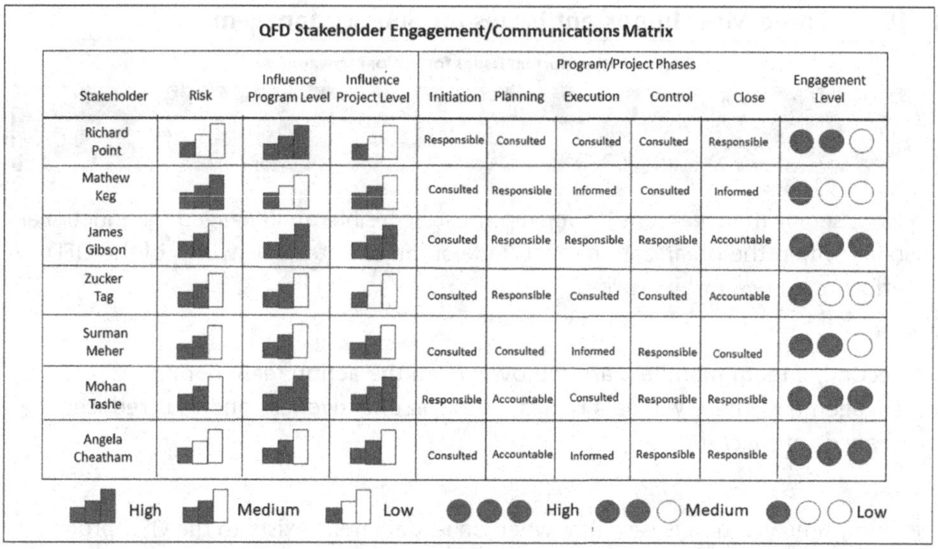

QFD Stakeholder Engagement/Communications Matrix

Stakeholder	Risk	Influence Program Level	Influence Project Level	Program/Project Phases					Engagement Level
				Initiation	Planning	Execution	Control	Close	
Richard Point				Responsible	Consulted	Consulted	Consulted	Responsible	
Mathew Keg				Consulted	Responsible	Informed	Consulted	Informed	
James Gibson				Consulted	Responsible	Responsible	Responsible	Accountable	
Zucker Tag				Consulted	Responsible	Consulted	Consulted	Accountable	
Surman Meher				Consulted	Consulted	Informed	Responsible	Consulted	
Mohan Tashe				Responsible	Accountable	Consulted	Responsible	Responsible	
Angela Cheatham				Consulted	Accountable	Informed	Responsible	Responsible	

Legend: High, Medium, Low (bar charts); High, Medium, Low (circles)

Figure 10.3   QFD Stakeholder Engagement/Communications Matrix.

engagement, it will have a strong negative impact and may jeopardize success. A process that is useful in assessing and monitoring overall stakeholder engagement is to develop a "Stakeholder Engagement Matrix," like the one presented in Figure 10.3.[38,73]

When executing the QFD process, especially during the translation of the VOC, there will be many more discoveries made than usual about how the customer "uses" the product or service and what they "want" in that product or service. This is often caused by the competitive analysis process when more research is done on current or potential competitors. With all this extra information, there is a strong temptation to include more features and functions in the QFD product or service than originally planned. The action team and management must resist this "scope creep" temptation and focus solely on the VOC analysis. In other words, concentrate on the "benefits" that the customer tells you they want, not on the "features and functions" of the competitive products and services already on the market.

This is not to say that the Action Teams' efforts to include "excitement quality" elements into the product or service should be restricted. This is why it was advocated that the Kano analysis process be executed during the discovery and design-to portion of the systems development process. It is intended to raise awareness that more features and functions do not necessarily translate into a more desirable offering in the marketplace. When management reviews the Action Team's progress, there must be a constant awareness of scope creed potential and a continuous refocusing of the team's activities.

Second Issue

To keep managers engaged in the QFD process and reduce chances that essential team members will be withdrawn, use the Stakeholder Engagement Matrix illustrated in Figure 10.2 as a communications tool. The matrix considers that different individuals require different levels of information (content and frequency) and often have different opinions on how they want to communicate. Experience has shown that an engagement matrix is a preventive measure essential for the success of a project such as QFD. Remember, the nature of projects is that they are easy to start but difficult to keep going and, most of all, keep on track!

When applied to a project such as QFD, a stakeholder matrix plan can maximize the utilization of the project's resources and hence its success. However, the ultimate is a planning approach that involves all the functions of the organization and tasks for a minimum of 12 months. This approach is often called Policy Deployment, also known as the Hoskin Kanri Planning Process or Management by Policy, which is an alternative to Management by Objectives. Figure 10.4 illustrates the seven steps involved in implementing the Hoskin Kanri Planning process.[69]

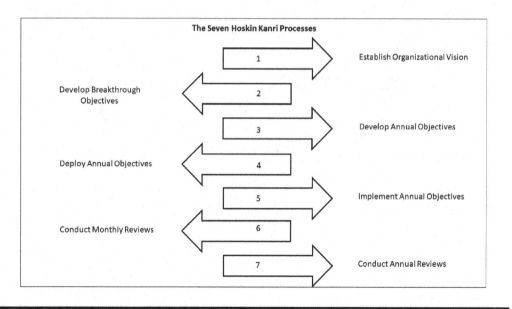

Figure 10.4   The Seven Hoskin Kanri Processes.

From the offset of planning, senior staff sets certain goals for the organization based on its mission and vision and shares them with subordinate functional areas. Each functional area then takes those organizational goals and determines what they must do to support higher-level goals. Resources are also determined for the functional area to attain the goals. Functional areas then return their statement of goals and resources to senior management. Suppose the next higher level is able to allocate any functional area resources required. In that case, a contract is established, and resources are assigned to the functional area to accomplish the functional area goals.

Third Issue

This all works fine until senior management cannot provide resources to the functional areas when required. When this happens, a series of processes known as "catch ball" occurs in which the two levels in negotiation go back and forth, trying to strike a balance between what resources can be allocated and what accomplishments need can be committed to. A typical "catch ball" process is illustrated in Figure 10.5.[69,74]

Once agreement is reached between each functional area and its next higher level, then within each functional area, going down into the specific tactical level, "catch ball" is played until all higher-level goals have been

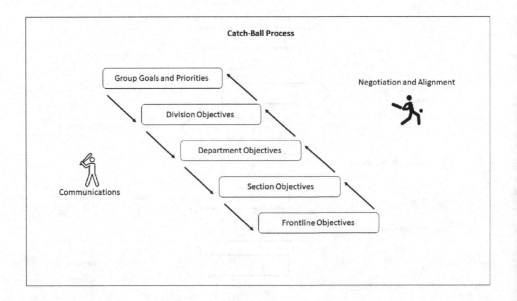

Figure 10.5   Typical Catch Ball Process Flow.

deployed to the lowest levels of the organization. It is at this point everyone within the organization has agreed on what their goals are and the resources they will have available to reach those goals. Of course, there will be many targets, or *hoshins*, (which means bright shiny objects or targets in Japanese), that the QFD action will be monitoring closely.

Typical QFD Project Schedule

The Stakeholder Engagement/communications Matrix presented in Figure 10.2 does not outline the entire action team/management interface. Both action team members and management will be involved in additional activities at different times as warranted for a specific QFD project. Figure 10.6 provides an example of a typical QFD project with details of actions taken during each step of the process.[69,74]

Scoping and operations review activities should be planned for 1 or 2 days. This step is done by the project-designated team leader and trainer/consultant, either internal or external (we will discuss these two roles more in-depth in the next section). The purpose of this step is to gain an understanding of the organization and product or service that will be the subject of the QFD project.

An overview session with management normally takes roughly half a day (approximately 4 hours). Therefore, it is vital that managers who will

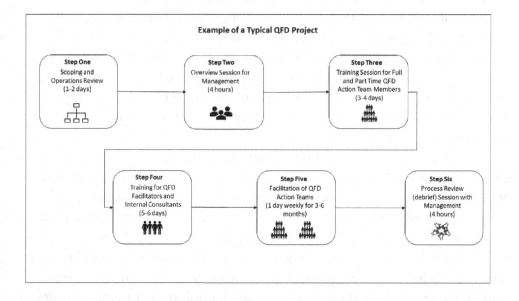

Figure 10.6   Example of a Typical QFD Project.

have subordinates taking part in the QFD Action Team attend this session. The goal of this step is to inform managers what QFD is, what it can and cannot do, what benefits can be derived from its use, what it requires of them (cooperation between functions), and what are the correct questions to ask, and at which points in the project to ask them to manage the process correctly. It can also be used to identify potential champions for the QFD activity within the organization.

Training sessions for full- and part-time QFD Action Team members are scheduled for between three and four days. All persons assigned to work on the action team go through the same training time or ad hoc members, such as those from key suppliers, customers, or corporate staff, will receive the same training as a full-time member. This step aims to inform all team members and interested managers about the elements of the QFD process and what to expect as they go through the process both from an analytical/technical standpoint and from a behavioral/team-building perspective.

Training for QFD facilitators and internal consultants normally requires five to six days. Training for facilitators working with the initial QFD projects and persons responsible for managing the QFD techniques within the organization is performed at this time. This step aims to have a cadre of personnel familiar with the QFD technique who can perpetuate it after the pilot consultant/trainer-facilitated project is concluded. This training can also serve those interested in championing the QFD process.

The facilitation of QFD Action Team generally lasts for between three to six months. Typically, one day weekly is devoted during the elapsed time. The step goal is to take QFD team members, facilitators, and propagators through a complete program from concept to product/service design-to. During this step, a postmortem review structure for future updating of matrices and setting up how to conduct feedback to organizational participants is created.

The process review session with management normally takes around one-half day (approximately 4 hours). Its goal is to go over the just completed QFD project with the management team, point out lessons learned, and share the outcomes (in terms of both the new product/service designed and the now-trained action team member). It is also here that the team building and design skills of the action team can be showcased. Side benefits of this step are increased awareness of QFD, reinforced convictions by current champions, and the creation of additional champions. All managers should attend this four-hour debriefing meeting.

Management's Nine Actions for QFD Analysis

Management responsibilities to the QFD analysis team can be summarized into nine actions. Each has been instrumental in assisting action teams regardless of focus (product or service) during their QFD execution journey. These management responsibilities are explored in the following paragraphs, along with several types of documentation that can aid action team organization and subsequent review process.

Action 1: Study and Fully Understand From Beginning to End

QFD is best understood if it is studied and discussed with experienced subject matter experts (SMEs) before involvement. Experience in its application is a major time and cost saver for the QFD neophyte. Management must listen to and work with external and internal QFD consultants before initiating any QFD projects within an organization. Because QFD is concerned with the conceptualization, design, development, production, assembly, packaging, shipping, and functioning of new and enhanced products or services, there must be a clear understanding of the VOC. Other voices also require attention: those of the engineer, the process, all the support functions, and society as a whole. However, QFD is not a panacea that can be expected to resolve all of management's concerns and solve all of an organization's issues and problems. Fortunately, QFD does interface with a variety of TQM tools. Figure 10.7 illustrates some of these quality interfacings.[17]

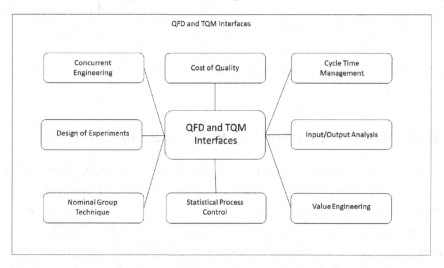

Figure 10.7   QFD and TQM Interfaces.

QFD acts as a framework and catalyst for Concurrent Engineering (CE) by providing a systematic methodology for integrating interdisciplinary inputs and facilitating better interdepartmental communications. As to the cost of quality (COQ), QFD focuses on creating the least cost products to meet customer needs. It supports QFD by highlighting the cost of not doing it "right" the first time. It also identifies the cost of conformance (prevention and appraisal) and nonconformance (internal and external failures). Regarding cycle time, QFD is concerned with improving designs in less time. It also provides project teams with a methodology needed to clearly define process purpose and objectives, identify process start and end points, highlight value-added and non-value-added activities, and identify tasks time, choke points, and duplicative operations.[17,36]

Design of Experiments (DoE) supports QFD through its capability to identify controllable factors and efficiently and effectively conduct experiments to discover interactions and effects between factors. Input/Output (I/O) analysis supports QFD because it provides clarification of roles and responsibilities, resolves roles and responsibilities, eliminates duplication, and opens new lines of communication. The Nominal Group Technique (NGT) supports QFD because it provides the generation and presentation of ideas, clarification of logic and data analysis, and development of action plans.[17,75]

Statistical Process Control (SPC) ensures that the gains achieved through QFD are not lost. It also helps to identify areas for performance improvement. Discovers common and special cause problem sources and prioritizes those problems and causes. QFD supports Value Engineering (VE) by providing a mechanism to identify required functions, analyze current configurations, identify costs associated with each part, determine the cost to perform required functions and develop alternative configurations.[17,75]

Action 2: Identify and Prioritize Projects Requiring QFD

At any given time, organizations have a multitude of projects that could benefit from analyses by QFD. A facilitated brainstorming session composed of management drawn from across a broad spectrum of the organization often is used to generate a comprehensive listing of potential QFD project candidates. Another method often used is a prioritization matrix. Generally, prioritization is required because most organizations do not have the necessary resources to do everything at the same time. Of course, there are

QFD Project Prioritization Matrix									
Criteria	Value		Risk		Effort		Cost		Weighted Score
Weights	.40		.20		.20		.20		
Options									
Project 1	675K	270K	5	1	4	.8	3	.6	277.8	2
Project 2	650K	260K	1	.2	2	.4	1	.2	260.8	1
Project 3									
Project 4									
Project 5									
Project 6									
Project 7									
Project 8									
Calculation: Value+Risk+Effort+Cost Note: R+E+C = 60% of weight			1 low – 5 high		1 low – 5 high		1 low – 5 high		

Figure 10.8   QFD Project Prioritization Matrix.

several prioritization processes, ranging from a simple voting technique to a more rigorous pairwise comparison process.[17,75]

On several QFD projects, I have found that using a hybrid type prioritization method where pairwise, weighted scoring and ranking give a well-rounded assessment for consideration. Figure 10.8 is an example of this QFD project prioritization matrix.

A weighted total score is computed for each project under consideration. Then the projects' scores are rank order to assist the management team members in deciding on the most important projects to pursue. The process develops a team consensus about the path to follow and instills a sense of ownership in the paths chosen. This ownership creates the will or spirit in the team to follow through.

Action 3: Define the Purpose and Plan Resource Allocation for the QFD Project

Each QFD project must have a specific, well-stated purpose. The creation of this statement of purpose is as much for the management that defines it as for the QFD analysis team that will ultimately use it to form the team charter. A statement must precede any other statement relative to the creation of the QFD Action Team. Figure 10.9 shows a typical QFD analysis team charter document.[4,17]

It is understood that they are a finite number of human resources available to be allocated to an infinite number of projects, QFD or otherwise. The question management must answer is how much of each personnel resource will be allocated to any QFD project. Figure 10.10 is a matrix analysis form designed to help management plan this allocation of human resources to the selected QFD projects.[5,17]

Typical QFD Analysis Team Charter Document			
QFD Project Name	Project Purpose		Date
Objectives	Assumptions	Deliverables	KPIs
	Financial: Non-financial:	Phase 1: Phase 2: Phase 3:	
Team members and % of time		In-scope	Out-of-scope
Role % time			
Sponsor: Longshore 100			
Leads: Cheatham, Gibson 100			
Team Members: TBD 100			

Figure 10.9 Typical QFD Analysis Team Charter Document.

Typical Resource Allocation Matrix Form

	Resource Name	Skillset	Daily Rate	Total Cost	Allocation			
					Sept-22	Oct-22	Nov-22	Dec-22
1	Angela Cheatham	Master Analyst	$1,000	$475,000	☑	☑	☑	☑
2	James Gibson	Formula Wizard	$2500	$675,000	☑	☑	☑	☑
3	John Longshore	QFD Process Analyst	$1,750	$500,000	☑	☑	☑	☑
4								
5								
6								

Figure 10.10 Typical Resource Allocation Matrix Form.

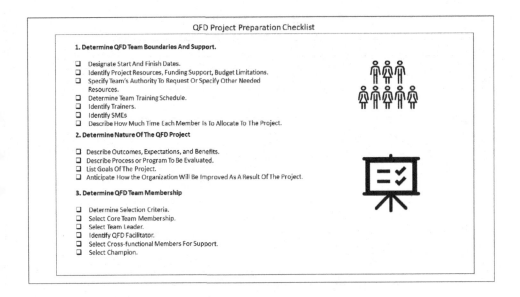

Figure 10.11 QFD Project Preparation Checklist.

The personnel resource allocation matrix is a systematic way to compare potential QFD staffing requirements. The left-hand side of the matrix contains the human resource name followed by the required skillset. This is followed by the daily rate and the resource's total cost based on time allocation.

It is recognized that personnel's responsibilities relative to preparing for a QFD project are broad and deep. As such, a detailed checklist is recommended to be used like the one presented in Figure 10.11 to ensure steps are not overlooked.

Action 4: Develop the Goals, Objectives, Scope, and Expectations (Project Parameters Report) for Each QFD Project

The Project Parameters Report (PPR) document must be developed for each QFD project before personnel is identified for assignment to the project. An example is shown in Figure 10.12.[17,76]

This document contains pertinent information for the project, such as the business case rationale, for example, "reduce the development time." It also has measurable objectives derived from overarching goals, for example, "reduce product development time by 40% from the current average of 240 days." "The scope of the project is also defined; for example, the project will

QFD Project Parameters		
Project Name:		
Business Case: :		
Opportunity/Problem:		Scope, Constraints, Assumptions :
Goals/Expectations: :		Key Resources:
Key Project Phases:	Target Date:	Actual Date:
Define Phase:		
Measure Phase:		
Analyze Phase:		
Improve Phase:		
Control Phase:		
Prepared by:	Approved by:	

Figure 10.12   QFD Project Parameters Report.

address W, X, Y, but not Z." It also makes clear management declaration of its expectations for the project, for example, "a justification for adaption of a new concept and/or technology will result." And finally, it is framed around the Define, Measure, Analyze, Improve, and Control (DMAIC) process, which makes it easily adaptable to ongoing Lean and/or Six Sigma initiatives.

Action 5: Appoint a QFD Project Manager

Every QFD project requires a project manager who will interface with management and provide the leadership necessary to ensure the successful completion of the project. The appointment of the right person to fill this position is a critical juncture in the chronology of the QFD project.

This project manager will be responsible for steering the QFD Action Team's efforts and integrating the project's results into the overall product or service development process. They will also be responsible for developing the Stakeholder Engagement/Communications Matrix illustrated in Figure 10.3.

Figure 10.13 lists the various roles and responsibilities the project manager will be required to perform.[1,17]

The management team can use this listing as a guide in evaluating the suitability of prospective project manager candidates.

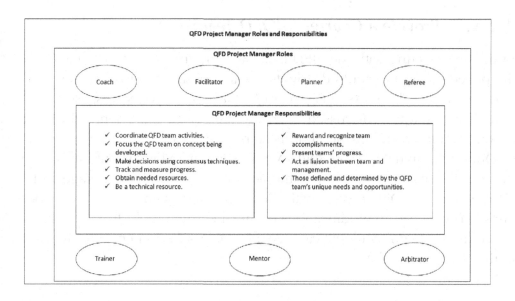

Figure 10.13 QFD Project Manager Roles and Responsibilities.

Action 6: Appoint a QFD Facilitator and a Cross-Functional Analysis Team

The newly appointed QFD project manager, along with the management team, must select a QFD facilitator as well as other members of the action team. Some of the facilitator's functions are:

- Ensure the team performs its assignment smoothly.
- Coordinate and set up meetings.
- Help the project manager overcome barriers.
- Prevent team discouragement and frustration due to lack of progress.
- Help keep the project on track.

In many ways, the facilitator is both a gatekeeper and a timekeeper, a QFD parliamentarian. Team members should not be lower-level staff personnel with little knowledge of existing organizational commitments. Specifically, they should be:

- Knowledgeable, technically or in the customer/marketing aspects of the QFD.
- Ready to articulate their capability to perform and act, be a dependable spokesperson for the functions they are presented.
- Able to make decisions that do not have to be reviewed.

Action 7: Provide a Charter to QFD Team

At the first meeting with the QFD facilitator and the other team members, the project manager should distribute the team's statement of purpose reflected in the Charter (see Figure 10.7). All should review this; the statement of purpose discussed to ensure the charter statement affords the action team to create individual indicators of success.

During the initial session, QFD Action Team members should review the stakeholder engagement and communication matrix and the linkage and alignment of the QFD project with the organization's goals. Team members' questions can lead to modifications of initial entries. Table 10.3 lists eight concerns that team members can use as a QFD selection checklist to assist in this reviewing task.[1,17]

Action 8: Enable, Empower, and Encourage QFD Teams

Enablement of a QFD Action Team goes beyond understanding and agreement with the project parameters. It also includes encouragement, meeting Expectations, and individual and team empowerment provisions. Figure 10.14 illustrates how these three "E's" work together to provide the action team with a needed boost toward successful project completion.

Table 10.3   QFD Project Selection Checklist

		QFD Project Selection Checklist
Yes	No	
☐	☐	1. The QFD project is related to key business issues.
☐	☐	2. The product/process targeted for improvement has direct impact of the organization's external customers.
☐	☐	3. The QFD process/project has visibility throughout the organizations.
☐	☐	4. All mangers concerned with the process/project agree that it is important enough to study.
☐	☐	5. Managers, supervisors and operators will cooperate to make this QFD process/project a success.
☐	☐	6. The process is not currently under a change, nor is it scheduled for such within the next 6 months.
☐	☐	7. The QFD project objectives are clearly defined with a defined start and end date.
☐	☐	8. The QFD team's charter clearly defines a problem or improvement opportunity to be addressed.

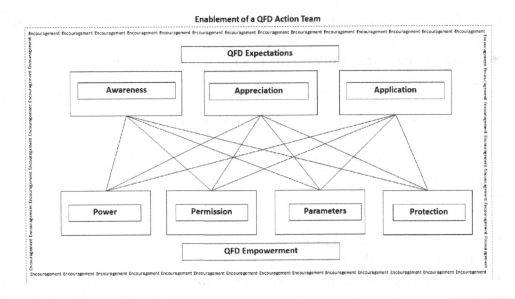

Figure 10.14 Enablement of a QFD Action Team.

The three As help the QFD Action Team to be aware of the expectations, appreciate what QFD can do to enhance a team's decision-making ability, and apply the QFD methodology to the selected project.

The four Ps help the action team be aware of the process of yielding power to act and decide by management permission to take whatever actions are necessary to achieve the project's parameters and be protected from possible management intervention.

Surrounded by encouragement, the action team can establish and maintain an appropriate managerial climate, organizational culture, and the spirit of cooperation between team members and non-team members.

Action 9: Provide Commitment and Involvement to QFD Teams Using a Management MAP Process

To maximize QFD Action Team output, management must provide both its commitment and involvement. An effective way of doing this is to use the monitor, audit, probe (MAP) process:

■ *Monitoring* of the QFD Action Team by management to ascertain team progress with respect to its anticipated completion date and resource consumption.

■ *Auditing* of the action project parameters provides periodic updates on the team's progress.
■ *Probing* demonstrates management's commitment to and involvement in various QFD projects.

There should be periodic probes with question such as:

■ Timeliness of the QFD process
  o Personnel appoints
  o Assignments
  o Research
■ Customer identification process
■ Timeliness of the VOC acquisition process
■ Demanded quality identification process and
■ Timeliness and accuracy of the competitive analysis process

Figure 10.15 is a MAP example template that the management guidance team can use when reviewing the QFD project team's progress.[77]

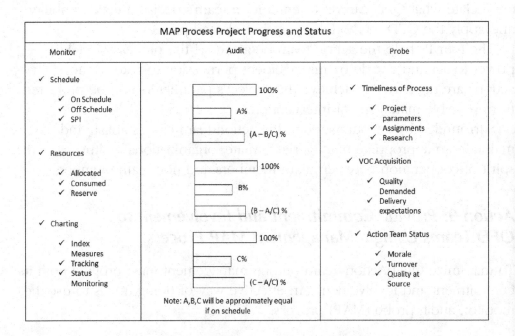

Figure 10.15   MAP Process Project Progress and Status.

Now that the QFD process is progressing, besides asking the right questions, the management guidance team also needs to:

■ Create and sustain the cultural environment.
■ Maintain the right push by instilling a sense of urgency.
■ Provide the right training on a just-in-time basis.
■ Ensure the right resources are available when they are required.

Summary

This chapter addressed how an organization's management, both levels, and structure influence a QFD project execution. It began with a discussion of how the organization can prepare for a QFD implementation within their respective organizations. The reader was then walked through the development process step-by-step, and assessment examples were presented for each management level highlighting their influence and role during QFD deployment. It then guided the reader through the process of forming the "QFD Action Team." It presented nine actions that are collectively management's responsibility that needs to be taken in forming those critical action teams. The chapter concludes with a discussion of the QFD project review process and establishes with the reader that review is the common thread between the initiation and the successful completion of a QFD project. The reader was then provided with editable QFD review forms that their respective QFD Action Teams can use to implement, manage, and monitor QFD project execution.

Chapter 11

Beyond the House of Quality

In today's Lean Six Sigma and Design for Six Sigma environments, what happens beyond the HOQ depends upon many things is truly fascinating! There are more options than were available when QFD was originally introduced.

Most organizations generally stop after the development of their customized versions of the HOQ. Even partial use of QFD is better than nothing. There are some cases where groups have extended their analysis to an additional matrix in which performance measurements from the initial HOQ matrix are deployed against product or service features. In a few cases, organizations have gone further to construct matrices or tables that describe shop-floor processes and machine settings. This said it is still common to see that the majority of QFD applications stop with the initial HOQ.[69,78,79]

There are numerous reasons why QFD Action Teams do not use the full possibilities of QFD. One is the inherent problem with explaining how QFD works. First and foremost, it can become very complex quickly unless it is held in check by those trained in its use. Also, it can be time-consuming in its implementation and resource-draining unless managed correctly.

If you are fortunate enough to be working in an organization that supports and is actively developing QFD, then the HOQ is just the beginning of the deployment of the VOC into design activities. If Design for Six Sigma projects and roadmaps are employed, they will generally be matted with QFD and necessitate working matrices beyond the basic HOQ. Figure 11.1 illustrates the flow of CTQ items out of the initial

DOI: 10.4324/9781003336044-15

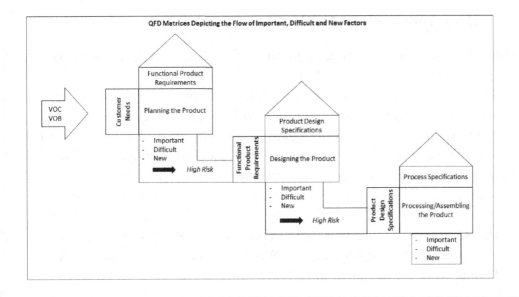

Figure 11.1 QFD Matrices Depicting the Flow of Important, Difficult, and New Factors.

HOQ, where they are deployed using the filters of Important, Difficult, or New.[13,80,81]

While the base HOQ and the accompanying matrices are the management tools for the deployment of the VOC, critical parameter management (CPM) is the technical accountability tool for the complex $Y=f(x)$ relationships for the HOQ process and component specifications. These complex parameters are singularly assessed via product mapping and CPM, which place greater emphasis than QFD alone on developing and detailing the product functions from the VOC. As such, part of the value of a process like DFSS paired with QFD is that pull is created from the QFD tool going beyond the basic HOQ.

QFD Alternative Approaches

Practitioners of QFD are generally flexible when applying it to their projects. However, most in the United States either use the original system developed by Professor Akao referred to as "Matrix of Matrices" or a simplified version developed by Dr. Fukuhara, called the "Four Phases of Matrices" and made popular by Dr. Don Clausing in 1994 with a 1994 publication titled *Total Quality Development*.

The Akao Approach to QFD

The Akao QFD model is huge and rather far-reaching. Figure 11.2 provides the 30-matrix approach to QFD.[6]

The 30 matrices are generally presented as a grid of matrices, charts, tables, or other figures, presented in a grid format. The first four rows are numbered 1 through 4, and the columns are labeled A through F. A fifth column, labeled G, contains six matrices labeled G1 through G6. Thus, any matrix can be referred to by its coordinates, for example, "B3."

Matrix A1 is the familiar HOQ depicted in the four-phase model (to be explained later in this chapter) except for the roof, which is Matrix 3. Other matrices correspond to tables used in the four-phase as well. Depending upon the practitioner's selection of "Whats and Hows" in each matrix, additional matrices are used to reflect:

- Competitive analysis versus cost
- Parts versus failure cost
- VOC versus failure modes
- Quality assurance planning by part
- Supplier versus manufacturing parts/materials and
- Process failure analysis

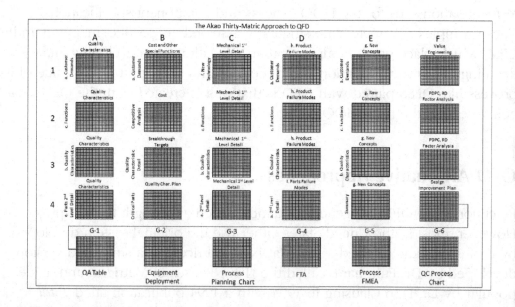

Figure 11.2   The Akao 30-Matrix Approach to QFD.

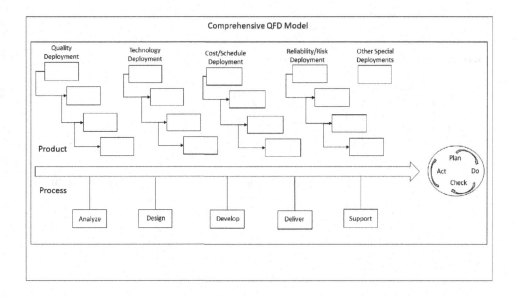

Figure 11.3   Comprehensive QFD Model.

The Akao Matrix of Matrices model is not intended to be used exactly presented. It is intended to open up possibilities to development teams. Because of its intimidating nature, there has been a subset of the 30 matrices proposed for those developers overwhelmed by the sheer number of matrices depicted in the model. This subset, called Comprehensive QFD, included 17 matrices generally based on the original 30, adding a VOC table and a concept-selection activity. Figure 11.3 is an illustration of a Comprehensive QFD model.[55,82]

The Comprehensive QFD model includes 17 matrices based on the original 30 in the Matrix of Matrices model. It adds the VOC via a customer table and a concept selection activity. The matrices are presented within a grid with product development phases along the left (moving from the VOC acquisition and proceeding to detail). In addition, elements of Continuous Improvement (CI) are included. This formulation of QFD creates a continuous improvement context for product development.

The Four-Phase Approach to QFD

The most described and used model in the United States is the Four-Phase model. Figure 11.4 illustrates this model.

Product Planning—System performance measures are the SQCs chosen for product planning. The prioritized performance measures are transferred to the

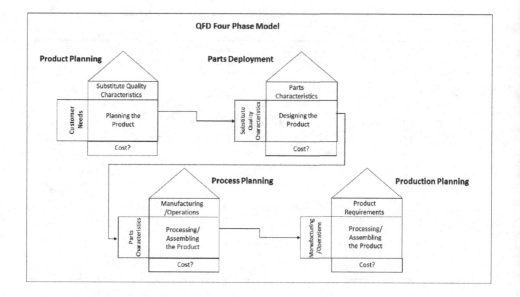

Figure 11.4   QFD Four-Phase Model.

left of the second matrix. It should be noted that design development work occurs between the matrices. A design concept is generally chosen after the product planning matrix is completed; however, this differs by organizational preference. Regardless of when design selection period, the concept should be fully developed before beginning the second phase matrix.

Parts Deployment—The first step in part characteristics deployment is to develop a function tree like the one depicted in Figure 11.5.[11]

In Figure 11.5, we see the total product first broken into subsystems, then the subsystems broken into parts. It is at this point the important characteristics of each part are enumerated. These are the descriptions of elements that are critical to the part's design. They will include measurements with directions of "goodness," which are specification parameters for the parts.

The part characteristics or equivalent elements are then placed on the top of the Design Deployment matrix. The action team then estimates the impact of each part characteristic on the performance measures. Priorities of the performance measures are then multiplied by their impacts to compute the Relationships; just as raw weights of customer attributes are multiplied by the impacts of SQCs. The relationships are then summed, and the resulting importance values prioritize the part's characteristics. This information tells the developers which part characteristics and parts will be customer satisfaction drivers.[83–86]

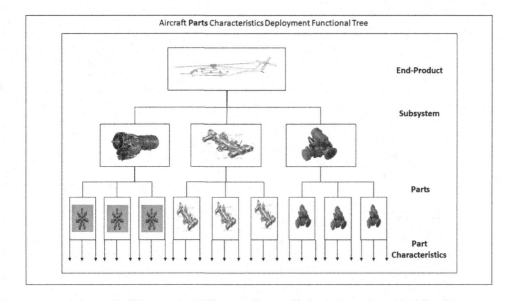

Figure 11.5 Aircraft Parts Characteristics Deployment Example.

Process Planning—The procedure for product planning is not exactly explicit in Figure 11.4. The recommended method for process planning that would result in process parameters is illustrated in Figure 11.6.[29]

The action team first lays out the main process flow, or system assembly process, and then decides on the subassembly processes needed to feed into the main flow. The operations required to produce each subassembly are next added to the matrix. This is generally done as a top-down process. However, any combination of top-down or bottom-up processes may be appropriate, including simply using existing process layouts.

Once the operation steps have been identified, the development team will use its expert knowledge and experimentation, to identify the key operations process parameters related to the sub-assemblies. Note these parameters are specific to the operations, not the products produced by the operations, so they will likely relate to such measurements as machine adjustments.

The selected process parameters now become the "Hows" at the top of the process planning matrix, where they are prioritized on the basis of their impacts on the part characteristics.

Production Planning—While this is depicted as a matrix with charts in Figure 11.4, it can be a table or list that constitutes a checklist of topics or

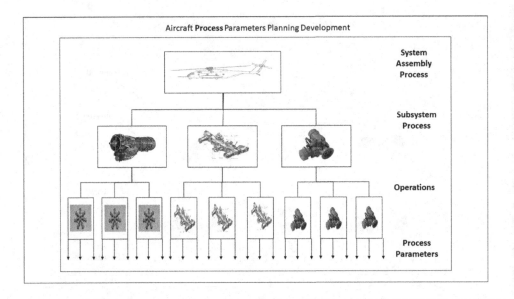

Figure 11.6   Process Planning Parameters Development.

issues that should be considered in planning production steps such as these listed:[29]

- Machine settings
- Control methods
- Sampling size and frequency
- Control documents
- Operator training and
- Preventative maintenance tasks

These or similar topics or issues are arranged along the top of the production planning matrix, and the most important parameters are arranged along the side. Then, the production planner fills the matrix table with comments, target values, or any other required data. This ensures production planning is linked back to the VOC, three levels (matrices) back.

QFD Model Conflict?

After reading through the design and development of the Akao Matrix of Matrices model and the Four-Phase Matrices model, a QFD practitioner, such as yourself, might construe they conflict with each other. There is an obligation to choose one over the other or each must be designed and executed as-is with little deviation in structure allowed. However, this is not the case.

There are several important reasons why they are not in conflict. The first is that neither model was intended to be used as presented. Because any complex idea such as QFD must be presented to a general audience, it must be specific enough to be understood. This specificity carries with it the suggestion that the way it is presented is the way it should be used. The intent behind both models is to present basic structures that can and should be customized for each application.

We have to prevail QFD models, each of which can be modified by adding or subtracting matrices or redefining those matrices to reflect what is germane to the practitioners' and organizations' needs. It would not be a stretch to say that a QFD Action Team could start with one model, add and subtract matrices as needed, and find itself using the other model.

The second reason the two models do not conflict is that the Four Phase model is contained within the Matrix of Matrices model. So, if the practitioner elects to implement the Four-Phase model, they have implemented a subset of the Matrix of Matrices model and if they elect to implement the Matrix of Matrices model, they have implemented all of the Four Phase models.

So, now that we have covered there is no conflict between the two prevailing QFD models, there are some differences that deserve mention.

The Four-Phase model is a blueprint for product development in a mature, efficient, disciplined organization. The Matrix of Matrices model is a blueprint for product development used in the same type of organization as well. Still, it is specifically designed to work within a TQM environment. This was mentioned in our discussion of the Comprehensive QFD addressed earlier in this chapter.

The Four-Phase model also covers basic product development steps, while the Matrix of Matrices model covers many activities that are not explicit in the Four-Phase model. These activities cover reliability planning, manufacturing quality control, value engineering, and cost analysis.

Having said all this about the differences between the two models, it can be summarized by saying that it is a matter more of style than of content that should drive the selection.

QFD Special Applications

Here we will examine some of the ways QFD is being extended beyond its original concept and integrated into the operational fabric of organizations daily. These three areas are: (1) *Design for Six Sigma using QFD*, (2) *Applying the Theory of Inventive Problem Solving (TIPS) using QFD*, and (3)

Integrating QFD into Business Process Re-engineering (BPR). Each is diverse in its application to each area. Each gives those organizations employing them a competitive advantage and enhanced strategic decision-making tool.

Using QFD in Design for Six Sigma Environments

Design for Six Sigma approaches can be approached with many roadmaps. Consulting groups specializing in Six Sigma each seem to have developed their roadmaps. Many are focused on product development, while others focus more on services. Those that currently are most popular and that have embraced and integrated QFD into their roadmaps are:

- *Concept, Design, Optimize, and Control (CDOC)*—This roadmap is utilized when a new product is developed and verified as meeting the customer's needs. An illustration of the CDOC roadmap is depicted in Figure 11.7.[56]

The concept phase of the CDOC roadmap also contains the Define components found in the DMAIC Six Sigma Road map. QFD, in the CDOC approach, begins in the Concept phase, where the HOQ is completed. This phase ends with requirements for the new product or service. It is followed by the Design phase, where the next matrices in QFD help manage the design-to process.

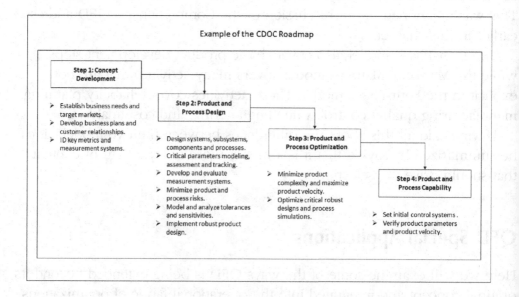

Figure 11.7   Example of the CDOC Roadmap.

■ *Concept, Design, Optimize, and Validate (CDOV)*—This roadmap often appears when a new product or service is to be developed and verified as meeting the customer's needs. It is a derivative of the CDOC methodology. The concept phase contains the Define aspects in the DMAIC Six Sigma roadmap, just like the CDOC roadmap. QFD, in this approach, begins in the Concept Phase where the HOQ is completed. The Design Phase follows where follow-on matrices held manager the overall design-to process.

■ *Define, Measure, Analyze, Design, and Verify (DMADV)*—The DMADV roadmap is used when a new product or process is developed and then verified as meeting the customer's needs. In the product-design area, it is used when performing product adjustments or redesigns where tolerancing or transfer functions are required for product design-to elements. In the approach, QFD resides in the Measure phase, except that the Measure phase begins the process by measuring the VOC and ends with requirements for the new product or process. It is followed by the Analyze phase, where the new concept options are analyzed to determine how well they will meet customer needs.

■ *Define, Measure, Explore, Develop, and Implement (DMEDI)*—The DMEDI roadmap is often where a new process is needed to develop and implemented. QFD, in this approach, resides in the Measurement phase, except that the Measure phase begins the process of measuring the VOC and ends with requirements for the new process. It is followed by the Explore phase, where new concepts are explored that have the potential to better meet the customer's needs.

■ *Identify, Design, Optimize, and Verify (IDOV)*—The IDOV roadmap is most often used when a new product is developed and verified as meeting customer needs. The Identify phase contains the Define phase aspects found in the DMAIC, DMEDI, and DMADV. The IDOV roadmap also contains the Optimize phase, the first to gain acceptance in DFSS. In this approach, QFD resides in the Identify phase, with the expectation that the Identify phase begins the process of identifying the measures and actions of the customer and ends with requirements for the new product. It is followed by the Design phase, where new concepts are designed according to customer needs.

The QFD practitioner may run across any of these roadmaps when working with an organization employing DFSS. However, most organizations would use their own NPD roadmap process phases augmented by DFSS. I have often followed this procedure when deploying DFSS, replacing the roadmap with a revised NPD phase gate process incorporating the sequence of tools of DFSS.

Applying the Theory of Inventive Problem Solving to the QFD Process

TIPS is a structured scientific method that can be described as the science of evolutionary technical systems. Only recently has TIPS become known in the United States. However, through its practice in Europe, it has proven to be extremely powerful in generating elegant solutions to complicated, paradoxical problems and predicting how technical systems evolve. It has also proven invaluable in solving difficult problems through identifying and eliminating conflicts present in all engineered systems.

The rigor and graphical format of QFD have proven to be an effective method by which product development teams organize and display correlations between product attributes. Unfortunately, these product attributes often are negatively correlated, presenting inherent paradoxes or system conflicts. Because QFD cannot have the ability to help resolve these conflicts, the development team is often frustrated. This is where TIPS comes into play with its conceptual solutions formulation ability.

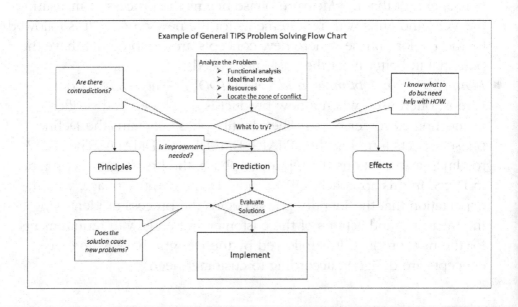

Figure 11.8   Example of General TIPS Problem Solving Flow Chart.

There are many ways to organize the tools and techniques of TIPS. A flow chart such as that depicted in Figure 11.8 is useful when working with TIPS and QFD, since it shows how the tools are related, as well as what they are.[87]

The first stage of the TIPS process is an analysis which is comprised of four components:

■ *Functional Analysis*—This should be familiar to QFD practitioners. Analyze the system, subsystems, and components in terms of the functions performed (not the technologies used.) One new technique in TIPS is "trimming"—examining each function to see if it is necessary and, if it is, whether any other system element could perform the function. Breakthrough designs and reductions in cost and complexity are frequent results of functional analysis and trimming.

■ *The Ideal Final Result*—This is familiar to QFD users as the customers demanded quality. Express the situation regarding why the innovation is needed, using technology-independent and implementation-independent language. Strategic breakthroughs frequently come from the insight gained at this step. Quality improvement opportunities can be identified by finding what elements make the system non-ideal. The progress that a design makes from a starting point toward the ideal final result is called "ideality" and is defined using the value equation as (Ideality = S Benefits/(S Costs + S Harm).

■ *Resource Analysis*—It is the Identification of the available things, energy sources, information, functions, and other elements that are in or near the system, which could be combined with the elements of the system to improve it. QFD practitioners will find that an awareness of the uses of resources in TIPS changes the way that they conduct customer observation visits.

■ *Locating the Zone of Conflict*—Those familiar with quality improvement use "root cause analysis." Understanding the exact cause of the problem. The "zone" refers to the time and place that the problem occurs. A new tool, "anticipatory failure determination," reverses the process and guides the developer to look for ways to cause failures to increase understanding of how to prevent the failures.

If the problem has been solved in the Analysis phase, developers frequently proceed directly to implementation. If it has not been solved, or if alternate solutions are desired for maximum creativity, the database tools of

Principles, Prediction, and Effects can be used. In many TRIZ applications, all three are used.[88]

- *Principles (also called resolution of contradictions)*—Technical contradictions are the classical engineering "trade-offs." The desired state cannot be reached because something else in the system prevents it. Physical contradictions are situations where one object has contradictory, opposite requirements. TIPS guides the developer to design principles that resolve the contradiction once the contradiction is defined in terms of standard parameters.
- *Prediction (also called Technology Forecasting)*—TIPS identifies eight patterns of technical evolution.
  o Increased ideality
  o Stages of evolution
  o Non-uniform development of system elements
  o Increased dynamism and controllability
  o Matching and mismatching of parts
  o Transition to the micro level and use of fields
  o Decreased human interaction and increased automation
  Designs of systems, subsystems, or components can be deliberately moved to the next higher stage within a particular pattern once the pattern is identified.
- *Effects*—Use scientific and engineering phenomenology and effects outside the discipline in which they were developed. Tools include databases, science encyclopedias, and technical literature searches to find alternate ways to achieve the functions needed to solve the problem. The last block in the flow chart is the Evaluation of Solutions. Solutions are compared to the Ideal Final Result to be sure that the improvements advance the technology and meet the customers' needs. Multiple solutions may be combined to improve the overall solution using a Feature Transfer similar to the Pugh concept selection and improvement.

The flow chart shows that the remaining problems are resolved by iterating the process. The advantage of TIPS is that the iterations are very fast, and many innovative ideas are developed at each stage. The flow chart shows that the remaining problems are resolved by iterating the process. The advantage of TIPS is that the iterations are very fast, and many innovative ideas are developed at each stage.

Table 11.1   TIPS Tools Used Throughout the QFD Process

TIPS Techniques	Product Planning	Visit the Gemba	Voice of the Customer	Demanded Quality Depoyment	Reliability Deployment	Functional Deployment	Concept Selection	Component Selection	Production Planning	Quality Assurance Plan
Ideal Final Result	X			X	X	X	X			
Technology Forecasting	X	X	X	X	X		X	X		
Resolving Contradictions	X	X		X	X	X	X	X	X	X
Use of Resources							X	X	X	X
Functional Analysis	X			X	X	X			X	
Trimming	X			X	X	X			X	
Scientific Effects							X	X	X	X
Feature Transfer							X	X		
Anticiatory Failure Deterination					X					X

Note: "x" indicates common use of TIPS techniques to solve problems that occur during the indicated stage of QFD process.

The general problem-solving process of TIPS can be used whenever the product or process developer has inventive problems. Specific tools that may be useful by themselves during QFD are listed in Table 11.1, and the stages of QFD in which they are useful are as indicated.[87]

The use of TIPS to enhance the practice of QFD is very new. However, research continues to find new ways to integrate these methods to help all product and process developers create innovative solutions that win market leadership by augmenting QFD, and better helping meet customer expectations.

Integrating QFD Into Business Process Re-engineering

The QFD structure and methodology have traditionally been used when designing and redesigning a product or service. It is also very useful when designing a system or a group of processes. The initial matrix help organize the VOC, the Whats, and show how it will be translated into technical requirements, the Hows. The later matrices, of course, address the process design used to deliver the product or service. In the case of BPR, it is the initial matrix that addresses the design of the process because the process is the product.

Combining QFD with BPR reduces the risk of failure during the BPR implementation process because there is a greater and continuing focus on the needs of the internal and external customers of the process being re-engineered. In addition, there is much involvement by the organizational personnel whose input is sought and deployed.

The inputs needed for using QFD are established at the outset of the BPR engagement and agreed to by the various sets. This early activity establishes the scope of the BPR project, which is important because "scope creep" is a major cause of BPR failure. Effectiveness is enhanced because the QFD matrices focus the BPR process on not just doing things right but doing the right things. The use of QFD to support an organization initial BPR process in a particular operational area not only allows for greater definition and control but offers the additional advantage that when re-engineering is initiated a second time, it can be accomplished considerably faster and more easily, thus gaining competitive advantage for the organization.

Numerous studies on BPR implementation have shown that the greatest gains and Return on Invested Capital (ROIC) organizations can achieve come when core processes are re-engineered companywide. Or even going beyond organizational boundaries, such as partnering with suppliers and/or customers. For this to occur, organizations must ensure that two structural dimensions are in balance: behavioral and analytical. Each of these dimensions has critical issues that must be continuously addressed as the organization executes the BPR process. Figure 11.9 provides a matrix showing the two dimensions and the

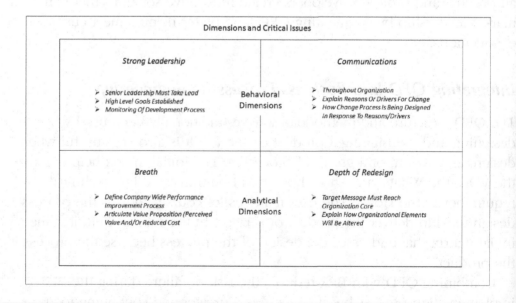

Figure 11.9 Dimensions and Critical Issues.

critical issues that comprise them that require addressing by the organization.[10,11,20,24,89]

The strength of using QFD to aid BPR during this evaluation process is its ability to define and integrate these dimensions and critical issues.

The Behavioral Dimension

- *Strong Leadership*—QFD can take the goals of senior leadership and use them as inputs. The development of new processes related to the BPR effort can then be monitored as the re-engineering team progresses through a series of matrices. The QFD matrices will show what has been accomplished and what still is required and, more importantly, shows the links between the different elements of the BPR process.

- *Communications*—QFD methodology uses the wants, needs, and requirements from the organization's customers to create new systems or processes. The QFD matrices explicitly show the progression from customer inputs (the Wants) to technical answers (the Hows and How Much) and, all of the elements of the technical answers. By picking the appropriate level and focus, the QFD matrices can be used to show:

  o To lower-level personnel, how they will fit in the new system proposed by the BPR process and why the processes they will work with when everything is changed are designed the way they are.

  o To senior executives how an overview of the BPR processes of the new system is integrated.

  o To middle managers and supervisors how they can highlight their own QFD matrices showing a linkage between high-level goals and low-level activities.

The Analytical Dimension

- *Breadth*—The QFD matrices can be set up to represent all of the processes in the system and have specific matrices for addressing high-level customer value issues for the proposed BPR system.

- *Depth*—The use of QFD matrices to describe the inner workings of key organizational elements and the linkages both feedback and feedforward between them helps the BPR design team organize the area(s) of greatest complexity.

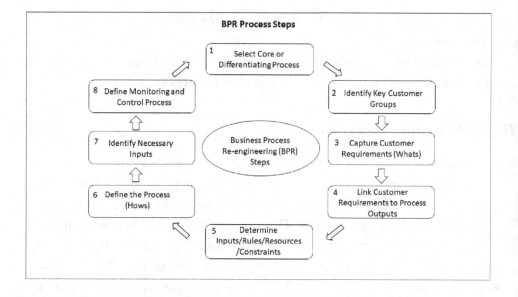

Figure 11.10 BPR Process Steps.

To understand the leverage that QFD gives the BPR effort, you should recognize the complexity associated with re-designing an organization's key core processes. The BPR team first must ensure that all BPR-related steps have been followed to align them into phases for subsequent integration in the QFD model. Figure 11.10 illustrates these steps.[10,11,24]

Step 1—Select a core process or system with sub-optimal performance or a competitive advantage in the marketplace; then discuss the issues around defining the scope of the process or system.

Step 2—Identify key customer groups of the process or system and establish the BPR effort's scope using internal and external customers.

Step 3—Capture the customer requirements (the Whats) for each group using various approaches such as surveys, focus groups, or interviews. Also, gather information on the different kinds of quality, expected, normal or exciting, using tools such as Kano analyses.

Step 4—Translate the customer requirements into the requirements for process output.

Step 5—Determine the following:

■ Relevant guides, rules, regulations, industry standards, processing guides, company rule, and government regulations.

■ The available resources include personnel, funding, time, and facilities. Also, assess constraints such as the number of personnel with unique skills or capacity limits on capital assets.

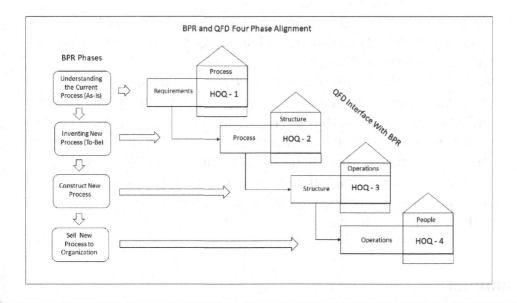

Figure 11.11   BPR and QFD Four-Phase Alignment.

Step 6—Define the process elements (the Hows) that can consistently
deliver quality output on time.

Step 7—Detail the necessary inputs needed to support the process.

Step 8—Create a means to monitor and control the process(es) or
system(s); then maintain the initial performance level and foster continuous improvement.

Once all BPR steps are actioned and in place, it is then time to align them
into phase alignment with the QFD process. Most organizations use BPR
and QFD Four-Phase Alignment like that illustrated in Figure 11.11.[10,11,24]

BPR Phase I, Understanding the Process (As-Is)—An (As-Is) model is developed, and the current process(es) is mapped. Root cause analysis is
conducted to define inefficiencies and identify problems and/or additional issues. Direct mapping into HOQ-1 is performed where requirements and processes are populated.

BPR Phase 2, Inventing New Process (To-Be)—Through Value Stream
Mapping, customer surveys, interviews, and so forth, a To-Be process
is developed. Direct mapping into HOQ-2 is performed, where the new
process and structure are defined.

BPR Phase 3, Construct New Process—All regulations, laws, rules, potential constraints, and so forth are identified, risk evaluation performed,

and mitigation strategies designed. Base disruptive technology assessment conducted. Direct mapping into HOQ-3 where overall new structure and operational design are integrated.

BPR Phase 4, Sell New Process to Organization—Perhaps the most important Phase during the integration process, during this phase, the "buy-in" from the people within the organization is emphasized. A clear vision must be developed and communicated to all organization members as to what will be "changed" and why it will be "changed." An overall communications strategy must be developed that targets each organizational member individually, answering the question, "Whats in It for Me" to ensure overall BPR success.

Summary

This chapter addressed what happens beyond the HOQ and pointed out that it will depend upon many converging initiatives, such as Lean Six Sigma and Design for Lean Six Sigma. It pointed out that most organizations that do employ QFD stop after developing their customized versions of the HOQ. It presented the prevailing "Four-Phase model" and the more intricate "Matrix of Matrices model" and then compared and contrasted them regarding the usability within their organizations. The reader was then presented with a discussion of QFD special applications in use today: (1) *Design for Six Sigma (DFSS) using QFD*, (2) *Applying the Theory of Inventive Problem Solving (TIPS) using QFD*, and (3) *Integrating QFD into Business Process Re-engineering (BPR)*. Each was elaborated on how it was being used and the benefits derived from its use.

References

1. Jaiswal, E. S. (2012). A case study on Quality Function Deployment (QFD). *IOSR Journal of Mechanical and Civil Engineering, 3*(6), 27–35. https://doi.org/10.9790/1684-0362735

2. Jui-Chin, J., Ming-Li, S., & Mao-Hsiung, T. (2007). QFD's evolution in Japan and the West. *Quality Progress, 40*, 30–37. http://ezproxy.libproxy.db.erau.edu/login?url=https://www.proquest.com/magazines/qfds-evolution-japan-west/docview/214768313/se-2

3. Vasiljević, D. (2009). Maintenance viewpoint of product-service bundle supportability. *The Yugoslav Journal of Operations Research, 19*(2), 315–321. https://www.researchgate.net/publication/47394058_Maintenance_viewpoint_of_product-service_bundle_supportability

4. ASQ. (n.d.). What is quality function deployment (QFD)? Retrieved September 21, 2022, from https://asq.org/quality-resources/qfd-quality-function-deployment

5. Wahel, P. (2021). An unmanned aerial vehicle sampling platform for atmospheric water vapor isotopes in polar environments. https://amt.copernicus.org/articles/14/7045/2021/

6. Akao, Y., & Mazur, G. H. (2003). The leading edge in QFD: Past, present and future. *The International Journal of Quality & Reliability Management, 20*(1), 20–35. https://doi.org/10.1108/02656710310453791

7. Younus, B., & Iqbal, A. (2011). Leveraging quality function deployment to enhance the productivity of an aviation maintenance repair and overhaul organization. In *2011 IEEE International Conference on Quality and Reliability* (pp. 115–119). https://doi.org/10.1109/ICQR.2011.6031692

8. Crow, K. Customer-focused development with QFD. *NPD Solutions*. https://www.npd-solutions.com/qfd.html

9. Devadasan, S. R., Kathiravan, N., & Thirunavukkarasu, V. (2006). Theory and practice of total quality function deployment: A perspective from a traditional pump-manufacturing environment. *TQM Magazine, 18*(2), 143–161. https://doi.org/10.1108/09544780610647865

10. Chan, L.-K., & Wu, M.-L. (2002). Quality Function Deployment: A comprehensive review of its concepts and methods. *Quality Engineering, 15*(1), 23–35. https://doi.org/10.1081/QEN-120006708

11. Cristiano, J. J., Liker, J., & White, C. C. I. (2001). Key factors in the successful application of Quality Function Deployment (QFD). *IEEE Transactions on Engineering Management, 48*(1), 81–95. https://doi.org/10.1109/17.913168

12. Ginting, R., Ishak, A., Fauzi Malik, A., & Satrio, M. R. (2020). Product development with Quality Function Deployment (QFD): A literature review. *IOP Conference Series: Materials Science and Engineering, 1003*(1), 12022. https://doi.org/10.1088/1757-899X/1003/1/012022

13. Dean, E. B. (1992). Quality function deployment for large systems. In *[Proceedings] 1992 International Engineering Management Conference* (pp. 317–321). https://doi.org/10.1109/IEMC.1992.225302

14. Delgado-Hernandez, D. J., Bampton, K. E., & Aspinwall, E. (2007). Quality function deployment in construction. *Construction Management and Economics, 25*(6), 597–609. https://doi.org/10.1080/01446190601139917

15. Dallosta, P., & Simcik, T. A. (2012). Designing for supportability: Driving reliability, availability, and maintainability in. https://apps.dtic.mil/sti/pdfs/AD1015901.pdf

16. Yazdi, M. (2018). Improving failure mode and effect analysis (FMEA) with consideration of uncertainty handling as an interactive approach. *International Journal on Interactive Design and Manufacturing, 13*(2), 441–458. https://doi.org/10.1007/s12008-018-0496-2

17. Matorera, D. (2015). A conceptual analysis of quality in quality function deployment-based contexts of higher education. *Journal of Education and Practice, 6*(33), 145–156. https://eric.ed.gov/?id=EJ1083530

18. Sireli, Y., Kauffmann, P., & Ozan, E. (2007). Integration of Kano's model into QFD for multiple product design. *IEEE Transactions on Engineering Management, 54*(2), 380–390. https://doi.org/10.1109/TEM.2007.893990

19. Almeida, M. F., & Martins, G. (2018). Fuzzy Quality Function Deployment (FUZZY-QFD) applied to new defense product development. In *International Association for Management and Technology IAMOT 2018 Conference Proceedings*. https://www.semanticscholar.org/paper/FUZZY-QUALITY-FUNCTION-DEPLOYMENT-(FUZZY-QFD)-TO-Almeida-Martins/5edfaeffb387f9 9ab9db574edf61d19a893dc240

20. Shad, Z., Roghanian, E., & Mojibian, F. (2014). Integration of QFD, AHP, and LPP methods in supplier development problems under uncertainty. *Journal of Industrial Engineering International, 10*(1), 1–9. https://doi.org/10.1007/s40092-014-0051-0

21. Pugh, S. (1987). Concept selection based on the work of professor Stuart Pugh: "Design decision–how to succeed and know why." *Xerox Corporation*. https://openlibrary.org/books/OL13931447M/Total_design

22. Hsu, J. C. (2006). Using system engineering on an aircraft improvement project. *Aeronautical Journal, 110*(1114), 813–820. https://doi.org/10.1017/S0001924000001688

23. Stylianou, A., Kumar, R., & Khouja, M. (1997). A total quality management-based systems development process. *ACM SIGMIS Database: The DATABASE for Advances in Information Systems, 28*(3), 59–71. https://doi.org/10.1145/272657.272691

24. Popoff, A., & Millet, D. (2017). Sustainable life-cycle design using constraint satisfaction problems and quality function deployment. *Procedia CIRP, 61*, 75–80. https://doi.org/10.1016/j.procir.2016.11.147

25. Dorst, K., & Cross, N. (2001). Creativity in the design process: Co-evolution of problem–solution. *Design Studies, 22*(5), 425–437. https://doi.org/10.1016/S0142-694X(01)00009-6

26. Mi, C., Chen, Y., Zhou, Z., & Lin, C.-T. (2018). Product redesign evaluation: An improved quality function deployment model based on failure modes and effects analysis and 2-tuple linguistic. *Advances in Mechanical Engineering, 10*(11). https://doi.org/10.1177/1687814018811227

27. Tuli, K. R., Kohli, A. K., & Bharadwaj, S. G. (2007). Rethinking customer solutions: From product bundles to relational processes. *Journal of Marketing, 71*(3), 1–17. https://doi.org/10.1509/jmkg.71.3.1

28. Rhodes, D. H., & Hastings, D. E. (2004). The case for evolving systems engineering as a field within engineering systems. https://www.semanticscholar.org/paper/The-Case-for-Evolving-Systems-Engineering-as-a-Rhodes-Hastings/48d8b72d2741b7eb206e32391069260b5f70464a

29. Shiu, M.-L., Jiang, J.-C., & Tu, M.-H. (2007). Reconstruct QFD for integrated product and process development management. *TQM Magazine, 19*(5), 403–418. https://doi.org/10.1108/09544780710817847

30. Department of Defense (DoD). (1986, May). Integrated logistics support guide (1st ed.).

31. Liang, G.-S., Ding, J.-F., & Pan, C.-L. (2012). Applying fuzzy quality function deployment to evaluate solutions of the service quality for international port logistics centres in Taiwan. *Proceedings of the Institution of Mechanical Engineers. Part M, Journal of Engineering for the Maritime Environment, 226*(4), 387–396. https://doi.org/10.1177/1475090212443615

32. Louw, L. (2022, January 7). What is Quality Function Deployment (QFD) and why do we use it? *Master of Project Academy Blog.* Retrieved September 21, 2022, from https://blog.masterofproject.com/qfd/#:~:text=Quality%20function%20deployment%20is%20a%20LEAN%20technique%20that,requirements.%20Quality%20function%20deployment%20is%20abbreviated%20as%20QFD

33. Mazur, G. Classical, blitz, or reverse QFD . . . which one for my project? *QFD Institute.* http://www.qfdi.org/newsletters/classical-qfd_vs_blitz-qfd_vs_reverse-qfd.html

34. Mazur, G. History of QFD. *QFD Institute.* http://www.qfdi.org/what_is_qfd/history_of_qfd.html

35. Alemanni, M., Destefanis, F., & Vezzetti, E. (2010). Model-based definition design in the product lifecycle management scenario. *International Journal of Advanced Manufacturing Technology, 52*(1–4), 1–14. https://doi.org/10.1007/s00170-010-2699-y

36. Lichtman, J. (2019). Breaking down the walls of product design with concurrent engineering. *Fictiv.* https://www.fictiv.com/articles/breaking-down-the-walls-of-product-design-with-concurrent-engineering#:~:text=Breaking%20Down%20the%20Walls%20of%20Product%20Design%20with,approach%2C%20also%20known%20as%20the%20simultaneous%20engineering%20approach

37. Abdelrazek, M. A., El-Sheikh, A. T., Zayan, M., & Elhady, A. M. (2017). Systems engineering management using transdisciplinary quality system development lifecycle model. *Zenodo*. https://doi.org/10.5281/zenodo.1339810

38. Franceschini, F., & Maisano, D. (2015). Prioritization of QFD customer requirements based on the law of comparative judgments. *Quality Engineering, 27*(4), 437–449. https://doi.org/10.1080/08982112.2015.1036292

39. Department of Defense (DoD). (2011, July). Logistics assessment guidebook. https://apps.dtic.mil/sti/citations/ADA606204

40. Davis, C. A. (2021). Understanding functionality and operability for infrastructure system resilience. *Natural Hazards Review, 22*(1). https://doi. org/10.1061/(ASCE)NH.1527-6996.0000431

41. Armacost, R. L., Balakrishnan, D., & Pet-Armacost, J. (2002). Design for remanufacturability using QFD. In *IIE Annual Conference. Proceedings*. https:// www.proquest.com/docview/192472069?parentSessionId=qHyAoSyMmmgRPMp Mp%2FQ4d4g0EklrkSciS7SVFyJdEJY%3D&accountid=27203

42. Bashier, F. (2017). Design process-system and methodology of design research. *IOP Conference Series: Materials Science and Engineering, 245*(8), 82030. https://doi.org/10.1088/1757-899X/245/8/082030

43. Basten, R. J., Schutten, J. M., & Heijden, V. D. (2009). An efficient model formulation for level of repair analysis. *Annals of Operations Research, 172*(1), 119–142. https://doi.org/10.1007/s10479-009-0516-5

44. Beshears, R., & Bouma, A. (2020). Engaging supportability Analysis through model-based design. In *2020 Annual Reliability and Maintainability Symposium (RAMS)* (pp. 1–5). https://doi.org/10.1109/RAMS48030.2020.9153646

45. Crooks, K. A., & Nanney, M. H. (2020). Reliability: Enablers for sustainment through supportability focused design influence. In *2020 Annual Reliability and Maintainability Symposium (RAMS)* (pp. 1–5). https://doi.org/10.1109/ RAMS48030.2020.9153654

46. Military Handbook. (1994, March). Logistic support analysis. https://www. hq.nasa.gov/office/ld/docs/MIL-HDBK-1388_HandBook.pdf

47. Department of Defense (DoD). (2021, November). Instruction 5000.91 product support management for the adaptive acquisition framework. https://www.esd. whs.mil/Portals/54/Documents/DD/issuances/dodi/500091p.PDF

48. Prasad, B. (1998). A concurrent function deployment process for product life. Cycle Management. Unpublished. https://doi.org/10.13140/2.1.1690.8805

49. Ryan, M. J. (2014). Design for system retirement. *Journal of Cleaner Production, 70*, 203–210. https://doi.org/10.1016/j.jclepro.2014.01.092

50. Schneider, S., Wollersheim, J., Krcmar, H., & Sunyaev, A. (2018). How do requirements evolve over time? A case study investigating the role of context and experiences in the evolution of enterprise software requirements. *Journal of Information Technology, 33*(2), 151–170. https://doi.org/10.1057/ s41265-016-0001-y

51. Seo, K.-M., & Park, K.-P. (2018). Interface data modeling to detect and diagnose intersystem faults for designing and integrating system of systems. *Complexity (New York, N.Y.), 2018*, 1–21. https://doi.org/10.1155/2018/7081501

52. Defense Acquisition University Integrated Product Support Element Guidebook. (2011, December). https://www.dau.edu/tools/Lists/DAUTools/Attachments/282/Integrated-Product-Support-(IPS)-Element-Guidebook.pdf

53. Dmitriev, A., & Mitroshkina, T. (2019). Improving the efficiency of aviation products design based on international standards and robust approaches. *IOP Conference Series: Materials Science and Engineering*, *476*(1), 12009. https://doi.org/10.1088/1757-899X/476/1/012009

54. Boyce, J., & Banghart, A. (2012). Performance based logistics and project proof point. Defense AT&L: Product support issue. https://www.dau.edu/library/defense-atl/DATLFiles/Mar_Apr_2012/boyce_bangheart.pdf#:~:text=27Defense%20AT%26L%3A%20Product%20Support%20Issue%20nMarch%E2%80%93April%202012%20%E2%80%98PMs,Defense%20AT%26L%3A%20Product%20Support%20Issue%20nMarch-April%202012%2028

55. Cruyt, A. L. M., Ghobbar, A. A., & Curran, R. (2014). A value-based assessment method of the supportability for a new aircraft entering into service. *IEEE Transactions on Reliability*, *63*(4), 817–829. https://doi.org/10.1109/TR.2014.2335972

56. Erkoyuncu, J. A., Roy, R., Shehab, E., & Wardle, P. (2009). Uncertainty challenges in service cost estimation for product-service systems in the aerospace and defence industries. https://www.semanticscholar.org/paper/Uncertainty-challenges-in-service-cost-estimation-Erkoyuncu-Roy/203b98d11b5f84978d3292c9e738bdbfa9acb7ed

57. Hu, Q., & Zhang, A. (2015). Real option analysis of aircraft acquisition: A case study. *Journal of Air Transport Management*, *46*, 19–29. https://doi.org/10.1016/j.jairtraman.2015.03.010

58. McMurtrey, M. E. (2013). A case study of the application of the systems development lifecycle (SDLC) in 21st century health care: Something old, something new? *Journal of the Southern Association for Information Systems*, *1*(1), 14. https://doi.org/10.17705/3JSIS.00002

59. Moisiadis, F. (2002). *The fundamentals of prioritising requirements*. Department of Computing, Macquarie University. https://www.researchgate.net/publication/228548912_The_fundamentals_of_prioritising_requirements

60. Sherrieb, H., & Stracener, J. (1992). R&M in conceptual aircraft design. *Combined Proceedings of the Leesburg Workshops on Reliability and Maintainability Computer-Aided Engineering in Concurrent Engineering*, 245–254. https://doi.org/10.1109/RMCAE.1992.245539

61. King, D. R., & Nowack, M. L. (2003). The impact of government policy on technology transfer: An aircraft industry case study. *Journal of Engineering and Technology Management*, *20*(4), 303–318. https://doi.org/10.1016/j.jengtecman.2003.08.007

62. Lager, T. (2019). The theory of QFD and related matrices, rooms and symbols—getting acquainted with the fundamental philosophy. In *Contemporary quality function deployment for product and process innovation towards digital transformation of customer and product information in a Ne* (pp. 5–21). World Scientific Publishing Co. Pte. Ltd. https://www.worldscientific.com/doi/pdf/10.1142/9789813279889_0001

63. Vaskic, L., & Paetzold, K. (2019). A critical review of the integrated logistics support suite for aerospace and defence programmes. *Proceedings of the Design Society, 1*(1), 3541–3550. https://doi.org/10.1017/dsi.2019.361

64. Verma, D. (1995). *Quality Function Deployment (QFD): Integration of logistics requirements into mainstream system design.* Stevens Institute of Technology. https://www.researchgate.net/publication/255584511_QUALITY_FUNCTION_ DEPLOYMENT_QFD_INTEGRATION_OF_LOGISTICS_REQUIREMENTS_ INTO_MAINSTREAM_SYSTEM_DESIGN

65. Wang, R.-T. (2007). Improving service quality using quality function deployment: The air cargo sector of China airlines. *Journal of Air Transport Management, 13*(4), 221–228. https://doi.org/10.1016/j.jairtraman.2007.03.005

66. Wen, J., Kang, R., Ma, L., & Wang, V. (2010). Operation and maintenance support resources forecast model based on support activity flow. In *2010 Prognostics and System Health Management Conference* (pp. 1–5). https://doi. org/10.1109/PHM.2010.5413617

67. Jessel, J., Hanley, G. P., & Ghaemmaghami, M. (2019). On the standardization of the functional analysis. *Behavior Analysis in Practice, 13*(1), 205–216. https://doi.org/10.1007/s40617-019-00366-1

68. Verma, D., & Plunkett, G. (2000). 6.1.3 Systems engineering and supportability analysis: Technology refreshment for COTS-intensive systems. *INCOSE International Symposium, 10*(1), 63–70. https://doi. org/10.1002/j.2334-5837.2000.tb00359.x

69. DRM Associates. Performing QFD step by step. *NPD Solutions.* https://www. npd-solutions.com/qfdsteps.html#:~:text=Performing%20QFD%20Step%20 by%20Step%201%20Gather%20Customer,block%20diagram%20and%2For%20 a%20preliminary%20parts%20list.%20

70. Murali, S., Pugazhendhi, S., & Muralidharan, C. (2016). Integration of IPA and QFD to assess the service quality and to identify after sales service strategies to improve customer satisfaction – a case study. *Production Planning & Control, 27*(5), 394–407. https://doi.org/10.1080/09537287.2015.1129463

71. Myers, M. D., & Maani, K. (1995). The use of quality function deployment in systems development: A case study. *Journal of International Information Management, 4*(1), Article 5. https://scholarworks.lib.csusb.edu/jiim/vol4/iss1/5

72. Nurmi, J., Pulkkinen, M., Seppänen, V., & Penttinen, K. (2018). Systems approaches in the enterprise architecture field of research: A systematic literature review. *EEWC.* https://www.researchgate.net/publication/330008469_ Systems_Approaches_in_the_Enterprise_Architecture_Field_of_Research_A_ Systematic_Literature_Review

73. Sivasamy, K., Arumugam, C., Devadasan, S. R., Murugesh, R., & Thilak, V. M. M. (2015). Advanced models of quality function deployment: A literature review. *Quality & Quantity, 50*(3), 1399–1414. https://doi.org/10.1007/ s11135-015-0212-2

74. Govers, C. P. M. (1996). What and how about Quality Function Deployment (QFD). *International Journal of Production Economics, 46*(1), 575–585. https:// doi.org/10.1016/0925-5273(95)00113-1

75. Sandborn, P., & Lucyshyn, W. (2019). Defining sustainment for engineered systems—a technology and systems view. *Journal of Manufacturing Science and Engineering, 141*(2). https://doi.org/10.1115/1.4041424

76. Wei-Guo, X., & Chuan-Min, M. (2013). Prioritizing technical requirements in QFD by integrating the grey relational analysis method and analytic network process approach. In *Proceedings of 2013 IEEE International Conference on Grey Systems and Intelligent Services (GSIS)* (pp. 33–37). https://doi.org/10.1109/GSIS.2013.6714737

77. Killen, C. P., Walker, M., & Hunt, R. A. (2005). Strategic planning using QFD. *The International Journal of Quality & Reliability Management, 22*(1), 17–29. https://doi.org/10.1108/02656710510572968

78. Affordable System Operational Effectiveness (ASOE) Model. DAU. Retrieved September 21, 2022, from https://www.dau.edu/acquipedia/pages/ArticleContent.aspx?itemid=553

79. Zave, P. (2001). Requirements for evolving systems: A telecommunications perspective. In *Proceedings Fifth IEEE International Symposium on Requirements Engineering* (pp. 2–9). https://doi.org/10.1109/ISRE.2001.948535

80. Antón, A., & Potts, C. (1998). The use of goals to surface requirements for evolving systems. In *Proceedings of the International Conference on Software Engineering* (pp. 157–166). https://doi.org/10.1109/ICSE.1998.671112

81. Ucler, C. (2017). Brainstorming the cryoplane layout by using the iterative AHP-QFD-AHP approach. *Aviation (Vilnius, Lithuania), 21*(2), 55–63. https://doi.org/10.3846/16487788.2017.1344138

82. Schroijen, M., & Tooren, M. (n.d.). Decision support framework for future aircraft development programs. In *9th AIAA Aviation Technology, Integration, and Operations Conference (ATIO) and Aircraft Noise and Emissions Reduction Symposium (ANERS)*. https://doi.org/10.2514/6.2009-6930

83. Dou, X. (2020). Big data and smart aviation information management system. *Cogent Business & Management, 7*(1), 1–14. https://doi.org/10.1080/23311975.2020.1766736

84. Erasmus, L. D., & Doeben-Henisch, G. (2011). A theory for the systems engineering process. *IEEE Africon, 11*, 1–5. https://doi.org/10.1109/AFRCON.2011.6071989

85. Gaffney, K. S., & Morones, P. (1994, January 24–27). Advanced-aircraft integrated-diagnostics system-concept evaluation. In *1994 Annual Reliability and Maintainability Symposium; Proceedings* (pp. 20–25), Anaheim, CA. https://ieeexplore-ieee-org.ezproxy.libproxy.db.erau.edu/document/291073

86. García, C., Dávila, A., & Pessôa, M. S. (2014). Test process models: Systematic literature review. *Spice*. https://www.semanticscholar.org/paper/Test-Process-Models%3A-Systematic-Literature-Review-García-Dávila/51cc8ce9fe38ab76d1bc0ca073bbbb9999de070f

87. Domb, E. (1997). QFD and TIPS-TRIZ. In *Proceedings of the 3rd International Symposium on QFD*, Linkoping. https://the-trizjournal.com/qfd-tipstriz/

88. Chaoqun, D. (2011). Research on application system of integrating QFD and TRIZ. https://www.semanticscholar.org/paper/Research-on-Application-System-of-Integrating-QFD-Chaoqun/f6da60057faf8ddfcf14ddb0739785dd1ddc073d

89. Ahmed, Z., & Moosa, A. (2009). An Intelligent Quality Function Deployment (IQFD) for manufacturing process environment. https://www.semanticscholar.org/paper/An-Intelligent-Quality-Function-Deployment-(IQFD)-Ahmed-Moosa/112e35097da3ba61c59a8601ed199958d26c4772

90. Dowie, U. (2007). QFD for services: The service matrix of matrices. Universität Stuttgart, Institute of Business Administration, Chair of Information Systems II (Business Software) Breitscheidstr. Stuttgart. https://www.semanticscholar.org/paper/QFD-for-Services-%3A-the-Service-Matrix-of-Matrices-Dowie/ee26022cc4be8f2da6907361c8e1e37c5d7fa10e

91. Ginn, D. (2005). The role of QFD in capturing the voice of customers. https://erau.primo.exlibrisgroup.com/discovery/fulldisplay?docid=cdi_econis_primary_507501748&context=PC&vid=01ERAU_INST:ERAU&lang=en&search_scope=MyInst_and_CI&adaptor=Primo%20Central&tab=Everything&query=any,contains,the%20role%20of%20QFD%20in%20capturing%20the%20voice%20of%20customers&offset=0&pcAvailability=true

92. Ginting, R., & Riski Satrio, M. (2020). Integration of Quality Function Deployment (QFD) and value engineering in improving the quality of product: A literature review. *IOP Conference Series: Materials Science and Engineering*, *1003*(1), 12002. https://doi.org/10.1088/1757-899X/1003/1/012002

93. Lee, Y.-C., Sheu, L.-C., & Tsou, Y.-G. (2008). Quality function deployment implementation based on Fuzzy Kano model: An application in PLM system. *Computers & Industrial Engineering*, *55*(1), 48–63. https://doi.org/10.1016/j.cie.2007.11.014

94. Tiwong, S., Ramingwong, S., & Tippayawong, K. Y. (2020). On LSP lifecycle model to re-design logistics service: Case studies of Thai LSPs. *Sustainability*, *12*(6), 2394. https://doi.org/10.3390/su12062394

Index

Note: Page numbers in *italics* indicate a figure and page numbers in **bold** indicate a table on the corresponding page.

Printed in the United States
by Baker & Taylor Publisher Services